D0479684

Apple Pro Training Series

Final Cut Pro 7
Advanced Editing

Michael Wohl

Apple Pro Training Series: Final Cut Pro 7 Advanced Editing
Michael Wohl
Copyright © 2010 by Michael Wohl

Published by Peachpit Press. For information on Peachpit Press books, contact:

Peachpit Press
1249 Eighth Street
Berkeley, CA 94710
www.peachpit.com
To report errors, please send a note to errata@peachpit.com
Peachpit Press is a division of Pearson Education

Apple Series Editor: Serena Herr
Editor: Stephen Nathans-Kelly
Contributing Writer (cameos): Serena Herr
Production Coordinator: Kim Wimpsett, Happenstance Type-O-Rama
Technical Editors: Brendan Boykin, Abba Shapiro
Technical Reviewer: Brendan Boykin
Copy Editor and Proofer: Dave Awl
Compositor: Chris Gillespie, Happenstance Type-O-Rama
Media Reviewer: Eric Geoffroy
Indexer: Joy Dean Lee
Cover Illustration: Kent Oberheu
Cover Production: Happenstance Type-O-Rama

ISBN 10: 0-321-63679-1
ISBN 13: 978-0-321-63679-9
9 8 7 6 5 4 3 2
Printed and bound in the United States of America

Contents at a Glance

Table of Contents

Finishing Techniques

Getting Started

Welcome to the official Level Two Apple Pro Training course for Final Cut Pro 7!

This book is an in-depth journey into advanced editing techniques and effects with Final Cut Pro. It uses diverse footage ranging from the feature film *The Genesis Code* to the music video *One Night in Jordan* (based on a live concert performance by internationally renowned artist Zade Dirani), and from the Blue Angels documentary *Bearcats* to various promotional spots and show bumpers to demonstrate both the features of the application and the practical techniques you'll use daily in your editing projects.

Whether you've been editing for years or are just beginning to work in film and video, this book will enhance your knowledge of Final Cut Pro while it advances your grasp of editing techniques. So let's get started!

The Methodology

This book takes a hands-on approach to learning the software. It's divided into projects—based on footage on the accompanying DVD—that teach you advanced techniques as you work through the lessons. Every exercise is designed to get you editing and creating effects professionally in Final Cut Pro as quickly as possible.

Each lesson builds on previous lessons to guide you through the application's functions and capabilities. If you're already familiar with Final Cut Pro, you can go directly to a specific section and focus on that topic, because every lesson is self-contained.

Course Structure

This book is designed to improve your skills both as an editor and as a Final Cut Pro operator. You'll begin by learning editing techniques designed to streamline your workflow and allow you to handle tricky situations and effectively perform complex editing tasks. Then you'll focus on sound editing and multicamera footage. Next, you'll explore the world of effects, covering such diverse topics as compositing, filters, keyframing, nested sequences, and speed modification. Finally, you'll finish your studies with two lessons dealing with the "nuts and bolts" of Final Cut Pro workflows, including working with widescreen sequences, media management, and exporting files. And there is a bonus appendix covering common workflows for footage shot using RED cameras.

The lessons are grouped into the following categories:

▶ Advanced Editing: Lessons 1–6

▶ Advanced Compositing and Effects: Lessons 7–11

▶ Finishing Techniques: Lessons 12–13

In addition to the exercises, some lessons include "Project Tasks" that give you an opportunity to practice what you've learned before moving on to new material. Throughout the book, other valuable sections will guide you in evaluating your project before moving to the next editing stage.

Using the DVD Book Files

The *Apple Pro Training Series: Final Cut Pro 7 Advanced Editing* DVD (included with the book) contains the project files you'll use for each lesson, as well as media files that contain the video and audio content you'll need for each exercise. After you transfer the files to your hard drive, each lesson will instruct you in the use of the project and media files.

Installing the DVD Lesson Files

On the DVD, you'll find a folder titled AdvFCP7 Book Files, which contains two subfolders: Lesson Files and Media. These folders contain the lessons and media files for this course. Make sure you keep these two folders together in the FCP7 Book Files folder on your hard drive. If you do so, Final Cut Pro should be able to maintain the original links between the lessons and media files.

1   Insert the *Apple Pro Training Series: Final Cut Pro 7 Advanced Editing* DVD into your DVD drive.

2   Drag the AdvFCP7 Book Files folder from the DVD to your hard drive to copy it. The DVD contains about 7.8 GB of data.

Each lesson will explain which files to open for that lesson's exercises.

Reconnecting Media

When copying files from the DVD to your hard drive, you may unintentionally break a link between a project file and its media files. If this happens, a dialog appears asking you to relink the project files. Relinking the project files is simple. Should the dialog appear when opening a lesson, follow these steps:

1   If an Offline Files dialog appears, click the Reconnect button.

    A Reconnect Files dialog opens. Under the Files To Connect portion of the dialog, the offline file is listed along with its possible location.

2   In the Reconnect Files dialog, click Search.

    Final Cut Pro will search for the missing file. If you already know where the file is located, you can click the Locate button and find the file manually.

3   After the correct file is found, click Choose in the Reconnect dialog.

4   When the file is displayed in the Files Located section of the Reconnect Files dialog, click Connect.

    When the link between the project file and the media file is reestablished, Final Cut Pro will be able to access the media within the project.

Changing System Preferences

A few editing functions within Final Cut Pro use function keys also used by other programs, such as Exposé and the Dashboard. If you want to use the FCP editing shortcuts, you will need to reassign the functions keys in these other programs.

1 From your desktop, open System Preferences.

2 In the Personal section, click Dashboard & Exposé.

3 Reassign the keyboard shortcuts for F9, F10, F11, and F12 to other keys.

Reassigning the shortcuts will allow Final Cut Pro to use these shortcut keys exclusively. At any time when using Final Cut Pro, you can return to System Preferences and change these key assignments.

About the Footage

Footage from eight diverse projects—which range from a feature film and a documentary to a concert video and various broadcast promos—is used throughout this book. Together, they represent a real-world sampling of the different types of projects and media formats you'll likely encounter as a working video editor. The exercises instruct you to edit the footage in a particular way, but you can use any part of this footage to practice editing methods. Techniques you've learned using one set of footage in a lesson can be practiced with a different set of footage to create a new project. Due to copyright restrictions, however, you cannot use this footage for any purpose outside this book.

System Requirements

Before using *Apple Pro Training Series: Final Cut Pro 7 Advanced Editing,* you should have a working knowledge of your Macintosh and the Mac OS X operating system. Make sure that you know how to use the mouse and standard menus and commands; and also how to open, save, and close files. If you need to review these techniques, see the printed or online documentation included with your system.

For the basic system requirements for Final Cut Pro 7, refer to the Final Cut Pro 7 documentation or Apple's web site, www.apple.com.

About the Apple Pro Training Series

Apple Pro Training Series: Final Cut Pro 7 Advanced Editing is both a self-paced learning tool and the official curriculum of the Apple Pro Training and Certification Program.

Developed by experts in the field and certified by Apple, the series is used by Apple Authorized Training Centers worldwide and offers complete training in all Apple Pro products. The lessons are designed to let you learn at your own pace. Each lesson concludes with review questions and answers summarizing what you've learned, which can be used to help you prepare for the Apple Pro Certification Exam.

For a complete list of Apple Pro Training Series books, see the ad at the back of this book, or visit www.peachpit.com/apts.

Apple Pro Certification Program

The Apple Pro Training and Certification Programs are designed to keep you at the forefront of Apple's digital media technology while giving you a competitive edge in today's ever-changing job market. Whether you're an editor, graphic designer, sound designer, special effects artist, or teacher, these training tools are meant to help you expand your skills.

Upon completing the course material in this book, you can become an Apple Certified Pro by taking the certification exam at an Apple Authorized Training Center. Certification is offered in Final Cut Pro, Final Cut Server, Color, Compressor, Motion, Soundtrack Pro, DVD Studio Pro, and Logic Pro. Certification as an Apple Pro gives you official recognition of your knowledge of Apple's professional applications while allowing you to market yourself to employers and clients as a skilled, pro-level user of Apple products.

For those who prefer to learn in an instructor-led setting, Apple offers training courses at Apple Authorized Training Centers worldwide. These courses, which use the Apple Pro Training Series books as their curriculum, are taught by Apple Certified Trainers and balance concepts and lectures with hands-on labs and exercises. Apple Authorized Training Centers have been carefully selected and have met Apple's highest standards in all areas, including facilities, instructors, course delivery, and infrastructure. The goal of the program is to offer Apple customers, from beginners to the most seasoned professionals, the highest-quality training experience.

For more information, please see the ad at the back of this book, or to find an Authorized Training Center near you, go to training.apple.com.

Resources

Apple Pro Training Series: Final Cut Pro 7Advanced Editing is not intended as a comprehensive reference manual, nor does it replace the documentation that comes with the application. For comprehensive information about program features, refer to these resources:

▶   The Reference Guide: Accessed through the Final Cut Pro Help menu, the Reference Guide contains a complete description of all features.

▶   Apple's web site: www.apple.com.

Advanced Editing

1

Lesson Files	Lesson Files > Lesson_01 > Professional_Technique.fcp
Media	Genesis Code_Hockey
Time	This lesson takes approximately 30 minutes to complete.
Goals	Review three-point editing concepts and rules
	Perform insert and overwrite edits from the keyboard
	Limit which tracks are affected by an edit
	Learn effective Timeline editing

Lesson 1
Professional Editing Technique

One of the most powerful aspects of Final Cut Pro is its flexibility. You can perform basic edits in no fewer than five ways. Edits can be trimmed (as you'll learn in Lessons 3 and 4) in no fewer than 11 ways, and so on. Some people work in list view, others in icon view; some people drag and drop, others exclusively use the keyboard.

There isn't one "proper" way to use the program; however, there are clearly faster, more efficient ways of working and slower, less efficient ones. In some cases, that might mean performing one complex operation instead of three or four simple ones (such as performing a ripple instead of using the razor blade). In other cases, it might mean taking a little more time to do things once the right way, instead of making a sloppy first pass and then spending much more time cleaning up the mess.

The more effectively you work, the more time and energy you can spend on the creative decisions—how best to tell the story—rather than where to click the mouse and what keys to press. Good editing requires a sense of rhythm and timing, and it's very hard to get in the flow when you're constantly stopping and starting, redoing the same operations, and making and cleaning up messes (such as extra junk in the Timeline, gaps, overlapping clips on multiple tracks, and so on).

The more complex your project, the more energy you'll waste by working inefficiently. Forcing yourself to instead edit in a more streamlined way has another important benefit: You'll be finished sooner, or at least you'll be able to achieve a much greater level of polish in the same amount of time.

This lesson covers some of the most fundamental aspects of professional editing technique in Final Cut Pro. It might seem very basic for some readers, and such people are encouraged to skip it and begin with Lesson 2. However, all of the advanced techniques covered throughout the rest of the book assume mastery of these fundamentals, so if you have any doubts, this lesson will get you up to speed in a hurry.

How the Pros Do It

Editing should be an iterative process. Little by little you chip away at the slab of raw footage until the story emerges, and you refine and trim away at it until each detail comes into relief, communicating its nuance as sharply and effectively as possible. Then you pass over it again, with a finer and finer grain, until it's polished and glistening with life.

The analogy to sculpting is accurate: cut too much too fast, and you risk ruining the form and structure needed to hold the story together. Skip those polishing passes and your film won't have the lifelike appeal that is the magic of the medium.

Because of this, editing takes a long time. A typical Hollywood film editor is given 8 or more months to finish the edit. Does it take that long for them to put all the pieces together? No! The *assembly* is typically done within a few weeks. The bulk of that time is spent exhaustively experimenting with different ideas, whittling away at the footage until all the texture and nuance is just right.

However, time is still money, and at the professional level no one can afford to waste either. So editors strive to work as efficiently as possible. This starts with organizing and categorizing all the raw footage, and extends into creating those first sequences.

Some of you may be fond of editing by dragging clips willy-nilly into the Timeline and then trimming and rearranging them there like the tiles of a mosaic. Final Cut Pro allows this workflow and there are often times where that approach yields great results. But it is rarely efficient.

Instead of just stuffing your sequence full of extraneous bits and pieces that you're later going to have to remove or rearrange, strive to add only the exact bits of the clips you plan to use, and ideally in your desired order. Make the edits "work" right away. Either way you're going to keep trimming, finessing, and refining those edits, but this way, you're already starting with something close to finished.

This takes discipline. It means forcing yourself to make decisions straightaway about what works and what doesn't, what's essential and what's expendable. By doing this hard work right away you yield significant benefits.

For one thing, the further along you start, the further along you'll finish. A film is never complete; it's just abandoned at some point when time runs out. If you waste your first few days (or hours or weeks depending on the scope of your project) fiddling around with too much junk in your sequence, you rob yourself of time you'll desperately want back later.

Following the techniques in this lesson, you also eliminate the likelihood of mistakes such as black flashes, (unintentionally) overlapping dialogue, and bad edits, all of which take more time to fix later than they do to just get right in the first place. Finally, and perhaps most importantly, this approach allows you to get directly to the place where you're evaluating the overall story, instead of wasting energy on putting individual shots together.

Three-Point Editing

The best way to accomplish these goals is to employ the editing technique known as three-point editing. If you're unfamiliar with it, that name may seem complicated (who wants to keep track of three things at once?), but in truth, it really means forgetting about the *fourth* point inherent in every edit.

Every edit requires four pieces of information: Where does the source clip start and end, and where in the sequence should it begin and end? That's two pairs of In and Out points—one in the Viewer, and one in the sequence.

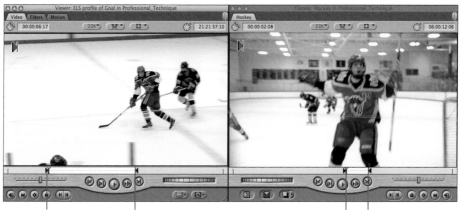

Source In point   Source Out point   Sequence In point   Sequence Out point

Once you set these points, you can perform insert or overwrite edits by dragging to the Canvas, clicking one of the Edit buttons, or quickest of all, pressing a keyboard shortcut.

There is one problem, however. If you set all four of these points you create a potential dilemma: What if the marked area of the source is of a different duration than the marked area in the sequence? You just can't stuff a ten-second peg into a four-second hole. So you have two options. You could count frames and ensure before performing the edit that both marked areas are exactly the same length (which would be tedious and inefficient), or you could simply forget about one of the four points. Voilà! Three-point editing.

If you set an In and an Out point in the Viewer, you need only set an In *or* an Out in the sequence. If you set an In and an Out in the sequence, you need only one point in the Viewer. Any three points can be used and Final Cut Pro will automatically calculate the fourth one.

1   Open Lesson Files > Lesson_01 > **Professional_Technique.fcp**.

The *Hockey* sequence should already be open in the sequence. This is a staged hockey game from the film *The Genesis Code*. There's one shot already in the sequence and you're ready to add a second shot.

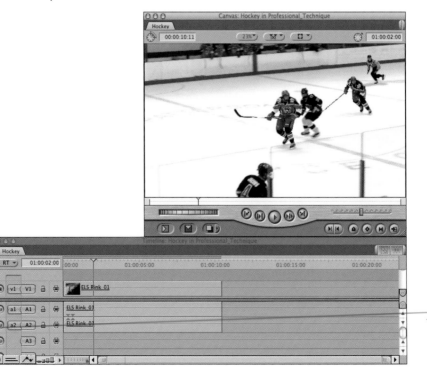

2 In the Browser, open **WS_Rink_02** into the Viewer and play the clip.

3 Mark an In point as the puck is being passed to the forward (at approximately 21:21:38:00).

4 In the sequence, find the frame where the same action is happening, where the puck is being passed (around 03:18), and set an In point there.

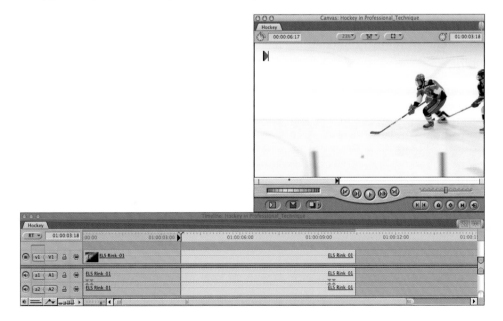

5 Play forward until after the goal is scored and the players start to pile up against the rink wall and set an Out point there (at approximately 8:00).

With three points set, you can perform the edit, and Final Cut Pro will use as much of the source clip as needed to fill the marked section of the sequence.

6 Drag the clip from the Viewer to the Canvas, and when the Edit Overlay appears, drop the clip onto the Overwrite target.

7 Play the sequence.

The first edit is pretty smooth, and the movement of the puck helps guide the audience's eyes past the edit point. The second edit (where it cuts back to the wide shot) is also pretty smooth. Both edits might need a little finessing, but that's what trimming is for.

TIP ▶ If it's more important that the ending edit is precise, you can set two Out points and one In point, and Final Cut Pro will back-time the clip to figure out where the In point should wind up.

Furthermore, Final Cut Pro makes it extra easy for you to do three-point editing even when you don't know you're doing it. If you don't set any points in the sequence, Final Cut Pro uses the playhead position as the In point.

8 In the Browser, open **Team Hug** into the Viewer and play it.

9 Mark an In point just before the fourth player joins the pile (at around 03:26:17:06).

10 Mark an Out point right as the player punches Thomas (at approximately 03:26:22:00).

> **TIP** ▶ Press Shift-\ (backslash) to play the clip from the In to the Out point to see exactly what portion of the clip will be edited into the sequence. It's a good idea to do this every time you set an In and Out point together.

At this point you've set two points, but you still need to set a third point before Final Cut Pro knows what you want to do. In this case all you need is an In point in the sequence, and Final Cut Pro can calculate the Out point automatically.

This situation is by far the most common three-point edit, so Final Cut Pro makes it extra easy. If you don't explicitly set an In point in the sequence, Final Cut Pro will use the sequence playhead as the third point.

11 Position the sequence playhead on the first frame of the last clip (at 8:01).

> **TIP** ▶ Use the Up Arrow and Down Arrow keys to navigate from edit to edit in the sequence.

12 Press F10 to perform an overwrite edit.

The clip is overwritten into the sequence, beginning at the playhead position and extending to the Out point specified in the Viewer.

TIP After a successful three-point edit Final Cut Pro automatically clears the points in the sequence and moves the playhead to the frame just past the last edit. This enables you to quickly add one shot after another without having to set any new points in the sequence.

▶ Enabling Function Keys

Few Mac programs use the function keys (often called F-keys) located above the number keys on a standard keyboard. Because of this, Apple has commandeered those keys to automatically control system volume, iTunes playback, and other system functions on many keyboards. Although it's handy to have one-key access to those system functions, this limits some convenient functionality in Final Cut Pro. Fortunately, you can wrest control back from the system in just a few clicks.

1   Open the System Preferences and click the Keyboard icon.

Continues on next page

▶ Enabling Function Keys *(continued)*

○ ○ ○   Keyboard
◀ ▶   Show All   🔍

[Keyboard | Keyboard Shortcuts]

Key Repeat Rate   Delay Until Repeat

Slow   Fast   Off Long   Short

☑ Use all F1, F2, etc. keys as standard function keys
  When this option is selected, press the Fn key to use the special
  features printed on each key.

☑ Illuminate keyboard in low light conditions
Turn off when computer is not used for:

5 secs   10 secs   30 secs   1 min   5 mins   Never

☐ Show Keyboard & Character Viewer in menu bar

(Modifier Keys...)

(Set Up Bluetooth Keyboard...)   (?)

2   Select the checkbox for "Use all F1, F2, etc. keys as standard function keys."

This allows those keys to do whatever any individual program intends.

3   Close the System Preferences window.

TIP ▶ You can also press the Fn key plus the function key to get the inverse of this setting (that is, when the setting is selected, pressing Fn and F8 simultaneously will start and stop iTunes and when the setting is disabled, you can press Fn and F10 simultaneously to perform an overwrite edit in Final Cut Pro).

Alternatively, you could customize your Final Cut Pro keyboard layout and reprogram the Edit functions to different keys on the keyboard.

Three Rules for Three-Point Editing

You exercised the first rule of three-point editing in the previous steps: *If you don't set an In or an Out point in the sequence, the playhead is used as the In point.*

The second rule is that *if you don't set an In or an Out in the Viewer, Final Cut Pro uses the beginning or end of the source media.* This is almost never desirable, because proper filming technique would always yield at least a little bit of *handles* around the section of the clip you plan to use. For this reason you almost always want to set at least one point in the Viewer.

The third rule is that *if you do accidentally set all four points, Final Cut Pro will always ignore the Out point in the Viewer.* If you went through the trouble to explicitly set an In and Out point in your sequence, the software assumes you must have done it deliberately; plus, the sequence is the part of your file that contains your creative work, whereas the Viewer just contains raw footage that never changes. The Viewer Out point is therefore deemed the least important of the four.

▶ Keep Your Clips on One Track

Another reason professionals use the editing method described in this lesson is because it tends to keep all the video on track V1. Less experienced editors frequently get in the bad habit of spreading their clips across many different tracks.

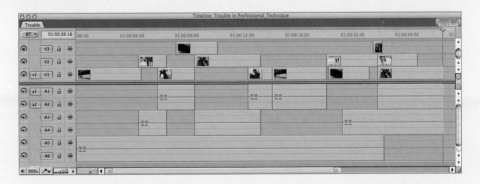

Although there's nothing technically incorrect about this, using multiple tracks for straight edits increases the likelihood of unintentional errors, because it may not be entirely obvious exactly where edits occur. It's also more difficult to effectively use transition effects, which will have a different result if applied to two adjacent clips on one track than to a clip on a different track. Finally, and most importantly, all of the amazing trimming tools that you'll learn in Lessons 3 and 4 are far easier to use when your clips are on the same track.

Continues on next page

▶ **Keep Your Clips on One Track** *(continued)*

Multiple tracks are intended to be used when compositing: when you want a title to superimpose over some video, or when you want to create a picture-in-picture effect, and so on. You'll learn all about making the most of multiple video tracks later in this book.

Using multiple video tracks for basic editing most often is nothing less than a fear of commitment. That's right! (You single video editors out there might do well to begin your road to recovery by putting your video items on a single track.) Although putting that alternate angle on V2 seems like it's saving you the time or hassle of getting back to the original if you change your mind, in fact it has the opposite effect. Rather than accepting the new shot into the edit, you're keeping it (and a tiny slice of your attention) on hold. Cumulatively, that can add up to a very distracting Timeline, and a very distracted mind.

If you're really not sure that you want to commit to the new shot (and you don't trust Final Cut Pro's 99 levels of Undo), duplicate your sequence before making the edit. You can always go back to the old version, and then you can compare them side by side. Otherwise, overwrite it into your sequence and live with it for a few days. Changing it later is as easy as a three-point edit.

Insert Editing

When editing using the professional technique described throughout this lesson, 90% of your edits will be overwrite edits. If you mark the points to determine where you want the clip to go, it only makes sense to put the clip *exactly there*. Furthermore, one of your priorities when editing this way is to keep the timing of the action in the scene consistent. Overwriting ensures that a new edit never upsets the timing already established in the sequence.

Still, there are some occasions where you want to add a clip to your sequence and push everything out of the way to make room for it. This is exactly what *insert* editing is good for. But remember, inserting still follows the rules of three-point editing.

1   Play the sequence and find the moment where you can see the player clearly just after the goal is scored (at around 6:00).

2   Set an In point there.

3   In the Browser open **Crowd** into the Viewer.

An In point and an Out point have already been set for you.

4   Drag the clip in the Viewer to the Canvas and when the Edit Overlay appears, drop it
     on the Insert target (or press F9).

The clip is inserted at the In point you specified in step 2.

5   Play the sequence to see how the crowd shot fits into the sequence.

In fact, inserting that clip did change the timing of the sequence. It now takes the skater an extra-long time to get from the goal to the back of the rink, but this is an example where you can fudge the actual timing in order to better tell the story.

Audio-Only and Video-Only Editing

When you make all of your edits using audio-only and video-only editing, you can also easily control which tracks (audio and/or video) are included. This enables you to quickly perform audio-only or video-only edits, or to overlap multiple audio tracks in a single step.

The Timeline track headers contain a patch panel where you specify which source tracks are included in the edit, and which tracks they'll be placed on.

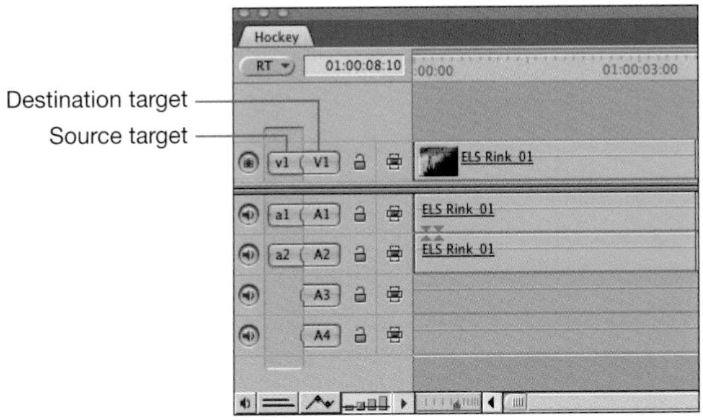

Destination target
Source target

The clip currently open in the Viewer determines which source icons, and how many of them, appear on the left side of the patch panel.

1   Open **scoreboard** from the Browser.

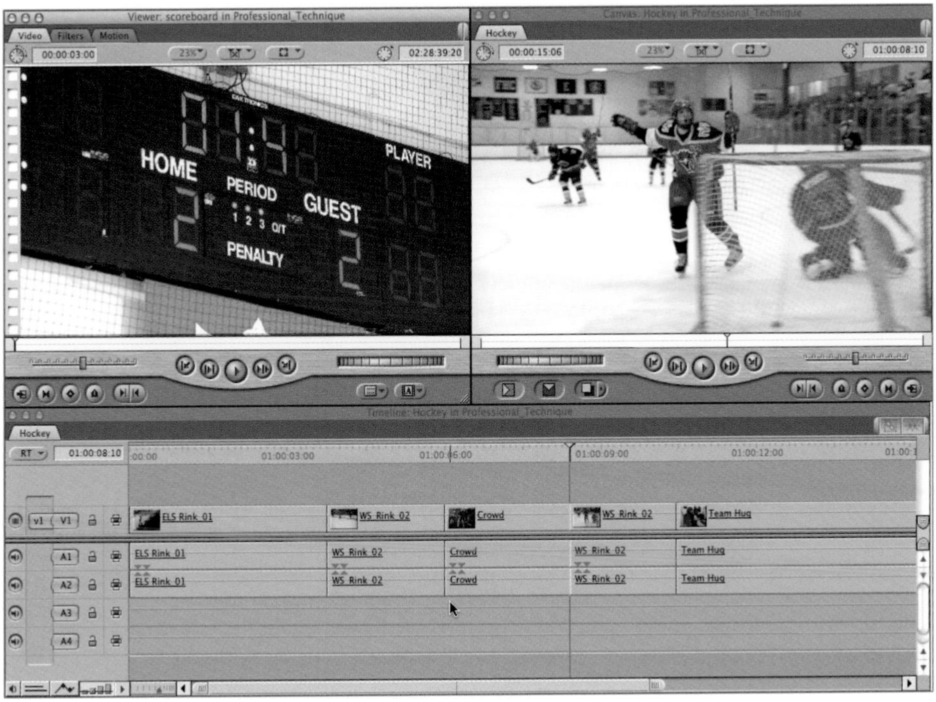

This shot has no audio. Look at the patch panel in the Timeline. There are no audio source icons.

2   Double-click **LS_Collision_01** in the Browser.

This shot has four audio tracks (as seen by the four Mono tabs present in the Viewer). Correspondingly, there are four audio source icons in the patch panel.

TIP▶ You can perform an audio-only or video-only edit by disconnecting the patches on the tracks you don't want.

3   In the patch panel, click the a3 and a4 source icons to disconnect them.

4   Move the sequence playhead to the end of the sequence so you don't accidentally overwrite any of the shots already in the sequence.

5   Drag **LS_Collision_01** from the Viewer into the Canvas and perform an overwrite edit.

TIP▶ Because overwrite is the default edit type, dragging a clip onto any portion of the Canvas not covered by the Edit Overlay will perform an overwrite.

Tracks V1, a1, and a2 of the source clip are added to the sequence.

You can also redirect the tracks to control exactly where the source audio is placed during the edit.

6   Open **MS Collision_01** into the Viewer.

In and Out marks have already been set.

7   Press Shift-\ (backslash) to play from In to Out.

This shot has two tracks of audio (as evidenced by the stereo tab in the Viewer).

8   In the sequence, set an Out point midway through the player's flip (at around 16:04).

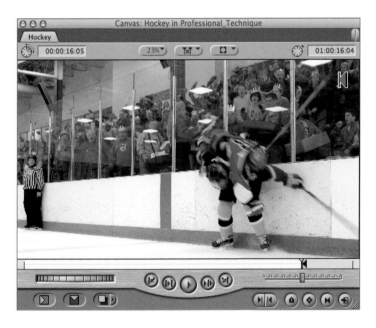

In this example you'll do a back-timed edit so the action of the flip lines up, regardless of where the beginning of the shot starts.

9   In the patch panel, drag both audio targets so they go to tracks A3 and A4.

NOTE ▶ Be sure not to disconnect the patches while reassigning them.

10 Press F10 to perform an overwrite edit.

11 Play the sequence.

The audio from both shots is audible where they overlap.

Dragging to the Timeline

Okay, so hopefully now you're convinced that editing by dragging to the Canvas (or better yet, using the keyboard shortcuts) is faster, more precise, and more fun than dragging clips to the Timeline. But you may slip back into your old habits now and again, and there's nothing wrong with that.

The biggest drawback to dragging clips to the Timeline is that it's imprecise. You can easily alleviate this by following the same procedure you did for the three-point edit exercises above.

Rather than blindly dragging a clip down there, unsure of where it's going to wind up, first play the sequence and put your playhead (or an In point in more complicated situations) on the frame where you'd like the edit to start or end. That way, when you drag to the Timeline, you have something to snap to and ensure that the new clip goes just where you want it.

1   In the Browser, open **MS Collision_02**.

In and Out points have already been marked on the clip.

2   Press Shift-\ (backslash) to play from In to Out.

You can use this third angle to add excitement to the action of the collision.

3   Play the sequence and stop the playhead on the frame just after the player's shoulder lands on the ice (when he's still mostly upside down) around 16:15.

4   Drag the clip from the Viewer to the Timeline, lining up the beginning of the clip with the playhead.

TIP   Turn on snapping (press N) if it isn't already turned on.

5   Make sure the edit is set as an overwrite edit (not an insert) and release the mouse button.

TIP   Drag above the dividing line to perform an insert edit and below the line to perform an overwrite edit.

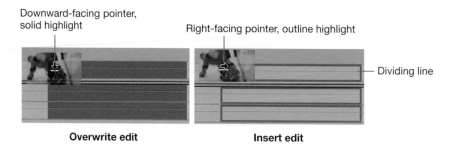

Downward-facing pointer, solid highlight

Right-facing pointer, outline highlight

Dividing line

Overwrite edit   **Insert edit**

The clip is edited into the sequence with the same precision as if you had done a standard three-point edit using the Canvas. Once you get comfortable with the workflow, you'll likely migrate toward using the F10 key, as that's faster than any dragging and dropping.

Handling Target Track Settings

One other obstacle to dragging to the Timeline instead of to the Canvas is how to manage the target tracks to perform a video-only or audio-only edit, or an edit where the audio overlaps (rather than overwrites) the existing tracks.

Dragging to the Timeline does observe the settings in the patch panel, but you can override those settings by dragging directly to a non-targeted track, although the edit will still follow the pattern of the patch panel.

1 Open **WS_Rink_02** into the Viewer.

2 Mark an In near the end of the clip when the players begin skating away from the rink wall (approximately 21:21:50:05).

TIP ▶ Because you didn't set an Out point, Final Cut Pro will use the clip all the way until the end of the media.

3   In the patch panel, disconnect the patches for sources a1 and a2.

This prepares you to make a video-only edit.

4   Drag the clip to the Timeline at the very end of the sequence, but before you drop it, look at the feedback you see when you put your pointer over different tracks.

If you drag to track V1, the patch panel is observed, and you get a video-only edit.

However, even though the audio is disconnected, putting your pointer over the audio tracks will allow you to make an audio edit.

Final Cut Pro will allow you to drop the clip there, but notice that the video is no longer part of the selection. With more complicated patch panel settings (especially with more tracks involved) the results can seem especially confusing.

For best results when working in complex situations, you're better off dragging to the Canvas instead of the Timeline. In that case the patch panel will always be observed and you can control exactly what will happen when you perform the edit.

Lesson Review

1. What is three-point editing?
2. True or False: If no In or Out point is set in the Viewer, the playhead is used as the In point.
3. If you set four points what happens?
4. How do you perform a video-only edit?
5. How many audio source tabs appear in the patch panel?
6. When inserting, are the rules of three-point editing observed?
7. Is dragging to the Timeline less precise than dragging to the Canvas?
8. True or False: When dragging to the Timeline, it's impossible to guarantee whether you'll get an insert or an overwrite edit.
9. True or False: Dragging to the Timeline ignores patch panel settings.

Answers

1. The act of setting In and Out points in the source clip and the sequence before performing an edit.
2. False. The beginning and/or end of the media is used.
3. The Viewer Out point is ignored.
4. Disconnect the audio source tabs in the patch panel.
5. As many as there are tracks currently open in the Viewer.
6. Yes.
7. Not necessarily. If you set an In point or position the playhead, you can achieve the same precision as when dragging to the Canvas.
8. Sometimes it seems true, but in fact it's based on where your pointer is when you drop the clip.
9. False. They aren't ignored, but they can be overridden.

Tapeless Groove— Steve Purcell

STEVE PURCELL IS ALL ABOUT MUSIC. For three decades, the Grammy- and Emmy Award-winning editor, director, and producer has been known

as one of the music industry's best. His credits, which include hundreds of concert films, music videos, and TV music specials (as well as feature films such as *Flatliners* and *The Last Confederate*), read like a Who's Who of the music world. Paul McCartney's "Get Back," B.B. King's "The Blues Summit," Alanis Morissette's "Jagged Little Pill – Live," Prince's "Sign O' the Times," John Lennon, Bette Midler, David Bowie, ZZ Top, Van Halen, K.D. Lang—the list is as varied as it is long.

Steve Purcell on location in Amman, Jordan, for Zade's One Night in Jordan.

But what really sets Purcell apart is the fact that he's always pushing the technological boundary in a quest to improve quality, save time and money, and enhance creativity. We asked him about his adoption of an all-digital workflow.

You work in a completely tapeless workflow. What are the benefits?

What it allows you to do is immediately start editing. There's no digitizing time. On a typical project I go out, shoot, download my files to a drive, make a backup of the drive, and then on the plane flying home I open Final Cut and start logging my material. That's a huge time-saver. In the past, if you shot 25 hours of footage, you're talking two days of digitizing time before you can even start working.

The other thing is, you're editing at full-res. So at any stage of the process, you can deliver. On the Jordan project [Zade's *One Night in Jordan*], we're delivering a 90-minute concert, but we also needed to release a trailer and a behind-the-scenes video. Because I have all the footage high-res in Final Cut Pro, I can switch gears at any point. I can go from cutting the concert to cutting a trailer, post it right out of Final Cut Pro to iWeb for approvals, do the color correction and mix, export a ProRes H22, and I'm done.

Are certain projects more suited to a tapeless workflow than others?

If I could, I'd shoot everything file-based. These days, the only times I shoot tape tends to be big concerts, where you've got 15 cameras and you're coordinating the shoot from a TV truck. Most TV trucks still have tape-based machines. But there's a show I'm doing next month with a truck that's all file-based, so even that's starting to change.

One of the long-standing benefits of tape has been that your source tapes serve as a reliable, master-quality backup. What's your recommended backup regimen?

When I get back from a shoot, I put all my media on the drive I'm going to edit with—right now I'm using eSATA G-Speed drives by G-Tech—and then I make a duplicate on the Drobo as a backup.

When I'm done with the project, I save the entire project. Drives are so inexpensive now that I buy removable drives of up to 2 terabytes and save the whole thing. Soup to nuts. All the dailies, the Final Cut project, music, graphics, all the render files go on that drive.

The great thing is that you archive everything, so you can come back at any time and pick up exactly where you left off. I did a show two years ago, and I just got a call from the producer last month asking for a couple minutes of the show. I pulled the drive out, opened the Final Cut project, took the 5 minutes they wanted, exported a ProRes QuickTime, and sent it to him. It was as though I'd turned on the computer exactly as I'd left it two years ago.

The concept of doing that at any edit facility on a tape-based show would be insane. It would take a day of locating the sequence, re-digitizing, outputting to tape, and converting to QuickTime, at a huge expense. Whereas for me, it took 15 minutes on a drive the size of a pack of cigarettes.

Are there any unexpected benefits to working in a tapeless world?

The huge creative benefit is that you're no longer taking your show and running it through various stages of completion at different facilities. You have the ability within one box to do your offline and online edit, color correct, mix, do your graphics, and final output.

So the real benefit is you can work at different stages. You can be creating a rough cut of certain portions of your show, while another section is locked picture and you're doing the color correction. So you can show clients 5 minutes of exactly what the final will look and sound like, while you're still working on the rest of the show.

Is there anything you miss from the "old days" of tape and film?

The camaraderie. In the old days of editing on tape and cutting on film, it put you in an environment where you were working with 20 other editors on a daily basis. We'd all go to the same big facilities to do what we do. That's how I met some of my best friends.

What's on deck for you?

I'm directing a PBS concert next quarter out of the Nokia Theater. I produce and direct about six music shows a year for Time/Life; the next one is in New Orleans. And I do a lot of work for Disney.

I'm also working on a documentary where we're following 3 pilots who fly WWII P-51 Mustangs in a three-ship aerobatic routine. We've been brought in to document the path they took from training in Texas to air shows all over the world. That will end up on Discovery as a series on aviation.

You seem to move easily between editing, directing, and producing on any given day. What's it like to wear all three hats?

I made the transition from editor to director in the late '90s, and after directing for 10 years or so, it really made sense to direct and produce. At this point, I probably edit about 20 to 30 percent of what I shoot.

To edit, you've got to shut the door, shut off the phone, and you can't really multitask. As a producer, you can keep multiple projects going at the same time, and there's just more work to go around for everybody. It allows me to stay busier and take on a larger volume of work.

Creatively, they're all different, but when you come from an editing background you just put that hat back on when you need to.

2

Lesson Files   Lesson Files > Lesson_02 > Workflow.fcp

Media   Poker, Genesis Code_Hockey, Genesis Code Cafeteria

Time   This lesson takes approximately 60 minutes to complete.

Goals   Improve overall editing efficiency and effectiveness

Use Final Cut Pro's sophisticated editing tools

Improve timing with replace edits

Access used source clips quickly with Match Frame

Gang (synchronize) the Viewer and Canvas

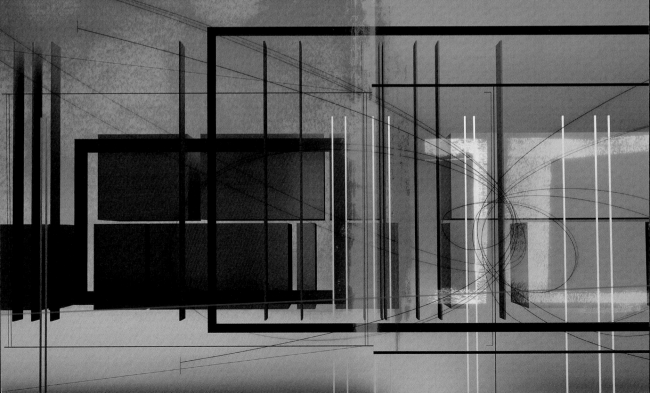

Accelerating Your Workflow

Although you can successfully edit projects in Final Cut Pro using only a few of the most basic tools, many other tools and techniques are available to speed your workflow and improve your final product. In most cases, these are compound tools or shortcuts that can perform several steps in a single action. Mastering these can significantly improve your editing experience and take you one step closer to that magical state in which you can operate the software as fast as you can think.

In most cases, these methods aren't difficult to use. They simply require a more sophisticated approach to editing, in which you foresee all your editing objectives at once, like a chess master planning three or four moves in advance. For example, if you know that you want to cut back and forth between two close-ups in a dialogue scene, Final Cut Pro has commands—such as Match Frame and Gang Sync—specifically designed to accelerate that workflow.

As you grow more comfortable with these advanced techniques, they'll become as familiar as three-point edits or the Blade tool, and you'll find that they're equally as versatile. This lesson covers a selection of the most useful features frequently overlooked or underused by self-taught editors.

Going Beyond the Double-Click

You already know that you can double-click a clip in the Browser to open it, or drag it from the Browser to the Viewer, or even select it and press Enter.

You also know that if you double-click a sequence clip in the Canvas or Timeline, it will open into the Viewer with sprocket holes displayed in the scrubber area to indicate that it's currently in use.

Clip opened from the Browser

Clip opened from a sequence

However, sometimes you want to quickly open a clip into the Viewer without going to the Browser, and without affecting the version of the clip currently in use in the sequence. For instance, you may have used a portion of a clip, cut away to another shot, and now want to use a different section of that first shot in another part of the sequence. Alternatively, you might have applied some effects to a clip in the sequence, and you want to use the original, unfiltered clip in a different way. In another example, you might have a title or graphic that you want to reuse in more than one place in your sequence.

In any of these cases, you could hunt through the Browser or Effects tabs looking for the original master clip, but this can be time consuming, and it takes you out of the flow of the scene you're currently working on.

Using the Recent Clips Pop-Up Menu

One place to find clips quickly is in the Recent Clips pop-up menu in the Viewer window. This menu shows the last ten clips opened into the Viewer. Selecting a clip from the menu will automatically reopen it.

This is especially helpful when you want to reexamine a clip that you viewed briefly but chose not to use. You can also populate this menu all at once with a group of clips.

1   Open Lesson Files > Lesson_02 > **Workflow.fcp**.

2   In the Viewer, click the Recent Clips pop-up menu.

It indicates that there are no recent items opened.

NOTE ▸ If you've opened any clips prior to beginning this lesson, the menu might not be empty.

3   Select the five clips in the Hockey Footage bin (do not select the *Collision* bin) and drag all of them to the Viewer window.

The first of these clips is opened into the Viewer, and the others are automatically added to the Recent Clips pop-up menu.

4 Click the Recent Clips pop-up menu and choose Scoreboard.

The shot of the scoreboard is loaded into the Viewer, and the In and Out points are displayed based on the last time the master clip was opened.

Additionally, you can customize the number of clips listed in the menu.

5 Choose Final Cut Pro > User Preferences and click the General tab.

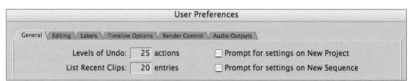

6 Set the List Recent Clips setting to *20* and click OK.

Now, the 20 most recently accessed clips will appear in the menu. They appear in the reverse order in which they were opened. Twenty is the maximum value for this setting (which is just as well—with any more than that, it would lose its benefit as a shortcut).

Using Match Frame

Another tool that opens a recently used clip is the Match Frame command. Match Frame automatically opens into the Viewer the master clip of the shot currently under the playhead, on the lowest Auto Select–enabled track.

The clip opens into the Viewer with the playhead parked on the same frame it was parked on in the sequence. Although this function may seem unimpressive, it's actually one of the handiest and most versatile shortcuts in Final Cut Pro. Throughout the rest of this lesson, you'll employ the Match Frame command for a variety of purposes.

> **NOTE ▸** If there is no video clip under the playhead, or if Auto Select is disabled on the video tracks, Match Frame will open the audio clips at the playhead position.

1   In the Browser, double-click the *Match Frame* sequence (if it's not already open).

2   Park the playhead anywhere in the second clip (**MS Collision_01**).

3   In the Canvas, click the the Show Match Frame button (or press F).

The unfiltered master clip is opened into the Viewer.

Note that the clip in the sequence has a Desaturate filter applied to it (making it appear black and white), but the clip in the Viewer—the original clip—has no filter applied. This was specifically done for this lesson to emphasize the difference between double-clicking a clip in the sequence and performing a Match Frame command. Also notice that there are no sprocket holes in the Viewer scrubber area. This also reinforces that the clip in the Viewer is not the same instance of the clip used in the sequence.

TIP ▶ There's also a Match Frame button in the Viewer. Clicking this button (or pressing F while the Viewer is active) will attempt to move the Canvas playhead to the frame currently active in the Viewer. If that frame appears more than once in the sequence, the first instance after the current sequence playhead position will be used. If that frame doesn't exist in the open sequence, Final Cut will just beep at you.

Matching Subclip Frames

You can also perform a Match Frame on a subclip; however, in that case, you can choose whether to match to the subclip or the original parent clip.

1 Position the playhead anywhere over the fourth clip (**Collision head-on**).

2 Press F to open the match frame in the Viewer.

The subclip is opened into the Viewer.

Although this can be useful in a variety of situations, you may also want to match back to the original clip.

3   Make the Timeline active, and choose View > Match Frame > Subclip Parent Clip.

The master clip is opened into the Viewer. Notice that in the scrubber area, the In and Out mark the same duration but as a smaller portion of the overall clip.

TIP   You can perform a similar match-frame-to-the-master operation when working with multiclips. You'll learn more about working with multiclips in Lesson 6.

Viewing Master Clips in the Browser

Match Frame will work even if the master clip you're looking for doesn't exist in the Browser window. For example, you may have deleted the clip from the project after placing it in the sequence, or you may have opened more than one project and dragged a clip from Project 2 into a sequence in Project 1, and so on.

If the master clip does exist in the Browser window somewhere, however, Final Cut Pro can find it.

1   Position the sequence playhead over the first clip (**ELS Rink_01**).

2   Choose View > Reveal Master Clip.

The Browser window takes focus and opens the bin containing that master clip and selects the clip.

Name	Duration	In	Out	Media Start
▼ 📁 Hockey Footage				
▶ 📁 Collision				
🎬 Crowd	00:00:02:00	19:00:00:01	19:00:02:00	19:00:00:00
🎬 ELS Rink_01	00:00:02:05	12:00:00:08	12:00:02:12	12:00:00:00
🎬 ELS Rink_02	00:00:01:02	12:00:03:14	12:00:04:15	12:00:00:00
🎬 scoreboard	00:00:01:13	02:28:40:12	02:28:42:00	02:28:39:20
🎬 Team Hug	00:00:14:02	Not Set	Not Set	03:26:12:00
▶ 📁 Las Vegas				
▼ 📁 Sequences				
📺 Gang Sync	00:00:00;00	Not Set	Not Set	01:00:00;00
📺 Match Frame	00:00:09:15	Not Set	Not Set	01:00:00:00
📺 Replace Edit	00:00:46:04	Not Set	Not Set	01:00:00:00

TIP ▸ If the bin containing the clip is open in its own tab, it will automatically be brought to the fore.

If the master clip doesn't exist in the Browser, Final Cut can automatically regenerate one for you.

3   Position the sequence playhead over the last clip.

4   Choose View > Reveal Master Clip (or press Shift-F).

A dialog appears.

5   Click OK.

The master clip is added to the Browser and selected.

This technique can be useful when you have more than one version of a clip in the Browser and you've lost track of which clip the affiliate clip in the sequence refers to.

Matching to the Source File

In some cases, rather than opening the master clip associated with the clip you're viewing, you may want to Match Frame directly to the original source clip. For example, you might do this if some parameters were modified on the master clip and you want to return to the unmodified footage.

First, you'll perform a standard Match Frame. The raw version need not be opened into your project. Final Cut Pro will look to the hard disk for the source footage and open a new version of the clip.

1   Position the sequence playhead over the fifth clip in the sequence (**ELS Rink_02**).

This clip has a Solarize filter applied, inverting the colors on the players' jerseys without affecting the ice or background.

2   Choose View > Match Frame > Master Clip (or press F).

The master clip is loaded into the Viewer, but the filter effect is still applied. This is because, in this case, the filter was applied before the clip was edited into the sequence.

3   Press Q to make the sequence active.

> **TIP** ▶ Pressing the Q shortcut key toggles focus between the Viewer and the Canvas.

4   Choose View > Match Frame > Source File (or press Command-Option-F).

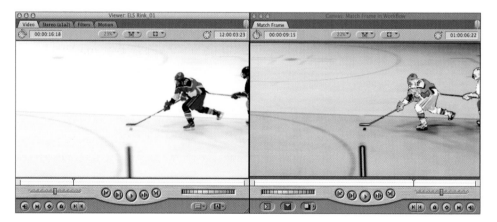

Now the original version of the clip is opened into the Viewer.

Using the Replace Edit

Overwrite and insert edits are probably second nature to you, in which you determine the edit points based on the In or Out points of the clip or the sequence. But often, the important moment in a shot isn't the first or last frame you see. Instead, the edit may hinge on a frame that happens midway through the shot, such as a lover slamming a door, a policeman shooting a gun, or a judge banging her gavel.

The replace edit allows you to make an edit based on just such an *anchor* frame, in which the In and Out points are set automatically based on the existing structure of the sequence. The replace edit is an invaluable tool for replacing a wide shot with a close-up of the same action—but without changing the timing that was already established. In another situation, you might replace a shot with itself to adjust the timing of an edit that wasn't quite working.

There are countless occasions when a replace edit is just what you need. The following sections show a few examples of how you can use it.

Replacing One Shot with Another

One of the most obvious uses of the replace edit is exchanging a shot with a different angle of the same action—without modifying the timing already established in the sequence; for example, if you have a wide shot and you instead decide to use a close-up.

1   Double-click the *Replace Edit* sequence to open it into the Canvas and Timeline.

2   Play the sequence.

   This is a comic scene about a poker game gone wrong.

3   Step frame by frame through the fifth shot, **3ShotFavorPaul**, and position your playhead on the exact frame where the chip falls into the pile (at approximately 06:14).

   This will be the anchor frame in the sequence. You don't need to set any In or Out points—just leave the playhead parked there.

4   In the Browser open the Las Vegas bin and double-click **Chip Falls Into Pot**.

5   Play the clip and park the playhead on the frame exactly where the same action happens (at approximately 47:09).

This is the anchor frame in the Viewer.

6   Drag the clip to the Canvas and drop it on Replace in the Edit Overlay.

7   Play the sequence again.

The shot is replaced, but the timing remains perfectly intact.

A replace edit doesn't base the edit on standard three-point editing rules in which In or Out points determine a clip's resulting position in the sequence. Instead, a replace edit uses the current frame in both the Viewer and the Canvas to define the edit.

Final Cut Pro will grab as many frames as are needed before and after the anchor frame to fill the duration of the clip in the sequence. If there are not enough frames before or after, the replace function won't work.

1   Reposition the sequence playhead on the same anchor, where the chip lands in the pile (06:14).

2   In the Browser, double-click **Drop chips from hand**.

3   Find the frame where the chip lands in the pile (23:04:48:16).

4 In the Viewer, drag the clip to the Canvas and drop it on Replace in the Edit Overlay (or press F11).

An error dialog warns you that there is insufficient content, which means that there aren't enough frames to replace all of the frames of the shot in the sequence.

Although the clip in the sequence is 17 frames long, and the clip in the Viewer is 18 frames long, the replace edit must match the position of the playhead in the Viewer with the playhead in the sequence. When it does that, there aren't enough frames remaining after the chip hits the pile to replace the similar frames in the sequence.

This is the most common problem that editors new to the replace edit function encounter. If you moved the playhead back a few frames in the Viewer, the replace edit would work, but you'd no longer be properly lining up the chip landing action.

Replacing Using In and Out Points

Although no In and Out points are necessary to use the replace edit, you can use sequence In and Out points to limit the effect of the replace action.

1   In the Timeline patch panel, disconnect audio a1.

2   Play forward through the new clips in the sequence, until the other poker player drops his chip into the pile.

3   Park your playhead directly on the frame where the chip hits the pile (approximately 10:08).

4   Press M to add a marker on that frame.

NOTE ▶ Although the marker isn't required, it will help ensure that you perform the edit on exactly the correct frame. While you're learning to master the replace edit, adding markers can help you keep track of anchor frames.

In this case, rather than replace the entire wide shot, you want to replace only the second half of it, without manually recalculating the precise timing already established in the sequence.

5 Enter –5 (minus five) to move the playhead backward five frames.

6 Press I to set an In point.

7 Press the Down Arrow key to move to the next edit point, and then press the Left Arrow key to step back one frame.

8 Press O to set an Out point.

9 Press Option-M to navigate to the marker you set in step 3.

Your playhead returns to the anchor frame.

10 **Drop chips from hand** should still be open in the Viewer; if it's not, use the Recent Clips pop-up menu to open it.

11 If the Viewer playhead isn't already parked on the frame where the chip lands in the pile, position it there (48:16).

TIP ▶ Marks in the Viewer will always be ignored during a replace edit.

12 Perform the replace edit.

In this case, the replace edit lines up the playheads, but limits the edit to the In and Out points set in the sequence. (In this case, you could even have omitted the Out point, and the end of the clip would have been used.)

13 In the Timeline patch panel, reconnect audio source a1 to track A1.

> **TIP** ▸ It's not necessary for the anchor frame to be within the In and Out points. This means you could use any frame anywhere in the shot to sync on, but replace an entirely different section. This expands the versatility of the replace edit enormously.

Replacing a Shot with Itself

Another common use for the replace edit is to quickly adjust the timing of a shot by temporarily loading a clip into the Viewer, adjusting the timing, and replacing the shot on top of itself.

1 Press End to jump to the end of the *Replace Edit* sequence.

2 Back up a few shots and watch the edit.

In the last shot, the girl's dialogue was edited to speed up the edit. This is frequently done with an *OTS* (over the shoulder) shot, but the timing seems slightly off. The girl makes a strong shrugging gesture that ought to coincide with the moment when she says, "…keep it DOWN?"

3 Play this part of the sequence again and find the frame right where she says "down" (approximately 41:15).

This will be your anchor in the sequence.

4 Press F to perform a Match Frame, opening the master clip into the Viewer.

5 In the Viewer, move the playhead to the apex of her shrug action (approximately 22:38:42:20).

6 Perform a replace edit (F11).

An error dialog appears warning that all target items need to be linked. This is because the audio under the playhead is from a different clip from the one you're replacing.

7 Click the a1 Source control to untarget that track, so only the video track is targeted.

8 Perform the replace edit again.

Nothing appears to be different in the Timeline, but the clip has replaced itself, and the timing of the shot has been improved.

9 Play the end of the sequence.

The shrug now lines up with the dialogue, and the edit feels much more natural.

Ganging the Playheads

One of the most common editing situations you'll encounter is when you have multiple angles of the same action, and over the course of the scene, you cut back and forth between those shots. The most familiar example of this is a typical dialogue scene, in which you have matching OTS shots or matching *singles* showing two sides of a conversation.

When building such a sequence, you can take advantage of the Final Cut Pro Gang Sync feature, which locks the playhead position of the Viewer to that of the Canvas and Timeline. That way, as you play forward (or backward) in one window, the playhead moves by the same number of frames in the others.

Once you establish a place where the Viewer and Canvas are in sync, you can lock that position, *ganging* the playheads together. As long as the action in both the sequence and the Viewer follows the same timing, you can freely edit pieces of the clip in the Viewer into the sequence and trust that they'll always remain in sync.

Although this may seem confusing in theory, it's extremely easy to do in practice and can be a huge timesaver.

1   Open the *Gang Sync* sequence.

2   Play the scene to get familiar with it.

    This sequence has begun to be edited, but it's fairly obvious that more editing is required to make full sense of the story. Because, like most dialogue scenes, the performance in each of the shots has (nearly) identical timing, this is a perfect opportunity to take advantage of the Gang Sync feature.

3   Position the sequence playhead anywhere over the first clip (**MCU Kerry_02**).

4   Press F to perform a Match Frame, opening the master clip into the Viewer.

At this point the Canvas and Viewer are obviously in sync (they're showing the exact same frame), so this is a good time to gang their playheads together.

5   In either the Canvas or the Viewer, click the Playhead Sync pop-up menu and choose Gang.

The icon in the Playhead Sync pop-up menu changes to show two parallel playheads enclosed in a box, indicating the Gang state.

6   Play the sequence until after Kerry says, "…don't mind if I sit down for a minute." (at approx 12:00).

This is an appropriate point to cut back to the OTS shot of Kerry.

7   Set an In point in the sequence.

The Viewer playhead has been moving along with the Canvas playhead, so it's already in the exact position for the In point.

8   Press Command-1 to make the Viewer window active.

> **TIP**   You can also press Q to toggle between the Viewer and Canvas windows.

9   Press I to set an In point in the Viewer.

10 Play forward until after the man says, "What are you writing, a book?" as he's taking the comic book back, and set an Out point there (at approximately 28:18).

11 Perform an overwrite edit.

12 Review the edit you just made.

You'll see that the timing of the edit is near-perfect.

> **TIP** When working with Gang Sync, you'll probably have to finesse most of the edits after the assembly is complete, but it's still one of the quickest ways to build a rough cut.

Because of the ganged playheads, you could make the edit just about anywhere and be assured that the clips will remain in close sync and the timing will be accurate. You can use any combination of three-point edits.

13 In the Sequence, play forward until after Kerry says, "super-jock," and set an In point there (around 25:00).

14 Play forward in the sequence until after Kerry says, "Where were you born?" at approximately 31:20 and set an Out point.

15 Press Q to switch to the Viewer.

The next step is extra-important. Because there were already In and Out points marked from the last edit, if you don't clear them you could accidentally edit the wrong portion of the clip into the sequence.

16 Press Option-X to clear the In and Out points.

17 Press O to set an Out point on the current frame.

TIP ▶ You needed to clear only the In point, because you set a new Out point, but it's good practice to always clear the points when working with ganged sequences to prevent you from ever accidentally editing the wrong section.

Now you once again have three points marked and so you're ready to edit the clip into the sequence.

18 Press F10 to overwrite the clip.

19 Play the sequence.

You've just added another clip to the sequence and you didn't even have to watch it in the Viewer! Because of the nature of dramatic coverage you can trust that the clips will line up (at least approximately).

Skipping the time-consuming steps of lining up the action in both Viewer and Canvas for each edit will speed your workflow dramatically. However, this method isn't magic.

If the performance in the two shots was different, even by a small amount, the new edit wouldn't be picture-perfect.

Nonetheless, ganging your playheads is a great way to take advantage of the similar timing in your shots, and it allows you to make a quick rough cut with little effort. This way you can rough your shots into the sequence with incredible speed, and you can use the Trim tools described in the next lesson to finesse and clean up the edits with frame-by-frame precision.

Lesson Review

1. What happens when you drag multiple clips into the Viewer?
2. What is the maximum number of clips you can show in the Recent Clips pop-up menu?
3. Does Match Frame load a clip from the Timeline into the Viewer?
4. How do you Match Frame to the clip's source file (instead of the master clip)?
5. When is a replace edit useful?
6. True or false: Replace editing observes three-point editing rules.
7. True or false: Replace editing will work as long as the new clip is longer than the clip being replaced.
8. True or false: Gang Sync locks the Canvas playhead to the Timeline playhead.
9. Gang Sync is most useful with what kind of footage?

Answers

1. The first clip is loaded into the Viewer, and the rest are placed into the Recent Clips pop-up menu.
2. 20.
3. No. Match Frame loads the master clip of a Timeline clip into the Viewer.
4. Press Command-Option-F.
5. When you want to perform an edit based on a frame between a clip's In and Out points.
6. Partially true: In and Out points in the Canvas are observed, but Viewer In and Out points are always ignored.
7. False: Even if the new clip is longer, there must be adequate frames before the playhead position to accommodate the In point, and after the playhead to accommodate the Out point.
8. False: Gang Sync locks the Canvas playhead to the Viewer playhead (the Canvas and Timeline playheads are *always* locked together).
9. Scenes in which you cut back and forth between multiple angles of the same action.

3

Lesson Files Lesson Files > Lesson_03 > Trimming_Concepts.fcp

Media Genesis Code_College Bar

Time This lesson takes approximately 60 minutes to complete.

Goals Master the Ripple and Roll concepts

Trim clips from the keyboard

Trim clips numerically

Use Extend Edit to roll an edit to the playhead

Split edits to hide edit points

Make complex trim operations using the Slip and Slide tools

Trimming Concepts

For most endeavors, the first 80 percent of the job takes only 20 percent of the time. That is to say, the last little bit of work—the finessing, refining, polishing, and so on—typically uses up a vast majority of the hours required to complete a project. Editing is a perfect example of this.

Roughing out a sequence typically happens very quickly (especially after you've mastered the techniques described in Lessons 1 and 2). Once you've roughed out your sequence, you can watch your program and get a feel for how it will look.

But that doesn't mean you're finished. You'll likely spend far more time tweaking and adjusting each of the edits in your show than you spent assembling that rough cut. This is what *trimming* refers to: the painstaking, detail-oriented, mind-numbing work of ensuring that each edit is perfect.

In some ways, trimming is very different from assembling. It uses a different part of your brain and requires that you pay attention to different aspects of your footage from those that preoccupied you during the first pass. An individual trimming task may seem unimportant; and yet, if one edit is off by a mere five frames, it can disrupt the flow of a scene, which in turn can sour an entire sequence and, by extension, undermine the flow and feeling of the whole show.

The Dynamic Art

Like most aspects of Final Cut Pro, using the trimming tools is not difficult to do, but understanding how and when to employ the myriad controls can be daunting.

Most trimming follows a predictable pattern: First, you *ripple* one or both sides of the edit point to get the timing to seem natural. Then, you *roll* the edit point, looking for the transitional moment that best hides the cut. Often, you roll the video or audio elements separately to create a split edit. Because these techniques are highly subjective (and typically gauged by nothing more than "feel"), it's very common to try a variety of approaches before settling on one.

The best and most useful advice about trimming is to *make your edit decisions while the video is playing*. It can be useful to study the symmetries or contrasting compositions of the frames at your edit point, but there's no substitute for experiencing the scene in exactly the way the audience will: moving by at 24 frames per second (or whatever your frame rate may be). Good edits are invisible; bad edits are jarring. It's nearly impossible to sense how successful an edit is until you see it in context.

The creators of Final Cut Pro understood this and developed a vast array of playback controls to facilitate playing your sequence in a wide range of contexts. Furthermore, there are many techniques and tools designed specifically for making edits while the sequence is playing. This lesson will familiarize you with these controls, get you thinking dynamically, and teach how you can make all of your edits on the fly. This type of editing is not only efficient and accurate; it's also exhilarating and fun.

Understanding Basic Trimming

The basis of all trimming is the ripple and roll functions. In order to master all of the more advanced types of trimming covered in this and the following lessons, you must have a complete and thorough understanding of these basics.

First of all, it might help to review the difference between rippling and rolling. Both are ways of changing the duration of a clip in the Timeline without creating any gaps, or needing to move other clips out of the way.

Rippling Edits

Rippling adds or subtracts frames from a clip, automatically moving all of the *downstream* clips right (for added frames) or left (for subtracted frames).

Before

After

Rippling the outgoing clip (the clip on the left side of the edit) is pretty straightforward; adding or subtracting frames from the end of the clip makes the right edge of the clip move to the right or the left. But you can also ripple the incoming clip, adding or taking frames away from the start of a shot. Some people find this more confusing, because the starting point of the clip doesn't change in the Timeline, even though the shot is getting longer or shorter. Instead the change in the clip's duration affects the clips downstream.

Before

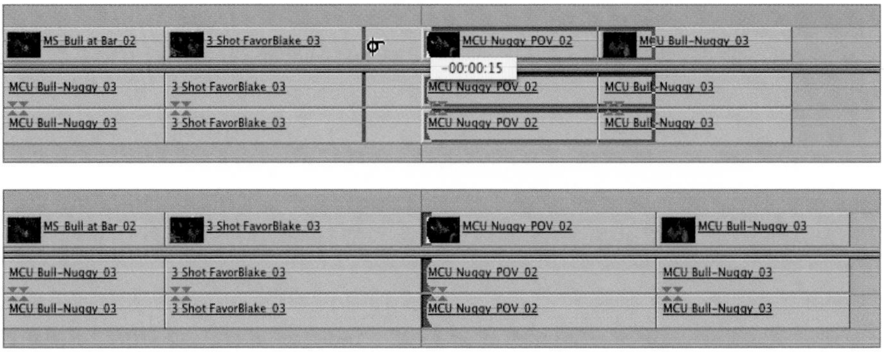

After

It's very important to understand that when you ripple a clip, you change the duration of the overall sequence. Everything downstream from the edit you're manipulating moves in time to accommodate the change. As long as none of the tracks are locked, everything will remain in relative sync, but by definition, rippling does affect the entire sequence.

Rolling Edits

Rolling an edit is a bit simpler visually, but is actually doing a more complex edit. When you roll an edit, as you add frames to one clip, the same number of frames is subtracted from the adjacent clip.

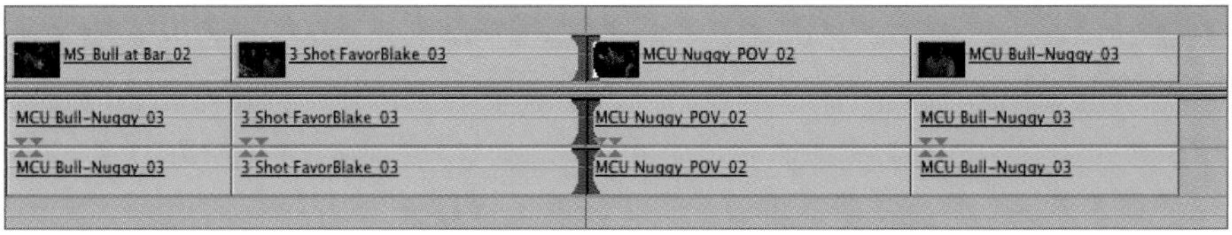

Before

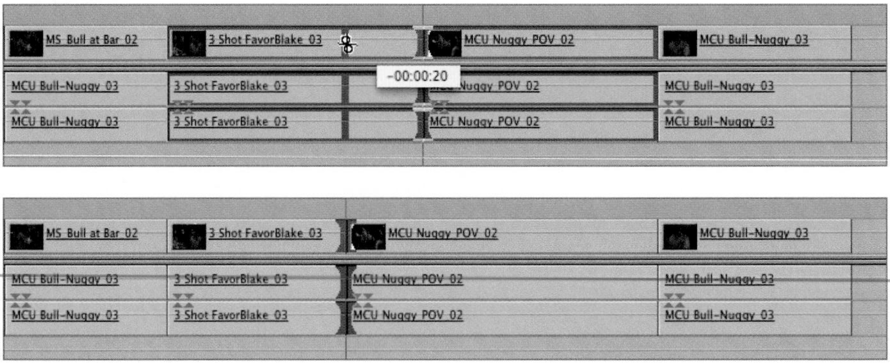

After

Unlike a ripple edit, with a rolling edit, the overall sequence duration doesn't change. You simply move one edit point's location in time. Whatever frames you add or take away from one clip are compensated for in the adjacent clip.

Furthermore, rolling never changes the timing of an edit, so if the action doesn't match already, rolling it will just make the mismatched timing happen in a new place.

Trimming in Practice

Both rippling and rolling are very efficient ways of working because they allow you to manipulate a specific edit without disturbing the rest of the sequence. Doing a simple ripple edit using the Blade tool would require no fewer than five steps, whereas with the Ripple tool, you can do it with a single drag.

But nothing will help you master these tools like putting them into action.

1   Open Lesson Files > Lesson_03 > **Trimming_Concepts.fcp**.

The *1. Basic Trimming* sequence should be open.

2   Play the sequence.

These two shots contain a simple action that serves as the cut point: two players exchanging a high-five. This is a very typical edit, and it has a very typical problem. The timing is slightly off, so there's an overlap of action.

3   Press the Up Arrow key or the Down Arrow key to move the sequence playhead to the edit point.

4   Press \ (backslash) to play around the edit.

Play Around is an essential tool to use while trimming, and you can customize how far before and after the current position it will play.

5   Choose Final Cut Pro > User Preferences, and then click the Editing tab.

User Preferences

General	Editing	Labels	Timeline Options	Render Control	Audio Outputs

Still/Freeze Duration: 00:00:10:00	☐ Dynamic Trimming
Preview Pre-roll: 00:00:02:00	☑ Trim with Sequence Audio
Preview Post-roll: 00:00:01:00	☐ Trim with Edit Selection Audio (Mute Others)
	Multi-Frame Trim Size: 5 frames

The Preview Pre-roll and Preview Post-roll settings default to 5 seconds before and 2 seconds after the current position. Although for slower-moving shows a 5-second pre-roll is useful, it can be far too long for quick-cut shows, and if it crosses over multiple edits, the pre-roll can prove more distracting than helpful.

6   Change the Preview Pre-roll value to *2:00*, the Preview Post-roll value to *1:00*, and click OK.

7   Play around the edit again.

With the shorter pre- and post-roll, you can focus more sharply on the edit point. And when you watch the edit, what do you see? The hands are slapped in the first shot and then again in the second shot.

In fact, the action is interrupted; the slap begins in the first shot, but isn't completed. Then, in the second shot, the whole action is repeated.

TIP ▶ Percussive actions like this are a great boon for an editor looking for a good place to cut. Always scan your raw footage for such events.

This is a perfect time to whip out the Ripple tool to add or remove frames from one shot without changing the duration of the other.

This task will be made even easier if you display the audio waveforms.

8   Press Command-Option-W to show audio waveforms in the Timeline and zoom in on the edit point.

Hand slap in outgoing clip   Hand slap in incoming clip

The waveform representing the sound of the hands slapping is visible in both shots.

9   Ripple the incoming shot to the right until the beginning of the clip lines up with the sound of the slap (3 frames).

10 Play around the edit.

The timing of the edit should now be perfect, but putting the cut precisely on the apex of the action draws unnecessary attention to the edit.

This is easily alleviated with the Roll tool. Because you've already established accurate timing, you can roll the edit as far as you want in either direction, and the timing within the scene will remain correct.

11 Press R to select the Roll tool.

12 Drag the edit to the right about 7–8 frames.

13 Play around the edit.

14 Drag the edit to the left about 12–14 frames and play around the edit there.

Although this position works visibly, it cuts off part of Blake's dialogue. This could be remedied by *splitting* the edit as described later in this lesson.

15 Experiment with different positions for the edit until you find one you like.

> **TIP** Editors most often choose to put the cut slightly before the action. That way, the viewer is so focused on the movement within the frame that by the time the action is complete, the edit has already happened, and the viewer didn't even notice.

Trimming from the Keyboard

Dragging the edges of clips is great if you want to get a tactile feel for the way trimming works, but it's probably the most inefficient way to trim. Because it's so important to make these decisions while the video is playing, the less often you have to stop playback to make the edit, the better. This is why learning a handful of essential keyboard shortcuts can vastly improve your performance.

Trimming from the keyboard is very easy. In fact, there are really only four keys you need to add to your arsenal of memorized shortcuts:

▶ V—Select edit

▶ U—Toggle edit type (ripple/roll)

▶ [(left bracket)—Trim one frame left

▶] (right bracket)—Trim one frame right

That's it! Of course, you'll also use a few shortcuts you already know. Most important is the \ (backslash) key to play around the edit and see the work you've done.

It's also vital to be able to tell at a glance whether an edit is selected as a ripple outgoing, a roll, or a ripple incoming.

Ripple outgoing   Roll   Ripple incoming

1   In the Browser, double-click the *2. More Trimming* sequence and play it.

    This is an expanded version of the same scene, and if you examine it you'll likely find several edits that need adjusting. Probably the most egregious is the one right in the middle where "Bull" is giving the nuggy.

2   Press the Up Arrow key or the Down Arrow key to navigate to the fifth edit, between **MCU Nuggy_POV_02** and **MCU Bull-Nuggy_03**.

3 Press \ (backslash) to play around the edit and figure out what you're going to do to fix it.

The problem is that Bull's arm is still above the guy's head before the edit, and it's already at his side after. Some frames need to be added to cover the missing action, and it's up to you to decide whether to add them to the outgoing clip or to the incoming clip (or both). Any of these solutions might work.

TIP ▶ Often the best solution may involve modifying both clips.

4 Press V to select the edit.

NOTE ► By default, selecting an edit always selects it as a roll. This is good because a roll is generally less destructive than a ripple. On the other hand, you generally want to ripple your edit to fix the timing before you roll it.

5   Press U twice to toggle the edit to a ripple outgoing.

Each time you press U, the way the edit is selected cycles among three states: roll, ripple incoming, and ripple outgoing. If you'd like, press U a few more times to see the state change. Make sure you return to the ripple outgoing selection.

6   Press] (right bracket) a few times to add frames to the outgoing clip.

If you press Shift-], you'll add five frames instead of one.

TIP ► You can customize your system so Shift-] will add up to 99 frames by changing the Multi-Frame Trim Size setting in the Editing tab of User Preferences.

TIP ► You can also simply hold down] (right bracket) and the edit will move along in near-real time.

7   Play around the edit by pressing \ (backslash) and keep adding frames and playing around until the timing feels right (about 11 frames). If you go too far, press [(left bracket) to move the edit point left.

Unfortunately, no matter where you place the edit, there's still a problem. The actor didn't repeat the performance exactly, so even though the timing is approximately right, the edit still looks wrong, because his arm rests in a different position.

In this case, it may be better to add frames to the incoming shot instead.

8 Press Undo to return the edit to its original position (or simply ripple left the same number of frames you rippled right).

9 Press U twice to switch the edit selection to ripple incoming.

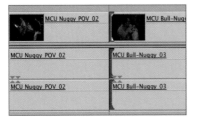

10 Press [(left bracket) until Bull's arm is back on top of Tim's head (about 14 frames).

11 Play around the edit frequently until you're satisfied with the edit.

> **TIP** Once you get the timing right, you can stop, but it's wise to keep working to make sure you've made the best edit possible. Every frame you change means compromising one thing or another and it's up to you to make the judgment call as to the best choice.

Because you established the timing using the ripple, you can roll to just about any position and the timing will remain accurate. However, rolling to different positions will produce different effects.

12 Press U to toggle the edit to a roll.

13 Press the bracket keys to experiment with different edit positions, and play around the edit frequently to "feel" the new edit.

> 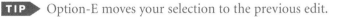 The technique employed in the first exercise is a great way to ensure accurate timing. That is, you add and remove frames from both shots until the action happens precisely on the edit, and then roll it for a less obvious cut.

Using Numerical Trimming

As you get even more comfortable with trimming, and when you're doing quite a bit of it, you'll be able to watch an edit and immediately have a sense of how many frames it needs to be adjusted by. In this case, rather than tapping the bracket keys repeatedly, you can simply enter a number to perform a trim by a precise number of frames.

The best aspect of numerical trimming is that no special mode or field entry is necessary. As soon as you type a number, or press the + (plus) or – (minus) key, Final Cut Pro automatically interprets that entry as a trimming instruction and applies the edit based on the current selection. If the edit is selected as a roll, the numbers will perform a roll edit. If the edit is selected as a ripple, you'll get a ripple edit. It's entirely context-sensitive. You'll see later that you can do the same thing with the Slip and Slide tools, and even with selected clips.

1 Press Shift-E to move the playhead to the next edit in the sequence between **MCU Bull-Nuggy_03** and **MS_Bull at Bar_02**.

> **TIP** Option-E moves your selection to the previous edit.

Notice that the edit selection moves along with you, so you don't need to reselect the edit point. This is because Final Cut Pro anticipates that you'll employ the common workflow of roughing all of your shots into the sequence, and then walk through them one by one, finessing each with the trim tools.

> **TIP** You can also use the Up Arrow and Down Arrow keys to navigate from selected edit to selected edit.

2   Play around this edit.

This is a very challenging edit. In this case, just getting the timing right may still result in a sort of jump cut, because the camera angles are so similar.

> **TIP** To avoid jump cuts, make sure the new shot is a clearly different framing from the previous shot. This is sometimes called the 30-degree rule: Make sure the new shot is at least 30° different along any axis (height, angle, zoom, and so on).

It may be possible to get a clean edit somewhere in the middle of Bull's exit, but a more guaranteed solution would be to end the first clip just as Bull exits the frame, and begin the second clip after Tim has been panned out of the frame. That way you're essentially cutting from a single of Tim to a single of Bull.

3 Press U to toggle to a ripple outgoing edit.

4 Type *+10*.

An information box appears in the Timeline, identifying the type of edit and the value you entered.

5 Press Enter (or Return) to perform the edit.

6 Play around to see the result.

The timing of the edit is still clearly off. Type a new number, positive or negative.

> **TIP** ▶ You don't actually need to bother typing the plus sign. Any positive number will move the edit to the right, and any negative number will move it left.

You can also press U to toggle to ripple incoming and adjust that side of the edit.

7 Press U to toggle to ripple incoming, type *18*, and then press Enter.

8 Play around the edit to see the result.

9 Continue experimenting with different edits by typing different numbers and playing around until the timing feels as good as it's going to get.

Remember, this is a challenging real-world example. You may have to try a variety of positions before you find one you're comfortable with.

10 Once the timing feels right, switch to a roll, type *5*, and then press Enter.

11 Play around the edit.

12 Type *–10* to move five frames before the original edit.

13 Play around again.

And so on. Bouncing back and forth like that helps you decide exactly where the best option for the edit is. You can continue to explore different positions for the edit until you find one that best tells the story of these particular shots.

TIP ▶   It's important to occasionally step back and play a longer section of your sequence. For example, if you had moved the previous edit too far to the right, moving this edit to the left could result in a very short clip in between. You need to consult the big picture to get a sense of the overall pacing of the scene.

Extending Edits

Now that you're comfortable with the trimming process, one more shortcut should further encourage you to make your editing decisions while the video is playing.

Rather than tapping the bracket keys or a specific number, playing around the edit, and then repeating this process over and over again, you can play the sequence and automatically roll the edit point to the current playhead position in one step. This is called an Extend Edit, and the keyboard shortcut is E.

1   Select the third edit in the sequence, between **MS_Bull at Bar_02** and **3 Shot FavorBlake_03**.

2   Zoom in on the Timeline and make sure the edit is selected as a roll.

3 Play around the edit.

This edit doesn't have any huge problems, but just before the edit, Bull raises his arm, and it's a little distracting. You should probably either include the whole action of him wiping his face, or cut before his arm begins to move.

4 Play the sequence until the playhead is just before the arm move begins.

5 Press E to roll (or *extend*) the edit to the current playhead position.

6 Play around the new edit.

The edit is much less distracting now.

This saves a little time, but the real power of the Extend Edit is that it enables you to make your edit decision entirely while playing. In fact, you don't even have to stop playback to use it.

7 Press the Down Arrow key (or Shift-E) to move the edit selection to the next edit (between **3 Shot FavorBlake_03** and **MCU Nuggy_POV_02**).

This edit is also fine, but there is a bit of a pause after we cut back to Bull, before he starts moving.

8 Press L to play the sequence forward, and then while it's playing, just before he begins to move, press E to roll the edit to that frame.

9 Play around the new edit.

> **TIP** ▶ Don't panic if you don't get the edit exactly right. You can always undo, or just play in the other direction and extend again.

Eventually, you'll get a feel for the technique and you'll be comfortable rolling your edits on the fly. Extend will always operate on the selected edit and only performs a roll. If the edit is selected as a ripple, pressing E will have no effect.

Extend works best with longer clips. The one caveat is that Extend will allow you to roll one edit right over another.

Before

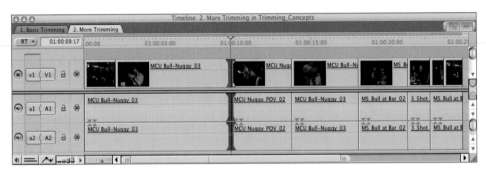

After

This allows you to completely eliminate a clip in your sequence, which is entirely appropriate in some instances. But if you do such an edit (and you didn't intend to), you can always undo it and return to the previous state.

Splitting Edits

Another way you can improve your edits with trimming is to use the Roll tool to offset the audio and video so they don't change at the same time, thereby creating a *split* edit. Remember, one of the fundamental goals of editing is to convey new information in a new shot without drawing undue attention to the change in framing required by an edit. In other words: Make the edits invisible. One of the most effective ways to do this is to split your edits.

An edit can be split in two ways. The audio can lead the video, creating a *J cut*, or the video can lead the audio, commonly called an *L cut*.

J cut   L cut

TIP ▶ J cuts tend to be much more common than L cuts, and for a good reason. In the real world, hearing a noise often prompts you to turn your head to see the source of the sound. If a viewer hears an offscreen sound in a film, she instinctively wants to turn her head to see what caused the noise. If the editor creates such a trigger with an audio cut, and then follows it with a video cut, the whole transition is hidden from the viewer, who is busy reconciling the sound and the picture.

1   Open and play the *3. Split Edits* sequence.

This is another version of the same scene with the previous exercises already completed.

2   Press A to make sure you have the Selection tool selected.

3   Play the sequence and find the spot where we cut to Blake and the two women snickering (at 7:00).

There are actually two things going on here that can both be resolved by creating a simple J cut.

First of all, Tim's line gets cut off. He says "I got your…" but the edit cuts him off before he can say "back." Also, the cut to the laughing friends feels a bit abrupt because we're cutting to them at the exact second we hear them begin to snicker.

By rolling the audio back, we can cover up the "I got your…" line, plus, we'll hear the laughter before we see who's laughing, creating a perfect, natural split edit that drives the story and engages the audience.

> **TIP** ▶ Remember, once you've used the ripple to get your basic edit timing right, you can generally roll with impunity—the action will always be smooth across edits.

4 Option-click to override the linked selection and select only the audio edit.

5 Press J to play the sequence backwards, and just before Tim says "I," press E (at approximately 6:03).

The edit is rolled to the playhead position.

6 Play around the edit.

The improvement should be quite evident.

There's another edit in this sequence that could benefit from being split: the high-five cut you played with earlier in the lesson.

7 Play the sequence to the end and watch the edit around the hand-slap a few times.

Right now, the slap comes in the first shot, which is acceptable, but as recommended earlier, it's often preferable to put a percussive action like this just *after* the cut, thereby holding your viewers' attention past the potentially distracting edit.

In this case, you can't simply roll the edit earlier because it would cut off Blake's "Thanks, Bull" line. But you can roll just the video, creating a J-cut that can greatly improve the sequence.

8   Zoom in on the edit between **3_Shot_FavorBlake_01** and **MS_Bull at Bar_02**.

9   With the Arrow tool, Option-click the video edit to select it without the linked audio clips.

10   Roll the clip to the left by 10–12 frames using any of the trimming techniques you've already learned.

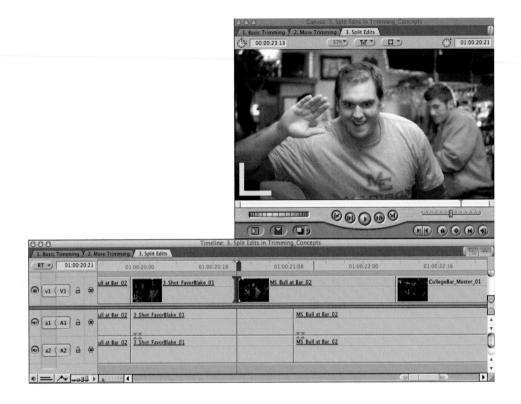

11   Play around the sequence.

The improvement is subtle, but not insignificant. The continuity of audio under the cut helps to hold the viewer's attention while the visuals are changing significantly, making the whole section seem smoother and more engaging.

You can probably see how you can quickly walk through almost any scene and split many edits in your show. And you should. Splits edits are just as appropriate for documentaries or training videos as they are for dramatic scenes.

Using Slip and Slide

Ripple and roll are powerful tools that allow you to perform multiple steps in a single operation. (Think about how many steps it would take to make split edits using the Razor Blade and track selection tools!) In that sense, slip and slide are even more impressive. These tools allow you to perform *two* roll or ripple edits in a single operation.

Slipping Clips

Slip simultaneously performs a ripple edit on both the incoming and outgoing edges of the same clip. This has the effect of changing the In and Out points of a clip in a sequence without modifying its duration or changing any of the surrounding clips.

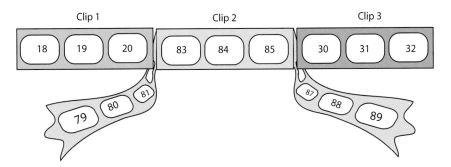

It's as if the media for the clip is *slipped* underneath the clip's position in the sequence.

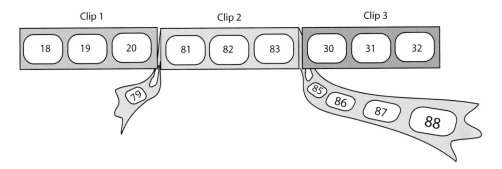

So, for example, in the preceding figures, clip 2 has been slipped by two frames. Its position in the sequence hasn't changed, and clips 1 and 3 haven't been affected, but different frames from clip 2's source footage are being used.

 The Slip tool never has an effect on the overall length of a sequence.

This is exactly what would happen if you rippled the incoming edge of the clip by two frames and then rippled the outgoing edge by the same amount.

1   Open and play the *4. Slip and Slide* sequence.

Again, this is an updated version of the same sequence.

2   Navigate to around 8:00 where Blake and his friends are snickering. Play around that area.

In this shot, Blake briefly looks up at Bull, but then looks back down before the end of the shot. The action of him looking up at Bull is actually a great motivation for a cut. Whenever a person looks offscreen, some part of the viewer's brain is wondering, "What's he looking at?" As an editor, it's your job to answer that question.

NOTE ▶ This shot has been flopped to make the screen direction appear correct throughout the sequence. For more on flopping a shot, see Lesson 8, "Mastering Filters."

Here you can use that eyeline shift to motivate the cut.

TIP ▶ Like percussive actions, eyeline changes are another of the things a trained editor learns to look for in her footage. Cutting on a look is one of the best ways to hide an edit.

3   Press S to select the Slip tool.

4   Drag the clip to the right about 22 frames.

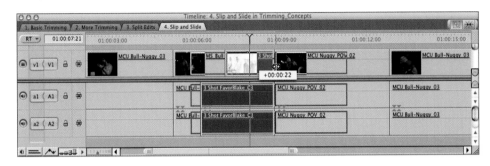

TIP ▶ You may want to press N to disable snapping so you can make more precise adjustments.

As you drag, feedback in the Canvas shows you the new In and Out points for the clip. Also, the Timeline shows the duration of the raw footage, so you can see which part of the raw source you're using.

Dragging to the right moves Blake's look to later in time; dragging to the left makes the look occur earlier.

5   Position the clip so the last frame (the frame visible on the right side of the Canvas) is the last frame before Blake looks back down.

TIP ▶ For this example make sure Linked Selection is on, so you're slipping both audio and video clips. Otherwise you can slip something right out of sync.

6   Play around the section to see how the change improves the sequence.

TIP ▶ You could have accomplished a similar edit using the Ripple tool, or in a number of other ways. One of the best reasons to use the Slip tool is that it doesn't disturb anything in the rest of the sequence. For that reason Slip (and Slide too) are typically used late in the editing process after the picture is nearly locked.

Sliding Clips

Slide is similar to slip, but it's generally used for a very different purpose. Sliding a clip is similar to the effect of rolling both its starting and ending edits by the same number of frames, although with a slide, the clip in the center is left untouched. Technically, what's happening is that each of the clips *before* and *after* your clip are being rippled.

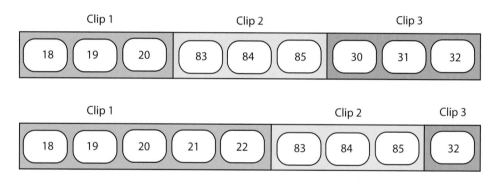

Whereas slip changes the content within a shot, slide changes the two shots surrounding a shot but leaves the shot itself unchanged. When sliding, you change the position of a shot without changing the rest of the sequence. This approach is most often employed on cutaways or B-roll footage.

1   Play the sequence a bit further.

A close-up of Kerry's reaction has been added to better smooth that awkward edit after the nuggy when Bull leaves Tim alone, but the timing of it isn't quite right.

2   Press SS to select the Slide tool.

3   Drag the **MCU_Kerry_02** clip to the left by about 12 frames.

TIP ▶ You may have to disable snapping (N) to effectively slide the clip by that number of frames.

The Canvas shows a two-up display, but this time it shows the two frames that are changing—the last frame of the preceding clip and the first frame of the following one.

4   Play around the new edit.

Slipping and Sliding from the Keyboard

Using the Slip or Slide tool you can drag to perform the edit, but when you release the mouse button the clip won't stay selected. You can also press the bracket keys to slip and slide one frame at a time, or directly enter a number; but in order to use these keyboard shortcuts, you need the clip to remain selected.

1   With the Slide tool still active, hold down Shift and click the **MCU_Kerry_02** clip.

Holding down the Shift key enables you to select the clip. After it's selected, you can slide it using keyboard shortcuts.

2   Press [and] (left bracket and right bracket) to slide the clip left and right.

As you might expect, holding down Shift allows you to slide by five frames (or by whatever number is set in the User Preferences, as described earlier in this lesson).

TIP ▶ It's very important to know which tool is currently active. After a clip is selected, the active tool (Slip or Slide) determines what happens when you use the trimming keyboard shortcuts.

You can also slip or slide numerically.

3   Press S to activate the Slip tool.

4   Type *–10*, and press Enter (or Return).

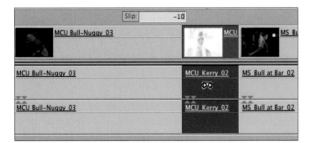

The clip is slipped by 10 frames.

Lesson Review

1. What's the most important advice about trimming?

2. Which is generally done first: rippling or rolling?

3. How do you control the amount of pre- and post-roll used when performing a Play Around function?

4. What five keys are essential to trimming from the keyboard and what are their functions?

5. True or false: Extend Edit can ripple an edit in either direction.

6. What is a split edit?

7. Why are split edits used?

8. Is a slip edit the same as two ripple edits or two roll edits?

Answers

1. Make your trimming decisions while the video is playing.

2. Rippling is typically done before rolling.

3. In the Editing tab of the User Preferences window.

4. V selects the nearest edit; U toggles the edit selection type; [and] (left bracket and right bracket) perform the trim one frame at a time; and \ (backslash) plays around the current playhead position.

5. False. Extend Edit rolls an edit in either direction.

6. A split edit is an edit where the audio and video edits happen on different frames.

7. Split edits significantly soften the jarring nature inherent in a cut, thereby making an edit point more "invisible."

8. A slip edit is the same as two ripple edits of the same amount on the beginning and end of the same clip.

4

Lesson Files	Lesson Files > Lesson_04 > Advanced_Trimming.fcp
Media	Poker
Time	This lesson takes approximately 60 minutes to complete.
Goals	Familiarize yourself with the Trim Edit window
	Learn different ways of trimming edits
	Use dynamic trimming
	Trim clips across multiple tracks
	Perform asymmetrical trims to maintain sync

Advanced Trimming Techniques

By now, you probably appreciate how powerful and essential Final Cut Pro's trimming tools are. Trimming is one of the most intensive aspects of the editing process, but with mastery of the tools it can be easy, and even fun. Still, no matter how you splice it, you're going to be trimming for quite a long time on each project. Although simple tasks like those in the last lesson are straightforward, you are likely to encounter more complicated scenarios.

Fortunately, Final Cut Pro is capable of far more sophisticated trimming techniques, and it includes a special interface just for trimming: the Trim Edit window.

Using the Trim Edit Window

The Trim Edit window is like a zoomed-in view on a single edit point. The left side of the window shows the outgoing clip, and the right side shows the incoming clip. The scrubber bars under each clip display provide essential information not available in the Timeline, such as how many frames are available beyond the current In or Out points.

You can also view the sections of either clip that lie beyond the edit points, which can be invaluable in determining the precise positioning of an edit. The J, K, and L keys not only control playback of each clip; when dynamic trimming is enabled, those keys perform trims.

1   Open Lesson Files > Lesson_04 > **Advanced_Trimming.fcp.** The sequence *Las Vegas Trimming* should be open in the Timeline. Play the sequence.

    This is another version of the sequence you used in Lesson 2.

2   Navigate to around 25 seconds into the sequence, where the players all get up from the table.

This is a great real-world scenario where all of these edits can be improved with a bit of fine trimming.

3   Using the Selection tool, double-click the edit point at 25:18, between **CU Paul 2-3** and **HH Fight angle2 15-2**.

Double-clicking an edit point selects it and automatically opens the Trim Edit window. By default, that window opens directly on top of the Viewer and the Canvas, and because it looks so similar, you might not even notice that anything happened.

Double-clicking the edit in the Timeline with the Selection tool selects the edit as a roll. If you double-click with the Ripple tool, the Trim Edit window will still open, but the edit will be selected as a ripple (based on whichever side you clicked).

TIP ▸ You can also press Command-7 to open the Trim Edit window. The nearest edit to the playhead will be selected as a roll.

In the Trim Edit window, the green bars above the video windows indicate which type of edit is selected. Currently, both sides are lit up green.

4   Press U three times to cycle through the edit selection states and observe the green bars in the Trim Edit window.

TIP ▸ You can also click the Trim Edit window directly to select the edit type. Clicking either window selects that side of the edit as a ripple, and clicking in the middle selects a roll. The pointer will change to indicate which edit type will be selected depending on your pointer position.

With the J, K, and L keys, you can navigate the clips in the Trim Edit window, but which clip they control is based on the edit type. If the edit is set to ripple outgoing, the J, K, and L keys will always control the outgoing clip. If it's set to ripple incoming, those keys will control that clip. When the edit is set to a roll, the keys will control whichever side your pointer is positioned over.

5 Position the pointer anywhere over the outgoing (left) clip. Don't click.

6 Press L or J to play the clip.

The clip on the left plays.

7 Press K (or the spacebar) to stop playback.

8 Position the pointer anywhere over the incoming (right) clip. Don't click.

9 Use J, K, and L to navigate through that clip.

This can be a little confusing, because nothing else in Final Cut Pro works merely because your pointer happens to be placed in one part of the screen. Once you get the hang of it, however, you'll find it a quick and efficient way to work.

10 Stop playback by pressing K, then press the spacebar.

Unlike in the Viewer or Canvas, in the Trim Edit window, pressing the spacebar performs the play around function—and regardless of the global looping setting, in the Trim Edit window, play around *always* loops.

11 Press the spacebar again to stop playback.

Part of the reason that playback always loops in the Trim Edit window is to enable you to make edits while the video is playing. As you make each adjustment, you can immediately see the result when the section is looped.

12 Press the spacebar again to begin looping.

13 Press [(left bracket) a few times until you eliminate the pause after they all stand up (about 10 frames).

Try a few frames, and then watch the loop play; then try a few more frames, and so on.

14 When the edit looks good, go a few extra frames just to make sure. Then, trim in the other direction until you're happy with the edit. Press the spacebar again to stop the looping playback.

15 Click the Go to Next Edit button to advance the selection to the next edit.

The tooltip lists three different shortcuts that also perform this task. Pressing the Down Arrow key works as well. Most importantly, observe that the edit stays selected, and the Trim Edit window stays open. This can really help speed your trimming workflow, but it also raises the question: How do you get rid of the Trim Edit window?

A close button is available in the upper-left corner, as in any window, and the standard keyboard shortcut (Command-W) will work as well.

> **TIP** ▶ The window will also close automatically if you simply move the sequence playhead off an edit point. The Trim Edit window can exist only if an edit point is selected.

16 Click anywhere in the Timeline ruler to deselect the edit point.

The Trim Edit window closes.

17 Double-click the edit (at 27:09 between **HH Fight angle2 15-2** and **HH Fight angle1 14-1**) to reopen the Trim Edit window.

> **TIP** ▶ You can also open the Trim Edit window by selecting the Edit Selection tool (G) and lassoing edits on the Timeline. This selects the edits and automatically opens the Trim Edit window.

18 Press the spacebar to play around this edit and assess what needs fixing. Press the spacebar again to stop playback.

Perhaps you observed that a bit of overlapping action occurs at the edit point: The man being forcibly seated in the chair starts sitting, and then sits down again. This means that there are extra frames, and you'll need to ripple one side or the other of this edit to correct the timing.

19 Press U twice to set the edit to ripple outgoing.

20 Use the J-K-L keys and the arrow keys to find the frame where the man appears to reach the nadir of his sitting action (about 22:42:46:22). This will be the new Out point for that shot.

Outgoing timecode

Just finding the frame doesn't perform the edit, however. Once you're parked on the correct frame, you must mark a new In or Out point.

21 Press O to set the Out point.

Indicates how many frames have been trimmed

The trim is applied. The Trim Edit window displays the *out shift*, indicating how many frames have been modified during the trim operation.

TIP ▶ If you were adjusting the Incoming clip, you'd press I to set an In point.

22 Press the spacebar to play around the edit again.

Now the timing is worse, but this will make it easier to line up the action precisely.

23 Press U twice to change the edit to a ripple incoming.

24 Use the J-K-L keys to find the approximate frame where the man is completely seated in this shot (22:40:02:18).

Incoming source timecode

This is a very typical edit in that it's difficult to tell exactly which is the perfect frame because part of the action happens offscreen. Remember that trimming is all about experimenting with different edit positions to gauge which one feels right.

25 When you've found a frame you think might be correct, press I to set a new In point.

26 Play around the edit (press the spacebar).

27 Press the bracket keys to experiment with different edit positions.

TIP ▶ You can also enter a specific number of frames, just as you did when trimming in the Timeline.

When you think you have the correct timing for the edit, it's time to switch to a roll edit and find the best placement.

28 Press U twice to toggle the edit selection type to a roll.

29 Position your pointer over the outgoing (left) clip. Don't click.

30 Use the J-K-L keys or the left and right arrow keys to find a frame when the man is halfway down in the chair (around 22:42:46:18).

31 Press O to perform the trim.

The edit is rolled to the new position.

32 Play around the edit.

33 Experiment with other edit positions to find an edit you're happy with.

Working in the Trim Edit window provides additional information to help you make trimming decisions. Being able to see the frames after the Out point in the outgoing clip and before the In point in the incoming clip can provide essential information that isn't available in the Timeline.

Trimming Dynamically

Once you've got the hang of trimming this way, you'll find it can work extremely fast, especially when you learn all the keyboard shortcuts and get used to looping the playback while you're making editing decisions. However, another step can be eliminated to further speed your workflow.

Currently, you use the J-K-L keys to find a new edit position, and then press I or O to confirm the edit. Final Cut Pro has a way to skip that step, so that as soon as you choose a frame, pressing K automatically sets the edit. This is called *dynamic trimming*.

1   Press the Down Arrow key to move the edit selection to the next edit in the sequence.

The Trim Edit window remains open, and the edit type remains set to roll.

2   Play around the edit and assess what needs to be done.

In this case, rather than overlapping action that indicates extra frames, there are missing frames. The man gets up from the chair in the outgoing clip, and on the other side of the cut, he's already crashed into the woman.

To fix this edit, you'll follow the same procedure you used in the previous exercises, only this time you'll employ dynamic trimming.

3   In the bottom center of the Trim Edit window, select the Dynamic checkbox.

TIP ▶ The Dynamic Trimming setting can also be selected in the Editing tab of User Preferences.

User Preferences

General	Editing	Labels	Timeline Options	Render Control	Audio Outputs

Still/Freeze Duration: 00:00:10:00   ☑ Dynamic Trimming

Preview Pre-roll: 00:00:02:00   ☑ Trim with Sequence Audio

Preview Post-roll: 00:00:02:00   ☐ Trim with Edit Selection Audio (Mute Others)

Multi-Frame Trim Size: 5 frames

Selecting this setting has only one tiny effect, but it completely changes the way you work. When this setting is enabled, every time you press K to stop playback (when using the J-K-L keys) the edit is performed.

4   Press U twice to switch to a ripple outgoing edit.

5   Press L to play the outgoing clip forward, and as soon as the man touches the woman under the arm, press K to stop (around 22:40:03:21).

That's it. The edit has been performed! If you don't like the frame you landed on, just use the J-K-L keys to choose a new frame.

TIP ▶ When you're still getting used to dynamic trimming, it can be fairly intimidating, but there's really nothing to fear. If you go too far forward, press J to go backward. If you go too far backward, press L to go forward again. Every time you press K to stop, the edit moves along with you. In the worst case, if you get yourself really confused, you can always undo.

Additionally, if you're pressing J and L to play back and forth and you want to stop without affecting the edit, just press the spacebar. This will stop playback and leave the edit point unchanged, just as if you had pressed the Esc (escape) key.

TIP ▶ It's also helpful sometimes to back up before playing forward, in order to give yourself more time to make the edit.

6   Press J to play backward; then, without pressing K, press L to play forward.

7   Again, try to find the exact frame where the man touches the woman's side, and press K to stop and perform the edit.

8   Play around the edit and keep working until you're happy with the edit.

Don't be confused by the audio jump-cutting (the woman's scream might get cut off). You can easily solve that by splitting the edit or rolling the whole edit to a new position once you've gotten the timing right.

Dynamic trimming is just one more way to help you follow that one essential rule advised at the very beginning of Lesson 3: Whenever possible, make your edits while the video is playing.

Trimming Across Multiple Tracks

Although there are many ways to perform a trim edit, it's a very straightforward process: Ripple to get the timing right, roll to position the edit. You can trim by dragging in the Timeline, using keyboard shortcuts, working in the Trim Edit window, or using dynamic trimming to make the process even more fluid.

But there are some cases when trimming gets a tiny bit more complex. In Final Cut Pro, you can trim one edit per track at the same time. This means that if you have a section of a sequence with many tracks, you can (and in many cases should) trim an edit on each of the tracks. Otherwise, you run the risk of knocking items out of sync.

It's important to understand that any edit to the right of the selected edit will automatically be rippled (as long as the track isn't locked) along with any trimming you do, but when there are edits that overlap clips on additional tracks, multitrack trimming is essential to ensure sync.

1   Press ' (apostrophe) to move the edit selection to the next edit.

2   Play around the edit.

In this case, there's some overlapping action, but there is also an extra audio clip on track A2 (the woman saying, "No, wait!") The editor carefully arranged it so that the woman's voice overlaps the edit, and her word, "wait," adds a percussive emphasis to the action of the man hitting the chair.

Your job is to fix the timing of the edit while keeping intact the relative timing of the A2 clip. To do this, you must trim that extra clip along with the main edit.

> **TIP** ▶ Any edit that begins after the rightmost selected edit will always automatically ripple and doesn't need to be added to the selection. It's only when the edit on another track overlaps the selected edit that you must explicitly choose it.

3 If necessary, use the U key to select the edit as a ripple outgoing.

4 On track A2, Command-click the edit at the head of the clip.

This adds the edit on that track as part of the selection. Right away, you should notice that the edit on tracks V1 and A1 is selected as a ripple outgoing, and the edit on track A2 is selected as a roll. Nothing prevents you from making this sort of complex selection (or selecting an edit containing a gap), and in some cases it may be just what you want, but in this case it will prove to be a problem.

5 Type –12, and press Enter.

The trim is applied, and as you might expect, the clips on tracks V1 and A1 are rippled, and the clip on track A2 is rolled.

6   Play around the edit.

At first it may seem that you have no additional concerns. Sure, the A2 clip got longer, but there were no undesired sounds in that earlier section, so no harm appears to have been done. The timing of the main edit has been fixed, and the scream stayed in sync with his rear hitting the chair.

But by rolling the clip on that track, and rippling the clips on the other tracks, you inadvertently allowed the clips that appear later in time (on track A2) to go out of sync.

In this case, it's imperative that you ripple all the tracks to ensure that everything downstream of the edit remains in sync.

7   Press Command-Z to undo the last edit.

8   Press RR to select the Ripple tool.

9   On track A2, Command-click the outgoing side of the edit to select that edit as a ripple outgoing.

TIP ▶ You can add an edit to the selection using Command, or Command-Shift. Command-clicking adds the edit in the same type as the existing edit or the selected tool (ripple or roll). Command-Shift-clicking adds the edit in the inverse (ripple or roll) of the selected tool. The pointer will change onscreen to help you anticipate what kind of edit will be selected.

It may seem strange to be trimming a gap, but in this case, it's exactly the right thing to do. Essentially, you're instructing Final Cut Pro to make the gap longer or shorter just as you'd do with a clip.

10 Type –*12* and press Enter.

11 Play around the edit.

The edit has been trimmed, and the downstream clips retain their original timings relative to the clips on the other tracks.

This is a very simple example of multitrack trimming, but illustrates the basic concepts. With a typical project containing 10, 20, or even more audio tracks, it becomes essential to fluidly employ multitrack trimming.

Trimming Asymmetrically

Once you understand that every track in your Timeline can be trimmed simultaneously (as long as you select just one edit per track), even more complex possibilities arise.

In certain instances, you may actually want to trim a clip on one track in one direction (such as ripple incoming) and another track in a different direction (such as ripple out-going). In such a case, it may still be critical to trim both tracks by the same number of frames to maintain a particular sync relationship. So it's ideal to do the trim as a single operation.

This may seem incredibly complicated, but it's not as bad as it sounds. In practice, it's even fairly intuitive. It's called asymmetrical trimming.

1 In the Timeline, click any blank area to deselect the current edit.

2   Play over the next video edit, where the man's head is slammed onto the table.

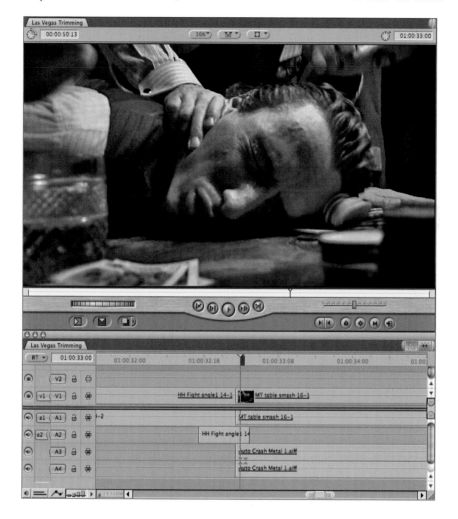

In this edit, the incoming clip (**MT table smash 16-1**) begins with the man's face already on the table. A few frames have to be added to the head of that shot to perfect the timing.

In this case, some extra audio clips have already been laid in: another scream from the woman on track A2 and a sound effect for the table smash on tracks A3 and A4.

3   Press RR to select the Ripple tool (if it's not already selected).

4   Press Shift-L to turn off linked selection.

5   Click the video In point of **MT table smash 16-1** on the the edit between it and **HH Fight angle1 14-1** as indicated in the figure.

6   Command-click the incoming edge of the audio edit directly beneath the video.

Command-clicking is how you add tracks to an edit selection.

For this edit, the timing of the audio on track A2 doesn't need to be precise, so you can ignore it. The sound effect on tracks A3 and A4, however, must line up precisely with the action in the video.

Furthermore, you don't actually want to modify the sound effect clip. Instead, you want to keep it where it is, which you can do by rippling the outgoing edge of the preceding gap.

7   Command-click the Out point of the edit on track A3 (selecting the gap).

The edit on track A4 is automatically selected because the sound effect is a stereo pair. Now you have an asymmetrical edit selection.

8 Drag the edit on track V1 to the left by about six frames.

The incoming edge of the edit on tracks V1 and A1 is trimmed, and the outgoing edge of the edit on tracks A3 and A4 is trimmed. The edits move in opposite directions. The result is that the sound effect remains in sync with the action in the video.

9 Play around the edit to see the results.

Although asymmetrical trimming is fairly rare, it can be a real time-saver in certain situations. The sound effect example here is one frequently encountered case; another is when a lower-third title is used over an interview.

It's common to have an interview subject's name appear one second or so after the interview clip begins. Once that title has been positioned, asymmetrical trimming can help to keep the lower third in position even when trimming the head of the interview clip is required.

TIP ▶ Asymmetrical trimming is also frequently used to create a split edit (described in Lesson 3) by rippling the video and audio of a simple edit in opposite directions.

Additional Practice

Many of the remaining edits in this sequence still need additional trimming. Experiment using the various trimming techniques covered in Lessons 3 and 4 to get the sequence as smooth and coherent as possible.

Compare your final work to the *Las Vegas Finished* sequence.

Lesson Review

1. How do you open the Trim Edit window?
2. How do you know what kind of edit is selected in the Trim Edit window?
3. In the Trim Edit window, which side of the edit do the J-K-L keys affect?
4. Is there a way to see how many frames have been cumulatively trimmed?
5. How do you navigate from edit to edit without closing the Trim Edit window?
6. When dynamic trimming is enabled, what changes?
7. How are edits added to an edit selection?
8. When is multitrack trimming important?
9. How many edits can be selected?
10. True or False: Asymmetrical trimming can be used to create split edits.

Answers

1. Double-click an edit point or press Command-7.
2. The green bar above the video windows shows whether the edit is selected as a ripple outgoing, ripple incoming, or roll.
3. It depends on the type of edit selected: In a ripple, the J-K-L keys will always control the clip on the selected side of the edit. In a roll, they will control the side where the pointer is located.
4. Yes. The lower-left and lower-right corners of the Trim Edit window show the number of frames that have been trimmed.
5. Press Shift-E, ' (apostrophe), or the Down Arrow key to move to the next edit downstream; or Option-E, ; (semicolon), or the Up Arrow key to move to the previous edit.
6. Pressing K performs the edit.

7. By Command-clicking an edit point.

8. When edits overlap clips on multiple tracks.

9. One edit can be selected per track.

10. True.

5

Lesson 5
Audio Sweetening

A show is only as good as its soundtrack. Although audiences will tolerate video with a wide variety of technical errors, we're much less willing to endure a program with poorly prepared audio. Fortunately you can perform a wide range of clean-up and improvements (known collectively as *sweetening*) right in Final Cut Pro, and what you can't do there, you can usually send right over to Soundtrack Pro where the changes you make are automatically updated back in your Final Cut Pro sequence.

Sound Editing is an incredibly rich and complex topic, and this lesson provides only a sampling of the most commonly needed advanced techniques available. If you're interested in learning more about all of the powerful sound editing and mixing capabilities available in Final Cut Studio, see *Apple Pro Training Series: Sound Mixing in Final Cut Studio.*

Mastering Audio Levels

There's really only one critical rule when working with audio, and that is to never, ever let the audio meters reach 0 dB (known as *peaking*). You'll find that almost everything you do when adjusting audio is, in one way or another, in service of this rule.

When audio peaks it can create distorted noise that not only sounds unpleasant (and invariably pulls the viewer out of the story), but also can damage equipment. Furthermore, even if you don't hear any distortion or cracking while monitoring your edit, when you later transcode the project to prepare it for DVD, web viewing, or another delivery method, a seemingly dormant peak can emerge and ruin your soundtrack. And it will be a lot harder to remove then.

Another important aspect of working with audio is to understand that levels are additive. When you play two sounds at the same point in time, the volume is louder than when you play them separately. A typical show has dialogue tracks, sound effects tracks, ambiences, sound design elements, and sometimes music all carefully woven together. However, if you're not careful, combining all this audio can increase your overall level and may bring you closer to that dreaded 0 dB.

> **TIP** ▶ Instead of turning up the elements you want to hear more clearly, turn down the other elements in the mix.

When setting your basic dialogue levels, the general rule is to use –12 dB as the target average level (the approximate position of the bouncing green bar in the audio meters) for common formats such as DV and HDV.

> **TIP** ▶ Other tape formats such as HDCAM SR or Digibeta have different recommended specs. The reason that we use a lower target level is that the noise floor is much lower and the dynamic range is much greater in formats like Digibeta.
>
> A good rule of thumb is to talk to your client – whoever you need to deliver your final master to, such as the post house or network, to see if it has any audio specification to which you need to adhere.

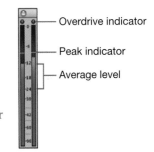

— Overdrive indicator

— Peak indicator

— Average level

However, it's important to know where this number comes from. The reason you set your dialogue to –12 dB is so that there's some room above that for intentionally loud sounds, such as screams, explosions, or music (when you want the music to be sweeping and "bigger" than the story). This way, those sounds can feel significantly louder than the average levels and still not touch 0 dB. If you were to set your dialogue to –3 dB, there wouldn't be any room for those other bits to sound louder.

This also makes your audio playable on lower-quality sound systems (such as built-in computer speakers, or old television sets), which can't reproduce a large *dynamic range* (the difference between the loudest and quietest parts of your program) without either the loud parts distorting or the quiet parts being inaudible.

> **TIP** When mixing for a theatrical environment you can set your average level as low as –20 dB or even –30 dB, which allows you to make those explosions mind-blowingly loud and still not touch 0 dB.

Matching Audio Levels

Now that you know what proper audio levels should be, you'll learn some of the many ways to control your clip's volume in Final Cut Pro.

1 Open Lesson_05 > **Audio_Sweetening.fcp**.

The *Interviews* sequence should be open.

2   Play the sequence to get familiar with it.

This documentary about the Blue Angels stitches together a group of interviews. Unfortunately each of them is at a different level.

NOTE ▶ This is a rough assembly, containing unprocessed greenscreen shots and some jumpcuts, all of which would presumably be cleaned up later in the editing process.

3   Play the sequence again, this time paying close attention to the audio meters.

The second clip is clearly too loud, coming dangerously close to touching 0 dB, and the third and fifth clips are obviously too low, but each clip needs a different adjustment. Fortunately, Final Cut Pro has a feature specifically designed to handle this situation.

4   Make sure Linked Selection is turned on (Shift-L) and make sure you have the Arrow tool (A) selected.

5   Select all the clips in the sequence by dragging a lasso around them or pressing Command-A.

6   Choose Modify > Audio > Apply Normalization Gain.

The Apply Normalization Gain dialog opens.

Here you set the maximum volume for each of the selected clips. Final Cut Pro will analyze the audio levels in the clips, identify the loudest frame, and change each clip's overall level to make that loudest frame match the value set here.

TIP ▶ You don't want your levels to ever hit 0 dB, so you might think that you should never leave the slider in its default setting here. However, Final Cut Pro dampens the result of this operation by 3–6 dB, so it will never actually make a clip hit 0 dB.

Remember that your goal is to get the average level to approximately –12 dB. Because this feature sets the loudest peak, the resulting average level will typically be significantly lower.

Also, if a clip contains one very loud sound, such as a cough near the mic, or a per-cussive noise of some kind, that loud sound will trigger the Normalization feature and the average level might not follow suit.

> **TIP** The Apply Normalization Gain feature analyzes the marked section of the clip. If you have a very loud sound in your clip, razor blade that sound into its own clip and apply the normalization to the remaining pieces.

7   Set the slider to –6 dBFS and click OK.

8   Play the sequence again, while watching the audio meters.

Now, the clips are all much closer to a uniform average level around –12 dB. Some clips were made louder and some made quieter to achieve this goal.

But how does it work? And how do you remove the effect?

9   Double-click the second clip, **Bearcat_engine**, to open it into the Viewer.

10   Click the audio (or Stereo a1a2) tab.

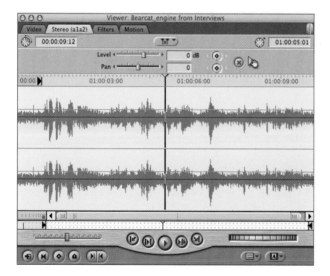

The audio level for this clip hasn't been modified from the default 0 dB setting. So how was the volume changed?

11   Click the Filters tab in the Viewer.

The clip has a Gain filter applied to the audio tracks. The value in the filter was provided by the Apply Normalization Gain operation. Because the clip was too loud, the filter is set to lower the audio by almost 5 dB.

Using a filter to change the volume of the clips has several advantages. Most importantly, it allows you to continue to use the clips' level sliders to make further adjustments, including fades in and out, boosting quiet sections, attenuating loud sections within the clip, and so on.

TIP You can manually add a Gain filter to any clip if you want to make an overall adjustment to an audio clip that already has level keyframes applied. To do so, just select the clip and choose Effects > Audio Filters > Final Cut Pro > Gain.

12 Double-click the third clip **Interview_03** to open it into the Viewer.

The Filters tab stays in front, but the contents now show the filters applied to the third clip. Because this clip contains two mono audio tracks, each was analyzed discretely and received a filter with a slightly different value. Because this clip was too quiet, the gain filters are set to add 13 and 11.5 dB, thereby dramatically increasing the volume of the clip.

> **TIP** ▶ Another reason the gain filter is useful is because it can be set far higher than the +12 dB available in the Audio tab in the Viewer. Use this filter to increase the level of very quiet clips.

Removing Normalization

The only possible downside to this effect being done using a filter is that you can't remove the effect by resetting a clip's audio level or by using the Modify Levels command.

However, there's an easy way to remove the normalization effect, and it can be done just as quickly whether you want to restore just one, or all of your clips to their pre-normalized settings.

1   In the Timeline, select all the clips by dragging a lasso around them or pressing Command-A.

2   Choose Edit > Remove Attributes.

3   Select Audio Attributes: Filters, then click OK.

All audio filters will be removed from the selected clips.

> **TIP** ▶ If you had other audio filters applied and didn't want them removed, you could simply open those clips into the Viewer and deselect or delete the Gain filter manually.

▶ **dB and dBFS**

You may find some of the audio measurements in Final Cut Pro confusing. You can have a clip set to 0 dB in the Viewer, but in the Audio Meters, it reads –12 dB. Furthermore, when you set a value in the Apply Normalization Gain dialog, the slider is measured in dBFS. What are these different audio measurements and how do they correspond with each other?

dB is shorthand for decibels, which is a logarithmic measurement of sound that corresponds with the way our ears hear and sound travels. A signal that is –3 dB is half as loud as one that is 0 dB, and –6 dB is half again as loud, and so on. When such signals are translated into digital form, there's a fixed range or scale in which audio can be measured (that is, how many bits represent silence, and how many represent maximum volume).

The audio meters in Final Cut Pro display an absolute value measuring that *full scale* (sometimes called *full spectrum* or *full code*) of the digital signal, or dBFS (decibels relative to full scale). The level sliders and gain filters all make relative adjustments, boosting or attenuating the level by a certain value, and so are measured in dB. In contrast, the Apply Normalization Gain dialog is setting an absolute level, and so is measured in dBFS.

Adjusting Levels Dynamically

Beginning editors frequently stop playback to adjust a level, then play the sequence again to see the results, then stop to make a change again, and so on. Advanced editors know that not only is this tedious, but it forces you to constantly interrupt the creative flow. Furthermore, it prevents you from having the same experience as your audience. The only way to accurately simulate your audience's experience watching your program is to see it play in real time.

> **TIP** Ideally you should always listen to your audio mix in the same environment and using the same type of speakers as your intended audience will.

Final Cut Pro is designed to facilitate making changes on the fly like this.

1   Open and play the *It's Perfect* sequence.

This is another section of the Blue Angels documentary where some B-roll shots have already been added to the interviews. You may notice that some of the airplane sound effects are too loud, overpowering the interviews.

TIP ▶ For best results when adjusting an audio setting, set the Sequence to loop around a certain clip or range of time.

2   Set an In point around the beginning of the **Prop Plane takeoff** clip and an Out point at the end of the clip.

3   Choose View > Loop Playback or press Control-L.

4   Select **Prop Plane takeoff**.

Selecting the clip will allow you to make changes to it while the sequence is playing.

TIP ▶ If you don't select a clip, the following commands will affect every clip under the playhead on a track with Auto Select enabled.

Auto Select

5 Pres Shift-\ (backslash) to play the sequence from In to Out.

Because Loop Playback is turned on, this section of the sequence will keep playing over and over again.

6 While the video plays, press Control-[(left bracket) to lower the clip's audio level by 3 dB.

NOTE ▶ Depending on how powerful your editing system is, you may experience a brief pause in playback when adjusting the levels this way.

7 If the clip is still too loud, press Control-[(left bracket) again.

TIP ▶ If you go too far, press Control-] (right bracket) to raise the level by 3 dB.

8 Continue adjusting the level of the sound effect until you're happy with it.

TIP ▶ Press Control-– (minus) to lower the volume by 1 dB or Control-+ (plus) to raise the volume by 1 dB.

Unlike the previous exercise using the Apply Normalization Gain these changes are applied to the clip's level.

9 Click the Keyframe Overlays button in the lower-left corner of the Timeline.

Pink lines appear to show the audio levels for the different clips. You can see that the music clip (on tracks A7 and A8) already has some keyframes applied.

10 Deselect **Prop Plane takeoff** and select **01 The Fish Eye.aiff.**

11 Press Control-– (minus) to lower the music track by 1 dB.

Observe that the entire pink line, along with all its keyframes, is moved uniformly.

12 Press Control-L to turn off Loop Playback, Option-X to clear the sequence In and
Out points, and Command-Shift-A to deselect the clip.

13 Use the same technique to adjust the levels of the other sound effects as needed.

Adding Fades

There are several different ways to add fade ins and fade outs to your audio clips. You can
turn on the Clip Overlays in the Timeline and add keyframes to the pink lines on the audio
clips, you can open a clip into the Viewer and add keyframes there, or you can apply audio
transitions to the edges of the clips.

You can use one of the built-in transitions, or you can create your own. This project contains a copy of the Cross Fade (+0 dB) transition modified so that it's only 10 frames long.

> **TIP** To learn more about using the two different Cross Fade effects in Final Cut
> Pro, *see Apple Pro Training Series: Sound Editing in Final Cut Studio*. But for a quick
> rule of thumb, use the 0dB version when fading to or from silence, and use the +3dB
> version when fading between two clips.

1 In the Browser, right-click (or Control-click) the 10 Frame Cross Fade and from the
shortcut menu, choose Set Default Transition.

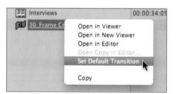

2 Drag a lasso in the Timeline to select all of the sound effects on tracks A3 through A6.

3 Press Command-Option-T to apply the default audio transition.

Transitions are added to the beginning and ending of each of the selected clips.

4 Play the sequence to hear how the effects sound with the transition effects applied.

Although the fades help smooth out the effects, several of them could benefit from adjusting the durations of the various transition effects. Some should be made longer and some shorter.

5 Zoom in and drag the edges of the transition effects to change their durations as required for the various different shots.

TIP ▶ Be careful not to roll the edit instead of trimming the transition.

You really must zoom all the way in, and turn off snapping, in order to modify some of the shorter clips.

NOTE ▶ Some clips are too short to have transitions applied. These edits will be left unmodified.

Fading Using Keyframes

You can create the same fade in and fade out effects using audio-level keyframes. Although this exercise takes more steps than the last exercise, it allows for more precision and customization.

1   Open the *It's Perfect 2* sequence.

This is a duplicate of the sequence you used in the previous exercise. The overall levels of the sound effects have been set, but they still need to be faded in and out.

2   Drag the track header for tracks A5 and A6 to give yourself more room to work.

3   Zoom in on the first half of the sequence.

4 Option-click four times on the pink line to add four keyframes to **Twirling Jets sound**.

TIP Adding multiple keyframes before setting any of them is quicker and easier than adding and moving them one at a time.

5 Turn off snapping.

6 Drag the first and last keyframes to the beginning and end of the clip and set their values to -inf dB.

This creates the desired fade in and fade out effect. You can add as many keyframes as you want to create a very specific or custom-shaped curve.

TIP If you can't select or drag keyframes near to the edge of clips (because your pointer keeps selecting the edit instead of the keyframe), press P to select the Pen tool, which will always adjust only keyframes. Be sure to press A to return to the Arrow tool when you're finished.

Once you've gotten one clip's fade in and fade out keyframes set, you can apply the same settings to the rest of the clips.

7 Select **Twirling Jets sound** and press Command-C to copy the clip to the clipboard.

8 Zoom back out (Shift-Z) and drag a lasso to select all of the clips on tracks A3 through A6.

9 Choose Edit > Paste Attributes or press Option-V.

The Paste Attributes dialog opens.

10 Select the checkbox for Levels, under the Audio Attributes heading, and click OK.

The keyframes are pasted to all the other selected clips.

> **TIP ▶** By default the keyframes are scaled to match the duration of each of the clips. You can override that and paste keyframes of a precise length by deselecting Scale Attribute Times in the Paste Attributes dialog.

11 Using the Arrow tool or the Pen tool, adjust the various keyframes to create the specific fades you think sound best.

> **NOTE ▶** You'll have to zoom all the way in to manipulate the keyframes on the smaller clips.

Making Uniform Changes

Once you've started adjusting audio levels, making additional changes can be tricky. For example, once you've added some keyframes to a clip, changing the relative volume of the clip might involve adjusting all of the keyframes individually. This would be tedious and prone to error. Similarly, you might want to modify multiple clips simultaneously, turning all of your sound effects up or down together, or even applying a single filter to a group of clips.

In this exercise you'll take the whole group of sound effects clips and attenuate their levels in one step.

1 Select all of the sound effects clips on tracks A3 through A6.

2 Choose Modify > Levels.

Gain Adjust
Adjust gain by: ◀ ⟼⟼⟼ ▶ 0 dB
Make Changes: Relative ⇕
Cancel   OK

The Adjust Gain dialog opens.

> **TIP ▶** ~~If you select video clips you can use the Levels dialog to adjust clip opacity.~~

You can choose whether to make a relative or an absolute level adjustment. A relative adjustment will add or subtract the decibels from the selected items, leaving all keyframes intact, but lowering or raising all the keyframes together. (Final Cut Pro is smart enough not to raise keyframes set to –∞.)

Alternatively, you can make an absolute change, which will force the levels of all the selected items to become exactly the value you select.

3   Set the pop-up menu to Absolute, set the slider to –5 dB, and click OK.

All of the clips' audio levels are set to exactly –5. Any existing keyframes are obliterated. In this case this is definitely not what you want.

4   Press Command-Z or choose Edit > Undo.

5   With the clips still selected, choose Modify > Levels again.

6   Leave the pop-up menu set to Relative, set the slider to –5 dB, and then click OK.

The clips are lowered to 5 dB below their previous settings. All keyframes remain intact.

Bussing in Final Cut Pro

Many dedicated audio editing tools provide a feature called *bussing* that allows you to direct multiple tracks to a single special track where you can perform one effect that modifies all of the bussed tracks. For example, let's say your show had several different shots that all needed to sound like they were coming through a telephone. You could apply an EQ filter to each of the clips individually, but if later you decided you wanted to change the "telephone" sound, you would have to go and adjust each clip's filter setting separately. It would be difficult to tell which ones had the new or old version of the effect and it would be easy to miss one. Using a bus, you could apply the filter once and then any settings you changed would affect all of the clips together.

Final Cut Pro doesn't specifically have this ability, but you can use the Nest Items command to achieve the same result.

1 Open and play the *It's Perfect 3* sequence.

This is another version of the *It's Perfect* sequence, with all the keyframes set on the sound effects tracks. In this exercise you'll nest all the sound effects tracks into one stereo track so you can perform a single volume adjustment on the group of tracks.

2 Select all of the sound effects on tracks A3 through A6.

3 Choose Sequence > Nest Items or press Option-C.

The Nest Items dialog appears.

4   Name the new sequence *Sound Effects*, leave the rest of the settings at their defaults, and click OK.

The group of sound effects is collapsed into a single clip.

Don't worry, this change doesn't do anything permanent, and doesn't modify your original clips. If you want to modify any of the original items individually, you can.

TIP ▶ This exercise works the way it does because all of these sound effects clips are not linked to any video. If you had video clips selected as well, those would also be added to the nest. See Lesson 10, "Nesting Sequences," for more information.

5   Double-click the Sound Effects "clip" in the Timeline.

A new tab opens in the Timeline containing all the clips inside the Sound Effects nest.

TIP ▶ You'll learn much more about working with nested sequences in Lesson 10.

6   Click the *It's Perfect 3* tab in the Timeline to return to the original sequence.

7   Option-click the pink levels line a few times on the Sound Effects clip in the Timeline.

8   Move the keyframes around to control the level of the group of sound effects.

In the following figure, keyframes were added to lower the sound effects track while the interviewees were speaking.

Filtering Audio

All of the exercises you've performed so far in this lesson have revolved around modifying the audio levels of your clips in one way or another. But there's a host of other types of adjustments you can make to your audio clips. Audio filters fall into one of three basic categories: dynamics, equalization, and effects.

Dynamics filters affect the volume of a clip. These include the *Gain* filter you applied earlier, which affects the overall volume; as well as filters like a *Noise Gate*, which turns down the volume of only the quietest portion of the clip; and a *Compressor/Limiter*, which turns down the volume of only the loudest portion of the clip.

Equalization filters also affect the volume of a clip, but they limit the adjustment to a selection of frequencies. All sounds are made up of many frequencies (colloquially called "pitch"). By boosting or attenuating specific frequencies you change the tone and tenor of the sound. Equalization filters can be multipurpose, allowing you to select a variety of frequencies and turn them up or down independently, or they can be special purpose like a *high-pass* (which allows the high frequencies to pass through the filter, effectively turning down the low rumbles) or a *Hum Remover* or *Vocal DeEsser* (which identify one specific frequency and turn the volume down).

Effects filters typically involve modifying or replicating portions of the audio signal and offsetting them in time, frequency, or volume. These includes common effects such as *echo* and *reverb*, as well as filters usually relegated to musical instruments such as *flanger, distortion,* or *chorus* effects.

Applying Audio Filters

Final Cut Pro contains many useful filters, but understanding how best to modify their settings to achieve your desired result is not always intuitive. In this exercise, rather than trying to accomplish a specific goal you'll get a chance to experience the audio filters workflow in Final Cut Pro. If you want to learn more about specific filters, please see *Apple Pro Training Series: Audio Editing in Final Cut Studio*.

1   Open and play the *Pretty big thing* sequence.

2   Click the Show Audio Controls button in the lower-left corner of the Timeline.

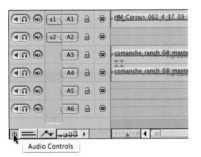

This adds Mute and Solo buttons to each of the audio tracks in the Timeline.

> **TIP**   Muting a track is different from turning off the audible button. For one thing, you can mute and solo different tracks during playback. Also, muting a track does not remove it from final output. Turning off a track's audible button turns the track off so that it's not part of the final output.

3   Click the Solo button for track A1 to hear the audio without the added airplane sound effects.

Fortunately, in this case, the added plane noises cover up the bad background noise in the interview, but you can still do whatever is possible to improve the sound in the main track.

4   Select the clip on A1 and choose Effects > Audio Filters > Final Cut Pro > Reverberation.

NOTE ▸ It's not likely you'd use reverb on this clip in a real-life situation, but it's an easy filter to adjust and hear the results in real time.

To make adjustments to a filter, it's best to loop playback.

5   Choose View > Loop Playback.

6   Double-click the clip on A1 to open it into the Viewer, and click the Filters tab.

Here you can adjust the filter's settings while listening to the clip play.

7   Play the sequence, and while it plays, experiment with the different filter settings.

Adjusting audio filter settings doesn't stop playback, so you can listen for gradual changes as you manipulate a slider.

> **TIP** If you find that you're adjusting a filter and it seems to have no effect, check that the clip you're changing is the one currently active in the sequence. Also, note that many audio filters create very subtle results or effects that won't have any noticeable result on certain clips (depending on the frequencies and levels of the clip).

8 When you're satisfied, turn off Loop Playback (Control-L).

The Final Mix

Before a show is finished, it typically goes through a process called the "final mix." This is basically the final opportunity to get all the sound just right before sending your project for final output. Mixing has an air of mystery to it, but it's really not as complex as you might think.

There is no secret sound-enhancing sauce that must be applied before you can call your audio "mixed," but there is a small checklist you can consider to be sure you've at least dotted the i's and crossed the t's.

1. Include All Elements

    The first step to making sure your mix is complete is to ensure that all elements are included. Obviously, your main dialogue is probably there, but have you gone through and added sound effects wherever possible? As a rule of thumb, anything that moves on screen should have a sound effect associated with it. Anything. That means footsteps, cars in the background, a dog walking by, and so on, but it also means titles or graphics.

Also, every scene should have some deliberately chosen ambience track. You can influence a scene quite dramatically by selecting one ambience over another. This is just as true for interviews in a documentary as it is for action scenes in a drama.

2. Check All Audio Levels and Pan Settings

    It's absolutely critical that audio levels are consistent and uniform. This primarily applies to your main dialogue elements (or whatever the primary sound in your program is), but it also applies to sound effects, music, and any other elements in your show.

    Furthermore, you should check to see that your tracks are all panned as desired. You don't want to leave some piece of dialogue unintentionally stuck coming out of the left channel, or a stereo piece of music accidentally panned mono. Typically, all dialogue should be panned to the center (unless something specific in the scene dictates otherwise).

    Be wary of overdoing pan settings. It's very rare that a sound should be panned 100% left or right. Even a sound coming from one side of you is usually audible by both of your ears, especially in interiors where sound bounces off of walls. You should strive to simulate such realistic pan settings when preparing your show for final output.

3. Audio Fades and Transitions

    Every audio clip in your Final Cut Pro Timeline should have a fade in and fade out applied to it. Every single one. Even though you may not be able to hear anything that sounds like a problem, small shifts in the natural background noise of a clip will kick in and drop out suddenly and can cause clicks, pops, or other unintended shifts that will stand out when your program is played in a quiet theater. These are also exactly the type of minor errors that can be amplified (literally) when you convert or compress your final movie into another file format for use on a DVD or on the web.

4. Equalization and Filters

    Ideally, some time has been spent evaluating every shot and applying equalization, compression, or other filters as needed to make the sound as clear, present, and sharp as you desire. This must be done before you confirm the final levels for such shots, as filters frequently will modify the volume of a shot.

5. Relative Audio Levels

    As a last step (usually), listen to the mix, turning on and off the different tracks or groups of tracks (music, sfx, vox, and so on) and confirming that the tracks' relative levels feel natural and realistic. Ensure that when combined, none of the levels rise too close to 0 dB. Getting those sound effects, ambiences, music, and other elements at the right relative level is the key to a professional-sounding mix.

Using the Audio Mixer Window

Let it be said here: There is no need to use Final Cut Pro's Audio Mixer window to "mix" your project; however, it does facilitate a few features that are unavailable in other parts of the program. For one thing, the Audio Mixer window is another place to access the Mute and Solo buttons. Most importantly, you can view individual audio meters for each track in your project.

1 Open the *It's Perfect 4* sequence.

This is a duplicate of the *It's Perfect* sequence you used earlier.

2 Choose Window > Arrange > Audio Mixing.

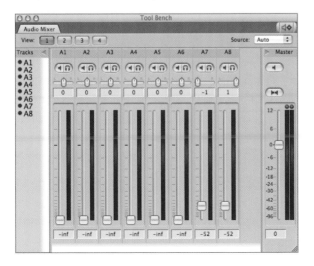

The windows are rearranged to make room for the Audio Mixer window which opens in the upper right.

TIP ▶ You can also access the Audio Mixer window without rearranging your windows by choosing Tools > Audio Mixer or pressing Option-6.

The Audio Mixer window displays audio level and pan controls for each track in the Timeline, as well as a Master level control. You can save four views containing different selections of tracks. In this exercise you'll organize these into dialogue, sound effects, music, and all tracks.

TIP ▶ Many programs use the four views to display dialogue, sound effects, ambiences, and music tracks.

3   Click the View 1 button if it's not already active.

This view will be used to show just the dialogue tracks, in this case tracks A1 and A2.

4   In the Tracks list on the left edge, click A3, A4, A5, A6, A7, and A8 to remove those tracks from the current view.

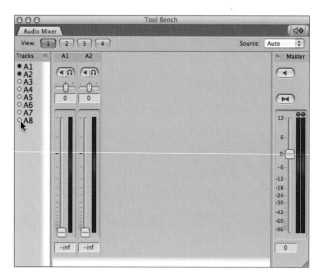

5   Click the View 2 button.

This view will be used for the sound effects tracks.

6   In the Tracks list, click A1, A2, A7, and A8 to remove those tracks from the current view.

7   Click the View 3 button.

This view will be used for the music tracks.

8   Turn off all tracks except A7 and A8.

You can leave view 4 showing all eight tracks.

> **TIP**   To make good use of the Audio Mixer window, you must first organize your sequence so similar clips are on consistent tracks. If your tracks are disorganized and you have a sound effect clip on a track that's primarily dialogue, or a snippet of dialogue on a music track, it will be very difficult to manipulate those elements here.

9   Play the sequence. While it plays, switch between the different views by clicking the View buttons at the top of the Audio Mixer window.

Recording Live Keyframes

One of the popular uses for mixing boards (like the one that Final Cut Pro's Audio Mixer window simulates) is for adjusting or *riding* the levels of the different tracks as you watch the program play. Although this technique makes most sense when using a physical mixing board attached to your computer through USB or a PCI card, you can perform a similar function without extra hardware by dragging the sliders right in the Audio Mixer window. The disadvantage is that you can only manipulate one track at a time. The advantage is that you can make dynamic adjustments to your audio levels on the fly.

> **TIP** ▶ Final Cut Pro will automatically recognize many third-party mixing consoles, mapping their sliders and dials directly to the corresponding controls in the Audio Mixer window. Consult the user manual for the hardware in question for configuration instructions.

1   In the Audio Mixer window button bar, click the Record Audio Keyframes button.

When this button is on, adjusting audio levels will automatically add keyframes to the audio levels for the tracks you adjust. This process is commonly called *automation*.

> **TIP** ▶ You can also enable or disable audio keyframe recording by clicking the Record Audio Keyframes checkbox in the Editing tab of the Final Cut Pro Preferences window. There you can also specify how frequently keyframes are added. For nearly all situations, the default setting of *reduced* is perfect.

2   Click the View 3 button and play the sequence.

3   As the sequence plays, grab the slider for either track 7 or track 8 and raise or lower the audio to better incorporate the music into the overall mix.

> **NOTE** ▶ Keyframes won't appear in the Timeline until playback is stopped.

TIP ▶ Because the clip in those tracks is stereo, adjusting either slider will affect both tracks.

4   When you're done recording the keyframes, play back the sequence again to hear how well you did.

There are a number of ways to remove the keyframes you added if you're unhappy with the result. Of course, you could always simply Undo, but you could also use the Remove Attributes command.

5   Select the clip (if it's not selected already) and choose Edit > Remove Attributes.

If you selected Levels under the Audio Attributes heading, you would reset the audio to its default (0 dB). But there's an even easier way, assuming you're planning to record a new automation.

6   Click Cancel to close the Remove Attributes dialog.

7   Move the playhead to the beginning of the sequence and play it again.

8   As it plays, grab the slider for either track and redo the level adjustments.

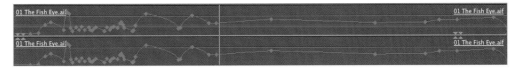

The new keyframes will simply replace the old ones. If you let go of the slider at any point, the old keyframes will remain. In this way you can replace only the portion of the keyframes that was unsatisfactory.

TIP ▶ You can also automate the settings of applied audio filters by making adjustments to the sliders in the Filters tab while playing with the Record Audio Keyframes setting enabled.

9   When you're satisfied with the audio level adjustments, click the Record Audio Keyframes button to deactivate it. Also, you may wish to return to the Standard window arrangement by pressing Control-U.

TIP ▶ Always remember to turn off the Record Audio Keyframes setting. Leaving it on allows you to later inadvertently make changes to your audio clips, even when the Audio Mixer window isn't open.

Lesson Review

1. Why are average levels typically set at −12 dB?
2. What does the value of the slider in the Apply Normalization Gain dialog determine?
3. How do you remove the Normalization effect?
4. Does the Modify Levels command make relative or absolute changes?
5. Do absolute level changes preserve existing keyframes?
6. What category of Audio filter is the Vocal DeEsser?
7. Does changing audio filter settings force playback to stop?
8. Which clips should have an audio fade applied to the beginning and end?
9. Why do you need to open the Audio Mixer window to complete your final mix?
10. Where can you find controls to mute or solo a specific track?

Answers

1. To allow enough headroom so sounds can be louder than average and still not hit 0 dB.
2. The intended level of the loudest moment in the clip.
3. Remove the Gain filter that is automatically applied.

4. Both.

5. No.

6. Equalization.

7. No, you can adjust audio filter settings while the sequence is playing.

8. Every single clip should ideally have a fade applied to its beginning and end.

9. You don't.

10. Mute and Solo buttons appear in the Timeline when the Audio Controls button is activated, as well as in the Audio Mixer window.

6

Multicamera Editing

Although traditional filmmaking is done with a single camera, some types of productions use more than one camera operating at the same time. Most often this *multicamera* technique is used when documenting a live event, such as a concert, theatrical performance, or sporting event. Shooting with multiple cameras is essential in these instances; otherwise there would be no way to edit the footage without automatically jump-cutting. Multiple cameras are also frequently used for complicated stunts or for action that is difficult to stage or repeat, such as improvisational performances.

It's true that sacrifices must be made when shooting with more than one camera. Framing options are severely limited if you're going to avoid showing other cameras in the shots, and lighting must be unnaturally even to ensure that all angles get an acceptable image. This explains the very formulaic and artificial look employed by many television sitcoms and soap operas in which three cameras are operated simultaneously and the show is edited on the fly using a broadcast switcher.

Editing Multicamera Footage

Although there are limitations for the production team, editing multicamera source footage is especially easy. When multiple cameras are capturing the same action at the same time, you can effortlessly cut from one angle to another without worrying about matching the timing. Not only will audio be in sync from angle to angle, but so will any action that happens simultaneously in all the shots. In many ways, multicamera setups are an editor's dream, except that the limited camera angles often mean that you may not have the exact close-up or insert that will most clearly tell the story.

Final Cut Pro has a special feature designed to take advantage of multicam footage and simplify editing such footage.

Using the Multiclip

Final Cut Pro can group multiple clips into a *multiclip*. A multiclip can hold up to 128 *angles* in a single clip; when the multiclip is used in a sequence, you can toggle between the angles to choose which one is currently visible.

Although you can create and use multiclips in a variety of ways, this lesson will focus on a recommended workflow that takes advantage of special features in Final Cut Pro and also serves the creative needs of multicam editing.

Creating a Multiclip

Although you can collect any group of clips into a multiclip, the feature is primarily designed for clips that are synchronous—especially clips that were photographed in a multiple-camera situation.

However, although the clips may all contain the same content, you must synchronize them somehow in Final Cut Pro. To do so, you'll need to identify some element that will link the clips together, such as matching timecode, a slate clap, or even a flashbulb going off.

1   Open Lesson Files > Lesson_06 > **Multicamera.fcp**.

   This project contains two sets of clips, each of which was created in a multicamera environment. First you'll work with a fairly typical three-camera shoot from a movie review podcast.

2   In the Browser, double-click **2_shot** in the *2MonkeysTV* bin.

3 In the Viewer, set an In point at the frame where the slate closes (05:04).

> **TIP** ▶ When looking for the frame where a slate closes, you should always step through the frames one at a time, moving backward and forward until you're sure you have found the exact frame where the clap stick has closed.

4 Double-click **Danik** to open it in the Viewer.

5 Set an In Point at the frame where the slate closes in this clip (08:00).

6 Double-click **Misha** to open it in the Viewer.

7 Set an In Point at the frame where the slate closes in this clip (04:02).

8 In the Browser, select the three clips and choose Modify > Make Multiclip.

	Make Multiclip		
Synchronize using:	In Points		
Angle Name	**Media Alignment**		**Sync Time**
☑ [1] – 2_shot			00:00:05;04
☑ [2] – Misha			00:00:04;02
☑ [3] – Danik			00:00:08;00
		Cancel	OK

The Make Multiclip dialog appears. You can see which sections of the clips overlap based on the sync point.

9 Verify that the "Synchronize using" pop-up menu is set to In Points and click OK.

A new clip appears in the Browser named **2_shot [1]-Multiclip 2**.

10 Double-click the multiclip to open it in the Viewer.

11 Play the clip.

All three angles play simultaneously.

12 Click each of the angles in the Viewer.

The active angle has a blue border around it. Notice that the multiclip name changes
in the Browser to reflect the currently selected angle.

13 In the Viewer View Options pop-up menu, choose Show Multiclip Overlays.

Editing with a Multiclip

Linking the clips together gets you prepared, but editing the multiclip in a sequence is where the real fun starts.

1   Click Angle 1.

2   Set an In point just before they say "Welcome to two monkeys" (at approximately 11:10).

3   Set an Out point just after they point at the screen (at approximately 53:17).

4   Create a new sequence, name it *Cowboys and Aliens,* and double-click it to open it in the Canvas and Timeline.

5   Option-drag the clip from the Viewer into the Canvas as an overwrite edit and click Yes to the Conform Sequence dialog.

> **TIP** ▸ You must hold down Option as you drag because otherwise clicking the clip in the Viewer changes the active angle.

After the multiclip is edited into the sequence, it looks like any other clip. But don't be fooled. It has special features that allow you to switch angles—even while it's playing back. However, to enable those features, you must first set two controls.

6   Check to make sure Linked Selection is turned on.

7   Set the Playhead Sync mode to Open.

The clip at the playhead position in the sequence will be opened into the Viewer. If you choose another option from the Playhead sync pop-up menu, you can still change angles. However, you won't be able to simultaneously play the multiclip in the Viewer and sequence.

8   In the Timeline, click the RT menu and verify that it is set to Unlimited RT, and that a checkmark is next to Multiclip Playback.

9   Make sure the Canvas or the Timeline window is active, and then play the sequence. While it plays, in the Viewer, click back and forth between the angles.

NOTE ▶ Be sure that the Canvas or Timeline window is active. If the Viewer window is active, the multiclip edits won't work.

Each time you click, you're creating a virtual edit point, temporarily indicated by a gray marker in the Timeline.

When you stop playback, the gray markers automatically turn into edit points.

You can continue to improve your sequence by modifying these edits. If you roll any edit point, both clips will remain in sync, but rippling, slipping, or sliding edits or clips will cause the affected clips to move out of sync.

NOTE ▶ Playing multiclips requires your system to read from multiple places on your hard disk simultaneously, and slower systems may drop frames during playback. If you get a dropped frames warning, deselect "Warn next time" and click OK.

Trimming a Multiclip Sequence

Although you can't ripple, slip, or slide a multiclip without introducing sync errors, you can make edits by removing a section of the source footage and covering the jump cut by switching angles.

For example, you can tighten this sequence by removing the mistake when Misha says, "I, uh, wait a second…"

> **NOTE ▶** Depending on where you made edits in the previous exercise, you may need to make additional edits or adjustments during the next few steps.

1   Play the sequence and mark an In point just after Danik says, "Cowboys" (at approximately 13:08).

2   Mark an Out point just before Misha says, "I really was psyched…" (at approximately 17:07).

3   Press Command-Shift-A to deselect all (just in case something was selected) and press Shift-Delete to extract the repeated line.

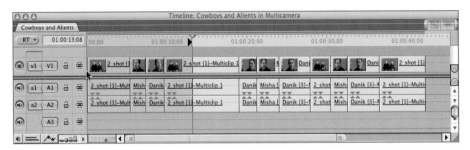

4 Press \ (backslash) to play around the edit.

The audio is clean, but because the same angle is used across the edit, it appears to be a jump cut.

While the playhead is stopped, clicking on a different angle in the Viewer doesn't add an edit, but rather changes the angle of the clip under the playhead.

5 Position the playhead over the clip after the newly created edit.

6 In the Viewer, click the CU of Misha's face.

7 Play around the edit again.

Now the jump cut is entirely hidden, and the sequence feels smooth.

If, in your sequence, changing one clip puts two identical angles next to each other, you'll see a thru-edit indicator.

This is harmless; it just means that the same angle is used twice in a row. When playing the sequence, no edit will be apparent.

TIP ▸ You can delete a thru-edit by selecting the edit and pressing Delete, or you can right-click on the edit and from the pop-up menu, choose Join Thru-edit.

Once your edits are roughed in, you can finesse the sequence by changing angles or rolling any edit point.

TIP ▸ Because you can be sure that the clips are always in sync, you can roll any edit by any amount, and the edits will always be smooth.

As in any project, choose the best places to put your edits; use movement in the frame, eyelines, and the natural phrasing of the dialogue to justify your cuts and create the smoothest possible edit.

Collapsing a Multiclip

After your angles have been selected, you may want to prevent further angle changes by collapsing the multiclip. When you collapse a multiclip, it's replaced by the active angle of the multiclip. This is useful when you send a sequence to a colorist or effects artist and you want them to focus only on the angles you chose during editing. Collapsing multiclips also improves performance because less video is streaming from disk.

Because the collapsing isn't permanent, you can uncollapse the active angle at any time and return to the full multiclip, even after you close and reopen a project.

1   Press Command-A to select all the clips in the sequence.

2   Choose Modify > Collapse Multiclip(s).

The angles are converted into ordinary clips based on the master clips to which they refer.

Notice that the clips in the Timeline now show just the names of the raw clips, not the multiclip. But Final Cut Pro never forgets that the clip was once a multiclip. You can always uncollapse it if you want to change to a different angle.

TIP ▶ To switch a clip back to the multiclip format in order to change its angle, select the clip and choose Modify > Uncollapse Multiclip(s).

You can continue to edit the sequence at this point, essentially forgetting that it once was a multiclip.

Working with Many Angles

The previous example was very simple, involving only two angles, but Final Cut Pro can accommodate many angles in a single multiclip, and the editing process can quickly get more complex.

1   Open the *One Night in Jordan* bin and select all seven clips.

This is footage from a music video based on a live concert performance by Zade Dirani. The clip called Concert_Footage1 is already edited (it was a multicamera shoot edited live to tape). The rest of the clips are from specially shot scenes in which Zade plays along to a click track to match his live performance.

2   Right-click (or Control-click) any of the selected clips and choose Make Multiclip from the shortcut menu.

The Make Multiclip dialog appears.

NOTE ▶ You can also right-click the bin and choose Make Multiclip to create a multi-clip that includes all the clips in the bin.

In this case, all of these clips share identical timecode, so you can sync to that, rather than syncing to an In point set on a slate clap as you did previously.

3   In the "Synchronize using" pop-up menu, choose Timecode.

The Make Multiclip window displays the way the various clips overlap. Some of the clips are significantly shorter than others. Selecting one of these angles in an area where there is no media will just display black.

4   Click OK.

The new multiclip is created in the *One Night in Jordan* bin.

Multiclip names always start with the name of the angle currently selected, but you can modify the rest of the name, just as you would change any other clip name.

5   In the Browser, select the multiclip, and then click it to edit the name.

When the clip name appears, only the editable part is visible.

6   Rename the multiclip *Fairytales Multi* and press Return.

The new name still includes the current angle, but it now ends with your customized name.

7   Double-click the multiclip.

The Viewer displays the **Fairytales Multi** multiclip.

8   Choose View > Show Multiclip Overlays to display the clip names and timecodes in the Viewer (if they're not already displayed).

9 In the Viewer, click the View Options button and choose Multiclip 9-Up.

Now all seven angles are visible at the same time.

TIP Shuttle through the clip so you can see video in all seven angles to match the picture above (at TC 1:00:13:15).

Although this looks impressive, it's a lot of information for you to monitor, and a lot of data for your computer to display at one time. In most cases, working in 4-Up is more manageable, but which four of the clips will you monitor? This choice is controlled by the order of the angles, and you can modify that order in a number of ways, as you'll see in the next section.

Setting Angle Order

The order of the clips initially is based on the value in the Angle field of each clip. The Angle field number can be entered when logging clips, or at any time in the Browser or Clip Properties windows.

1   Double-click the *One Night In Jordan* bin.

Name	Duration	In	Out	Angle	Ree
Camera_01	00:03:49:18	Not Set	Not Set		Mus
Camera_02	00:03:57:09	Not Set	Not Set	2	Mus
Camera_03	00:03:59:10	Not Set	Not Set	3	Mus
Camera_04	00:04:00:00	Not Set	Not Set	4	Mus
Camera_05	00:03:56:20	Not Set	Not Set	5	Mus
Camera_06	00:03:46:01	Not Set	Not Set	6	Mus
Concert_Footage1 [1]–Fairytales Multi	00:04:02:18	Not Set	Not Set		Mus
Concert_Footage1	00:04:02:18	Not Set	Not Set	1	Mus

The Angle field is visible to the right of the Out field.

Final Cut Pro works hard to determine how to arrange clips that don't have a value in that field. If the clip name is identified with an *A* followed by a number (such as A2 or A11), that number will be used to set the Angle number. Otherwise, the first number that appears in the clip name will be identified as the angle number. (For example, a clip titled CUPiano_7_01 would be identified as Angle 7.) If no number is identified, the reel name and the media file name are consulted.

TIP   If two clips have the same angle number and are included in the same multiclip, they appear in the order they were sorted in the Browser window at the time the multiclip was made, and they push other angle numbers down the list. (So if there are two Angle 5 clips, Angles 6 and 7 will become Angles 7 and 8.)

2   Close the *One Night in Jordan* bin.

3   In the Viewer window, Command-drag one of the angles to rearrange it in the
9-Up display.

TIP ▶ If you click without the Command key, you'll select the angle instead of
moving it (indicated by a colored box appearing). If this happens, don't fret, just
Command-drag the next time.

The other clips move to make room for the new clip.

4   Arrange the clips so that the first four clips are **Concert_Footage1**, **Camera_01**,
Camera_02, and **Camera_03**.

5   Choose View > Multiclip Layout > Multiclip 4-Up.

Now the first four clips are visible, and you can play the sequence and switch among them on the fly. The other angles are still viewable; you just have to scroll them into view.

6   Position the pointer in the lower-right corner of the Viewer window.

A small, boxed arrow appears.

7   Click the arrow to move **Camera_04** and **Camera_05** into the 4-Up display.

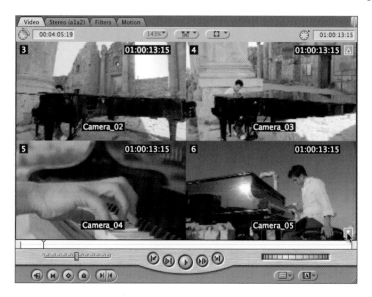

Each time you click that arrow, another row of angles is revealed. You can scroll up through the rows by clicking the similar arrow in the upper-right corner of the display.

Deleting and Adding Angles

After a multiclip has been created, you can change its number of angles by dragging into or out of the Viewer.

1   Scroll the view so that angles 1 through 4 are visible.

2   Click the **Concert_Footage1** angle to make it active (if it's not already).

3   Command-drag the **Camera_01** angle out of the Viewer window.

    This angle is removed from the multiclip.

NOTE ► You can't delete the active angle.

4   In the *One Night in Jordan* bin, select the **Camera_01** clip and drag it into the Viewer. Continue to hold down the mouse button until the overlay appears.

5   Drag the clip onto Insert New Angle and release the mouse button.

The angle is added back into the multiclip.

TIP ▶ If you drag the clip onto the active angle, a different set of options will appear.

NOTE ▶ In some versions of Final Cut Pro, this feature may not work as expected. In that case, simply press Command-Z to undo the removal of Camera_01.

Alternatively, you could have overwritten one of the existing angles or added a new *angle affiliate,* which would add the angle to the multiclip currently in the Viewer, plus would also add that angle to any other versions of that multiclip.

You would do this, for example, when adding an angle to a multiclip that had already been used in a sequence and was divided into multiple edits.

Editing the Multiclip

Remember that you must first put a multiclip into a sequence in order to edit it.

1   Create a new sequence, name it *Untold Fairytales* and double-click it.

The sequence opens in the Canvas and Timeline.

2 In the Viewer, click **Concert_Footage1** to make that angle active.

3 Set the Playhead Sync menu (in either Viewer or Canvas) to Video.

4 Play the clip until the first frame appears in that angle (just as the music begins). Set an In point there (at timecode 01:00:00:00).

5 Press the Down Arrow key to advance the playhead to the end of the clip.

6 Set an Out point there.

7 Option-drag the clip into the Canvas and perform an overwrite edit.

The familiar Change Sequence Settings to Match Clip Settings dialog opens.

8 Click Yes.

The multiclip is added to the sequence.

Preset Multiclip Button Bars

Final Cut Pro provides a preset button bar configuration to assist with multiclip editing. This provides shortcuts to the most common multiclip controls such as turning on multiclip display, switching the Viewer to 4-Up view, and even switching and cutting between angles.

You can further customize the button bars to suit your personal multiclip editing style if, for example, you often use the 9-Up display or frequently switch audio and video angles together.

> **TIP** ▶ Final Cut Pro doesn't include a choice to restore the default Button Bars set. Before you change from the original set, choose Tools > Button Bars > Save and name the preset *Default*. That way, once you've switched to the Multiclip button bar set (or any other set), you can get back to the pristine state without having to manually clear each window's button bar.

1 Choose Tools > Button Bars > Multiclip.

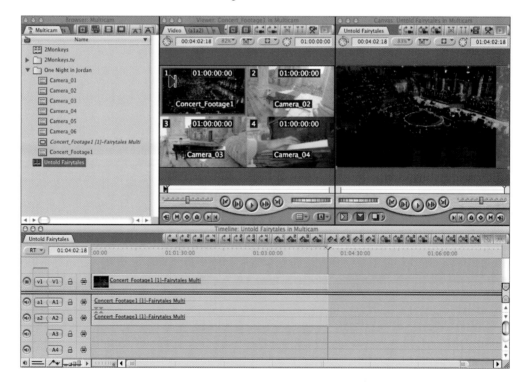

Dozens of buttons are added to all the windows. These buttons can be used to configure Final Cut Pro for multiclip editing and even to perform the edits.

2   Set the Playhead Sync mode to Open.

3   Switch focus to the Timeline or Canvas and play the sequence.

4   Instead of using the Viewer to cut between angles, click the cyan buttons in the Timeline button bar to cut between Angles 1 through 4. For this example, just make a few edits.

Temporary gray markers appear whenever you click one of the angle buttons, and when playback is stopped the markers are converted to edits.

As you can see, there are buttons for performing a variety of other actions, such as cutting the audio separately from the video (see "Separating Audio and Video" in this lesson) and switching between angles with effects on them (see "Applying Effects to Multiclips" in this lesson).

Switching Angles

After your multiclip has been divided into separate clips, you may change your mind and want to choose a different angle for a segment. This is called *switching* angles.

1   In the Timeline, right-click the second clip.

2   Choose Active Angle > Camera_05 from the shortcut menu.

That segment is changed to display the **Camera_05** angle.

TIP ▶ You can also use the buttons in the button bar to switch angles.

3   Deselect all clips, and then position the playhead over the third clip in the Timeline.

If a clip is selected, the buttons will switch the angle of that clip. If nothing is selected, they will apply to the clip under the playhead on the lowest auto-selected track.

4   In the Timeline button bar, click the Switch Video to Angle 2 button.

TIP ▶ You can also step through all the angles in order by clicking the Switch Video to Next Angle button or the Switch Video to Previous Angle button in the Canvas or Viewer button bars.

Using the Keyboard

You can work with multiclips most efficiently when you program keyboard shortcuts that help you quickly perform tasks at the touch of a key (or two).

Final Cut Pro has a keyboard layout specially designed for multiclip editing. This layout transforms the number keys on an extended keyboard so you can quickly switch and cut between angles.

To use this keyboard layout, choose Tools > Keyboard Layout > Multi-camera Editing. Although no obvious changes occur, your keyboard has been transformed into a multiclip editing console with the following multiclip-specific capabilities:

▶ Pressing the 1 through 0 keys (0 serves as angle 10) automatically switches the current video angle to the angle of the number you press.

▶ Pressing Option in combination with a number key switches the audio to the angle number selected.

▶ Pressing Command in combination with a number key *cuts* the multiclip, switching the new angle to the number chosen. This is equivalent to clicking the images in the Viewer.

▶ Pressing Shift in combination with a number key switches the video to the new angle number along with any applied effects.

One advantage to using keyboard shortcuts is that you can press keys to perform quick cuts or switches while the video is playing. Another advantage is that you can cut or switch among up to ten angles at once.

> **TIP** ▶ You can further increase the shortcuts' usefulness by rearranging the numbers so they match the relative positions in the Viewer. On the keyboard, the numbers 1, 2, and 3 occupy the bottom row, but in the Viewer, those angles are at the top. If you dare, arrange your shortcuts so the 7, 8, and 9 keys switch to angles 1, 2, and 3, and the 1, 2, and 3 keys switch to angles 7, 8, and 9. (4, 5, and 6 can be left alone).

If you forget what shortcuts are available in the Multicamera Editing keyboard layout, the tooltips on the button bar provide a quick reminder.

> **TIP** ▶ The Multicamera Editing keyboard layout is intended to be used on an extended keyboard with separate numerical entry keys. If you're working on a laptop or a condensed keyboard, you can still use the keyboard for switching and cutting between angles. Just make your own custom keyboard layout by choosing Tools > Keyboard Layout > Customize.

Separating Audio and Video

So far in this lesson, you've been cutting or switching multiclip angles with linked audio and video, or just changing the video (when using the buttons or keyboard shortcuts). So you've probably realized that you can switch the audio and video angles separately.

This is exactly what you would want to do with the current footage, in which the pre-recorded version of the song is attached to only one of the clips. All of the other video tracks include scratch audio, which is great for ensuring that all the clips are in sync but not ideal for a finished soundtrack.

When you edit a multiclip by clicking images in the Viewer, settings in the Playhead Sync menu control which channels are affected.

1 In the Timeline, press the Home key to move the playhead to the beginning of the sequence.

2 In the Viewer, click the Playhead Sync menu button and choose Audio > All.

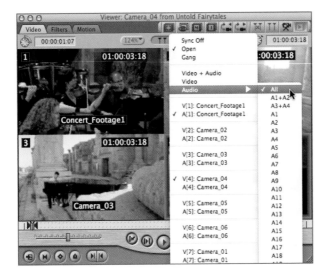

> **TIP** ▸ This setting can also be found in the View menu in the Multiclip Active Tracks submenu.

3 In the Viewer, click the **Concert_Footage1** angle.

A green border indicates which angle is providing the audio; a blue border indicates the selected video angle. These are referred to as the *active* angles.

> **NOTE** ▸ If the Viewer switches to the Audio tab, click back to the Video tab to select the desired angle.

4 Make sure that the Playhead Sync mode is set to Open and that Multiclip Playback is chosen.

5   Make the Timeline or Canvas window active and play the sequence.

6   As it plays, click between the different angles in the Viewer.

     This time, only the green box moves and, correspondingly, the edits you make in the
     sequence affect only the audio tracks.

7   Because in this example you don't want any audio edits, press Command-Z to undo
     and remove the edits you just made.

8   Click the Playhead sync menu and choose Video + Audio.

Applying Effects to Multiclips

You can apply filters, speed changes, and other effects to multiclips, just like ordinary
clips, but you must determine whether you want the effect applied to an individual angle
or to the whole multiclip, regardless of which angle is currently active.

After a filter or effect has been applied, you also must account for that effect when switching angles on the multiclip.

1   In the Effects tab, open the Video Filters bin and then open the Image Control bin.

2   Drag the Desaturate filter to the last clip in the Timeline. Continue to hold down the
     mouse button until the overlay appears.

     The overlay provides two choices: Apply to Source Angle or Apply to Multiclip. The
     first applies the effect to the current angle, and the second applies the effect to the
     clip, regardless of which angle is active.

3   Drag the clip onto Apply to Source Angle and release the mouse button.

4   Move the playhead so you can see the effect of the filter in the Canvas.

When a filter is applied to an individual angle, only that angle is affected. Switching to a different angle will leave that filter on the angle that is no longer in use, and the newly selected angle will be unfiltered.

If you choose Switch Video with Effects, the filter is applied to the new angle.

5   In the Timeline button bar, click the Switch Video with Effects to Angle 4 button, or press Shift-4.

The angle is switched, and the filter is applied to the new angle. Other effects, such as speed and motion effects, can also be moved from angle to angle in the same manner.

Bonus Exercise

Take the time to do a full multicamera edit for the Zade music video. Using the rhythm of the music to guide your editing, make sure that you never include a shot where you can see one of the other cameras, and never see a black screen (because the angle you chose had run out of footage). Use the close-up of the piano keys at the most opportune times. Have fun with it and try different versions to see how they have different impacts.

Lesson Review

1. What is a multiclip?

2. How do you create a multiclip?

3. How do you drag a multiclip into the Timeline or Canvas from the Viewer?

4. What are two settings you must activate before live multiclip editing is possible?

5. What does it mean to collapse a multiclip?

6. How do you rearrange multiclip angles in the Viewer?

7. How do you control which tracks are affected by multiclip edits?

8. Can filters and effects be applied to multiclips?

Answers

1. A multiclip is a special type of clip that contains between 2 and 128 angles, any one of which can be used at one time.

2. Select the clips in the Browser and choose Modify > Make Multiclip.

3. You must hold down the Option key to drag a multiclip in the Viewer.

4. In the RT menu, turn on the Multiclip Editing setting and set the Playhead Sync mode to Open.

5. Converting a multiclip back into individual clips after it has been edited in a sequence.

6. Hold down Command while dragging the angles to rearrange them in the Viewer. Command-dragging an angle out of the Viewer deletes it from the multiclip.

7. Choose the video and/or the specific audio tracks listed in the Playhead Sync menu.

8. Yes.

Digital Genesis— Edward R. Abroms

EDWARD R. ABROMS IS NO STRANGER TO TAKING RISKS.

With more than a decade of editing indie features under his belt (including *Brooklyn to Manhattan*, *Checking Out*, and *Point Blank*) plus dozens of episodes of fast-paced TV shows like *CSI: Miami, Law & Order, and Day Break*, Abroms is used to pushing the technological envelope to save time and money in post.

Even so, the all-digital venture he embarked on with *The Genesis Code* was a daring one. The film—in which a college hockey player and a female journalism student struggle to find common ground between faith and science—was shot on RED cameras and edited with the just-released Final Cut Pro 7. So Abroms was using a new workflow and new software, on location in Michigan, on a tight indie budget with no wiggle room. We asked him how it went.

Ed Abroms in his 2K edit suite for The Genesis Code.

Describe your ingest workflow—was there anything unusual about it?

We used the new log-and-transfer function in Final Cut Pro 7 for RED footage. With log-and-transfer, when importing RED .r3d files, you can transcode to any of the ProRes codecs on import. We decided to import directly into ProRes HQ at 2K resolution.

One nice feature is that FCP's log-and-transfer uses whatever metadata is on the RED files, including the color-space settings chosen by the cameraman. So the look they wanted when they shot the footage is baked into the ProRes HQ files.

What advantages do you see in working with RED source files versus other tapeless formats?

It's wonderful to have 2K files to work with. My cutting room was also essentially a dailies screening room. We had a 12- by 9-foot screen with a 2K Panasonic projection system set up in the editing room. We projected our ProRes HQ dailies directly out of the computer onto the screen after log and transfer.

It's been ten years or more since I was able to sit down every night with the DP and director on location and watch dailies. It was very refreshing. I didn't physically edit to that screen during the day, but I was able to look up from my two 24-inch displays and see my scene across the room in full 2K resolution. It was like having a DI suite right in the editing room.

Are there challenges unique to the RED workflow?

Even though ProRes HQ files are 10 to 15 percent larger than the RED files, we decided to go with them in order to maintain a 2K workflow from shoot through post.

A lot of Final Cut editors like the proxy QuickTime files that the RED camera generates, because they can be rendered dynamically in different resolutions. But they can be a pain to work with, and the performance isn't what we'd like. Occasionally, we'd use them to double-check some footage on a drive, but for the most part, the ProRes HQ codec gives you much better performance inside Final Cut Pro and lets you bring in multiple streams and do real-time effects, which is not possible with even the highest resolution proxy files.

Describe your output workflow from Final Cut Pro.

When the cut is delivered, the DI will be done in Los Angeles. We cut in 2K, which will be the actual resolution of the delivery. Rather than send the DI house an EDL or XML files, we're sending them the entire cut as a Final Cut Pro project file, along with the RED file backups that they'll be using for the actual DI, rather than using the Pro Res HQ material. It's a truly unique way of doing a DI.

Much of your editing is done remotely from your producer and from the set. How do you get feedback?

We used several remote review tools, one of which was the new iChat Theater, which lets people in different locations view and edit a Final Cut project in real time.

One of my producers works in Peoria, Illinois, so I used iChat Theater to let him see anything he wanted on my Canvas or Viewer. I could also switch the iChat view between clips and sequences while we talked, or turn on a timecode overlay to help identify specific frames. It worked great.

Are there any other new Final Cut Pro 7 features that helped your workflow?

One of the great new features in Final Cut Pro 7 is the ability to use different color-coded clip and sequence markers to indicate groupings and kinds of scenes or sequences. For example, we used purple to mark and number each line of dialogue, green markers to indicate gags, and so on.

I also liked the redesigned time-remapping feature, which allows clips to be played at variable speeds within a sequence. It made doing a speed ramp a very easy task. We also used Motion 4 to render the time-remapped clips using optical-flow interpolation. It can take a long time to render, but we sent a couple of clips directly from the Final Cut Pro Timeline to Motion in order to use this feature, and the result looked as though it had been ramped in-camera.

Advanced Compositing
and Effects

7

Lesson Files	Lesson Files > Lesson_07 > Compositing.fcp
Media	Surf Video
Time	This lesson takes approximately two hours to complete.
Goals	Use motion parameters to transform clips
	Create motion effects using the onscreen controls in the Canvas
	Reset attributes
	Apply composite modes to clips
	Copy and paste attributes from one clip to another
	Arrange multiple clips into a single composition
	Use the Crop and Distort tools
	Work with multilayered Photoshop files
	Construct Travel Matte effects

Advanced Compositing

Compositing is a general term that describes the act of combining multiple images onscreen at the same time. The result is called a *composition*. In Final Cut Pro, to composite images, you stack clips on multiple tracks at the same point in the Timeline. Compositing typically begins by modifying the scale, position, rotation, and other similar parameters of the clips involved.

Using motion parameters such as Scale, Rotation, Center, and Crop, you can create anything from a simple split screen to a multilayered motion graphics sequence that integrates video and graphics. By mastering these compositing techniques, you can create exciting visuals, as well as solve simple, everyday editing problems.

In this lesson, you'll learn the fundamentals of motion properties and then create a finished composition: an opening sequence for a program about surfing culture. Then you'll learn how to quickly reshape, distort, reposition, crop, and superimpose video clips; save time by reusing motion settings; and refine your effects for professional results.

Launching a Project

To begin, you'll open a project file and change the window layout to one best suited for this kind of motion graphics work.

1 Open Lesson Files > Lesson_07 > **Compositing.fcp.**

2 Double-click the *Surf Intro* sequence to open it into the Timeline, if it's not already open.

3 Choose Window > Arrange > Two-Up.

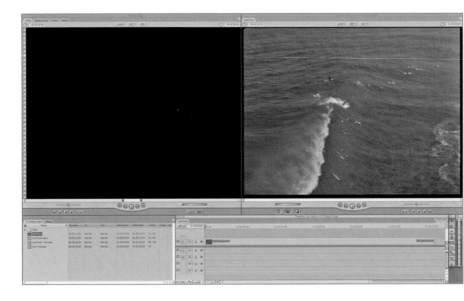

By default, the Final Cut Pro standard window layout maximizes the area available for the Timeline by shrinking the Viewer and Canvas and making room for the Browser. Although this is an excellent layout for editing, you may find that the two-up window layout is more useful for working on effects because it increases the size of the Viewer and Canvas while reducing the Timeline's width. Motion graphics and compositing tasks involve more activity in the Viewer and Canvas—such as adjusting parameters and onscreen controls—and less activity in the Timeline. So this redistribution of screen real estate makes sense.

TIP ▶ If your computer's display is big enough, you may want to increase the height of the Timeline so you can view more video tracks.

4 Move the pointer to the border between the Timeline and the Viewer or Canvas. When it becomes the Resize pointer, drag the border up to simultaneously resize all four windows in the interface.

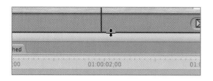

You'll find that different compositing tasks emphasize different parts of the interface. Some tasks require more room in the Canvas; others need more room in the Timeline or the Viewer. With the Final Cut Pro window resizing controls, you can quickly make room where you need it and keep your workspace organized.

5 To make even more room for your video clips in the Timeline, move your pointer to the divider between the video and audio tracks and drag it downward.

Using RT Extreme Settings

With a few exceptions, most of the effects you use in this book will play in real time on current Macintosh systems. You should be aware, however, that Final Cut Pro includes a few options to optimize real-time playback performance on your computer. These settings are located at the top left of the Timeline in the Real-Time Effects (RT) pop-up menu.

Clicking the RT pop-up menu reveals the options shown in the screen below.

```
    Safe RT
  ✓ Unlimited RT

    Play Base Layer Only

  ✓ Scrub High Quality

    Playback Video Quality
  ✓ Dynamic
    High
    Medium
    Low

    Playback Frame Rate
    Dynamic
  ✓ Full
    Half
    Quarter

  ✓ Multiclip Playback

    Record To Tape
    Use Playback Settings
  ✓ Full Quality
```

These settings allow you to maximize the real-time performance of your computer. The following settings are especially important:

▶ Safe RT restricts Final Cut Pro to displaying only those effects that can be played in real time at the current frame rate of your project. Sections of your Timeline that exceed your computer's capabilities are not displayed, and they're identified by a red render bar at the top of the Timeline ruler and the word "unrendered" in the Canvas during playback.

TIP ▶ By using Safe RT, you guarantee that whatever you see in the Canvas is an accurate representation of your finished program.

▶ Unlimited RT frees Final Cut Pro to attempt to process and play back effects that exceed the capabilities of your computer. In other words, if you're piling on more effects than your Mac can handle, Final Cut Pro will try to process them anyway. This may result in reduced frame rate or picture quality (or both), but you'll never see that annoying "unrendered" warning in the Canvas.

TIP ▶ Sections of your sequence that trigger this behavior are identified by an orange render bar in the Timeline.

▶ In both the Playback Video Quality and Playback Frame Rate sections, choosing Dynamic allows Final Cut Pro to reduce and increase the resolution and/or frame rate of the Canvas on the fly to continue real-time playback of effects. For consistency, if you want to fix the quality at which your images play back onscreen, you can choose one of the resolutions or frame rates that appear below in the RT pop-up menu.

> **TIP** ▶ Lower resolutions and frame rates exchange image quality for increased real-time playback capabilities when you're working with effects-intensive projects.

In the current project, the Browser contains a project file that shows Unlimited RT in action.

1   Double-click the *Unlimited RT Demo* sequence to open it into the Timeline.

   Depending on your computer's capabilities, the three sections of the sequence containing effects should have orange render bars.

2   Play the sequence, and watch the results in the Canvas.

   As the sequence plays, you should observe that playback is smooth in the sections of the sequence with no effects. You should also see varying numbers of dropped frames in each orange bar–marked Unlimited RT section. This is an exceptionally useful mode in which to work because you can see real-time previews of your compositions regardless of the type or quantity of effects you use. This defers the need to render a sequence until you have to see the final, full-resolution result.

> **TIP** ▶ The results of this exercise will vary depending on your Mac's speed, number of processors, and graphics card.

3   Position your pointer over the orange area of the render bar to activate the tooltip.

01:00:01:00	01:00:02:00	Video: Unlimited Audio: Gap A motion or compositing effect can not be played in real time.	01:00:0

   The tooltip indicates what effect is requiring Final Cut Pro to activate Unlimited RT mode.

4   Position your pointer over several areas of the render bar to see other indications that the Render Bar tooltip can display.

   Raw media files are indicated as such, as are areas that have already been rendered.

5   In the Timeline, Control-click the Unlimited RT Demo tab and choose Close from the shortcut menu.

Monitoring Canvas Playback Quality

One last note before you get started: The image quality of effects in the Canvas will vary depending on the effects you've applied and your computer's ability to keep up with the processing demands of Final Cut Pro.

Clips in the Timeline identified with green, yellow, dark yellow, or orange render bars are displaying *approximations* of their final appearance. This is useful for quickly seeing the results of your work, but when your project is complete you should always render these sections to verify the appearance of the final effect.

> **TIP** ▶ Effects in these color-identified sections of the Timeline are always rendered prior to being printed to video or edited to tape unless you override this behavior by opening the RT pop-up menu and choosing the Record to Tape > Use Playback Settings option. Video exported to QuickTime or that uses Compressor is always rendered at full quality.

Reviewing Motion Basics

Before diving into the Surf lesson, take a moment to review the most common ways you can transform clips. These techniques will be used extensively in later exercises.

1   Double-click **Surf_Background** in the Timeline to open it into the Viewer, and click the Motion tab.

The Motion tab contains motion parameters associated with every video clip. The controls in this tab are separated into groups, which you can open or close by clicking the disclosure triangles to the right of each group name. By default, the Basic Motion parameters are exposed, revealing the Scale, Rotation, Center, and Anchor Point controls.

2   Drag the Scale slider to the left until it's set at around 60.

As you make this adjustment, you can see the clip shrink in the Canvas.

The Scale parameter is a simple percentage, which can be adjusted from 0 (which makes the image non-existent) to 1000.

TIP Beware that enlarging an image beyond 100 may result in a softening of the image.

3   In the Canvas, click the View pop-up menu, and choose Image+Wireframe.

This option makes a wireframe appear over the selected clip in the Canvas. If you don't see the wireframe, either the playhead isn't over the selected clip, or no clip is selected. To select a clip, click it in the Canvas or in the Timeline.

TIP ▶ Double-clicking a clip, either in the Canvas (in Wireframe mode) or in the Timeline, opens that clip into the Viewer.

Wireframes serve two purposes. First, they let you know which clips are selected. Second, they provide you with onscreen controls to graphically adjust most of the motion parameters (displayed in the Motion tab of the Viewer) in the Canvas.

4   In the Canvas, move the pointer directly over one of the corner handles of the wireframe.

5   When the arrow turns into a crosshair, drag the corner point toward the center of the Canvas to shrink the clip.

TIP ▶ If your pointer changes to the Window Resize pointer instead of the crosshairs, dragging will resize the windows rather than resize the clip. Be sure to see which pointer is active before dragging.

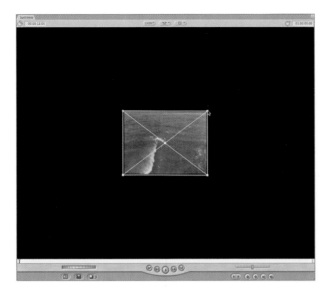

As you drag the clip's corner, notice how the Scale parameter updates in the Motion tab of the Viewer.

TIP By default, resizing is done proportionally, around the center of the clip.

6   Shift-click one of the wireframe corners, and drag it up and to the left.

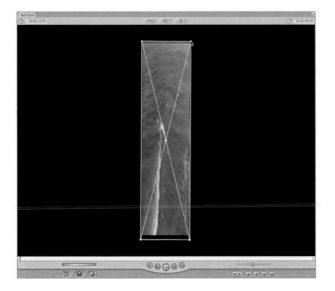

By holding down the Shift key while you resize an image in the Canvas, you can resize it freely, squeezing or stretching it out of its original proportions by simultaneously adjusting the Aspect Ratio parameter (currently hidden in the Distort parameter group in the Motion tab of the Viewer).

7   Position your pointer over any edge of the clip.

The Rotate pointer appears.

8   Drag the edge of the clip to rotate it.

9   Position your pointer anywhere over the body of the clip.

The Rotate arrow changes to a Move pointer (a crosshair with arrows on each end).

10 Drag the clip to change its position in the Canvas.

The Center Point control in the Viewer updates to reflect the new value.

11 Shift-drag the clip from anywhere in the body of the object, left to right or up and down.

NOTE ▶ Pressing Shift constrains clip movement to horizontal or vertical directions.

For every action you make in the Canvas, the values in the Motion tab are updated. And similarly, modifying the values in the Motion tab automatically updates the Canvas (assuming the Canvas is currently parked on the clip open in the Viewer).

TIP ▶ If you want to set precise numerical values, it's far easier to use the Motion tab, but if you want to observe the intuitive feedback and get a general feel for the effect, dragging in the Canvas is superior.

Resetting Attributes

Before you continue, it's critical to know how to undo all of these changes and reset the clip to its native state. Aside from manually returning each parameter to its default settings, there are two ways you can restore a clip's attributes.

1   To begin, click the Reset button, located in the Motion tab of the Viewer to the right of the Basic Motion section header.

This button resets all the controls in the Basic Motion section. However, it doesn't restore the Aspect Ratio parameter because that setting is part of the Distort parameter group (which has its own Reset button). Fortunately, another method for resetting a clip's parameters is more comprehensive.

2 In the Timeline, Control-click the **Surf_Background** clip, and choose Remove Attributes from the shortcut menu.

3 In the Remove Attributes dialog that appears, select the parameter groups you want to restore to their default settings and click OK. By default, the Distort setting is already selected.

The image is now returned to its default size and position, ready for you to create your first composition.

The Remove Attributes dialog displays checkboxes for every parameter group, filter, and speed setting that can be applied to a group. If you want to immediately set a clip to its default state, this is the way to do it.

> **TIP** ▶ You can also use the Remove Attributes dialog to remove attributes from multiple clips at once. For instance, one clip may have a filter and another clip may have an altered motion setting. Simply select all clips with effects, Control-click, and choose Remove Attributes from the shortcut menu. Then select the attributes you want to remove from all of the clips.

Creating a Multilayered Show Opener

In this exercise, you'll build on the previously described techniques to create an intro for a video program on surfing, imaginatively titled *Surf*. As is typical for many show opens, a wealth of unused B-roll was made available from the shoot, providing you with the opportunity to create a multilayered composition of surfing shots. A designer has also provided a multilayered Photoshop file that you'll use as the actual title and logo for the show.

The final composition will consist of a background clip, four foreground clips, and four graphics layers on top of that. In the process of marrying all of these elements together, you'll also be bringing together many different compositing techniques.

Previewing the Final Composition

Before you get started, take a look at the final product to orient yourself.

1   Double-click the *Surf Intro - Finished* sequence to open it into the Timeline.

2   Move the playhead to the beginning of the sequence and press the spacebar to play.

> **TIP** ▶ If your computer is dropping too many frames to keep up with all the effects in this sequence, render the sequence by making the Timeline or Canvas the active window, and choosing Sequence > Render All > Both (Option-R).

As you work on the exercises in this lesson, feel free to refer to the finished version of the project by clicking back and forth between the Surf Intro and Surf Intro - Finished tabs in the Timeline or Canvas. This should help guide your adjustments.

Editing Superimposed Video Layers

The first thing you need to do is edit in the clips you want to use in this composition.

1   In the Browser, open the Clips bin.

    There are two ways to edit superimposed clips into a sequence.

2   In the Timeline, click the Surf Intro sequence tab.

    There's a single item in the Timeline: the **Surf_Background** clip that happens to be the placeholder clip from your imaginary original program. You need to superimpose the clips that you'll arrange in the middle of this composition.

3   Press the Home key to move the playhead to the beginning of the sequence, and then drag the **Surf_Shot_02** clip into the Canvas and drop it onto the Superimpose Edit Overlay.

A new video track is created above track V1, and the clip is edited into it. You can also superimpose the clips by using keyboard shortcuts.

TIP To use the F9 through F12 keyboard shortcuts to make edits in this next step, you need to disable these keyboard shortcuts in the Dashboard and Exposé panels of the System Preferences window, as well as enable the "Use F1, F2, etc. keys as standard function keys" setting in the Keyboard panel of the System Preferences window.

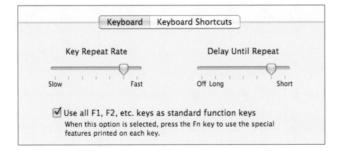

4   Press Command-4 to make the Browser active. Use the arrow keys to select the **Surf_Shot_01** clip, and press the Return key to open that clip into the Viewer. Press F12 to edit the selected clip into the sequence with a superimpose edit.

Notice that **Surf_Shot_01** has been superimposed over the track indicated by the source/ destination controls, which is still track V1. The first clip you edited in, **Surf_Shot_02**, moved up to a new video track to make room. This demonstrates that superimposed clips are always edited into a sequence above the destination track.

If there are clips already in the track above, they'll all move up one track to make room.

The second method of superimposing clips in the Timeline is a more hands-on technique (for those of you who prefer to keep your hands on the mouse).

5   Drag the **Surf_Shot_03** clip to the beginning of the Timeline and drop it into the gray area above track V3.

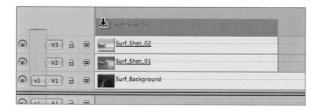

A new video track is created, and the clip is edited in above the other clips. One advantage to dragging a clip into place is that it spares you the step of changing the source/destination track pairing when you want to add a clip to the very top of a growing stack of clips.

TIP In this latest method, if snapping is turned on, the clip will snap , so you can use the beginning of the clip in the Timeline or the playhead for precise alignment.

6   Drag the **Surf_Shot_04** clip to the top of the superimposed stack of clips. These are all of the video clips you'll be using for this opening sequence.

Cropping Images

Cropping allows you to cut off part of the top, bottom, and sides of an image. You might do this to hide unwanted edges of an image, to eliminate all but just the portion of a clip you want for your composition, or to open up room for other images.

If you look closely in the Canvas in the following figure, you'll notice a thin black border at the edges of the image.

Borders such as these along one or more edges of the frame are commonly found in video from a variety of sources. Many camcorders record these black borders along one side of the frame. Some video capture cards introduce similar borders. In other cases, the equipment used to telecine film to video may introduce such borders.

In this exercise, you'll trim these unwanted borders from clips that are resized and superimposed into the overall composition. You'll also crop into some of the images to make room for other elements. Along the way, you'll turn on features in the Canvas that make it easier for you to perform these and other compositing tasks.

1   Move the playhead to the beginning of the sequence, and from the View pop-up menu, choose Show Overlays if necessary. If you don't see the title safe boundaries, choose Show Title Safe from the View pop-up menu.

The title safe boundaries appear in the Canvas.

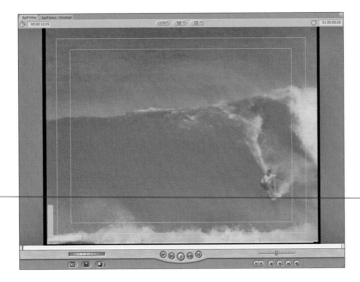

As you create compositing layouts for broadcast video programs, it's typical to refer to the title and action safe boundaries of the picture.

TIP ▶ Most televisions display a video image by overscanning it. In other words, approximately 10 to 20 percent of the outer parts of the image is "cut off" behind the bezel of the television, to provide a "full-screen" image. With older television tubes, this overscan hid significant distortion due to the curves at the edges of the screen. These problems are less severe or alleviated altogether with modern flat-screen and flat-panel TVs.

However, to give guidance to the motion graphics designer, the outer boundary indicates the action safe area. You can reliably expect everything outside this area (the outer 10 percent) to be cut off by most televisions. The inner boundary indicates the title safe area (which excludes the outer 20 percent of the picture) that should be visible and undistorted on virtually every television.

In this image, you can see a thin black border. Compared to the outer action safe boundary, you can assume that this part of the picture will be outside the area that anyone will see on television. On the other hand, if you intend to resize the image to fit within a composition (as in this example), you can't let the borders show.

2 In the Timeline, double-click **Surf_Shot_04** to open it into the Viewer. Click the Motion tab, and then click the disclosure triangle next to the Crop parameter group.

3 Drag the Left slider to the right until you've cropped the image all the way to the action safe boundary.

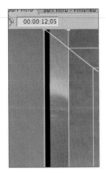

As you crop the top image, notice that the area being cropped is indicated by a separate crop wireframe, and the images that appear underneath start to peek through.

TIP The sliders are really useful when you need to make precise adjustments. However, there's a tool you can use to crop images directly in the Canvas that's a little more interactive.

4   Click the Crop tool.

5   In the Canvas, move the pointer to the right edge of the image. When the pointer turns into the Crop pointer, drag the edge to the left, all the way to the action safe boundary, to crop it.

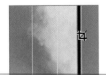

This would be useful if you just wanted to exclude the unwanted border around the image prior to shrinking it, but you actually want to crop in to isolate the surfer within the frame.

6   From the Zoom menu at the top of the Canvas, choose Fit All.

The image in the Canvas shrinks to display more of the gray border around the image. This makes it easier to manipulate the outer edges of wireframes located at the edge of the frame.

7   In the Canvas, scrub through **Surf_Shot_04** to get a sense of where the surfer goes in the frame.

In this clip, the surfer moves from his position at the right of the frame to a point just about halfway through the frame, before he "cuts back."

8   Use the Crop tool on the right edge of **Surf_Shot_04** to drag the crop wireframe to touch the surfer at the beginning of his motion, and drag the crop wireframe at the left edge of the clip to touch the surfer at the end of his motion. Also, crop just a little of the top and bottom of the image to get rid of the black border.

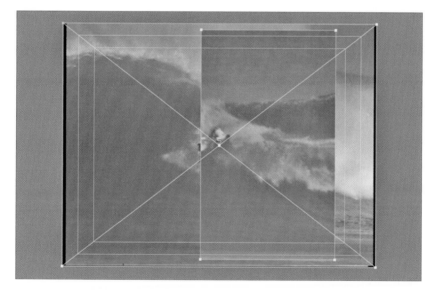

Next, you'll crop each superimposed clip to isolate the greatest area of motion.

TIP ▸ With so many clips in the Canvas, however, operating on the wireframe of a layer underneath can be difficult, so you should solo each video track containing the clip you want to work on.

9   Option-click the Track Visibility control for track V4.

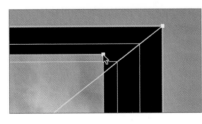

This control turns off the visibility of every other video track, leaving just the clips in the track you Option-clicked visible. Option-clicking the same Track Visibility control a second time makes all of the tracks visible again.

10   In the Canvas, click the clip.

Notice that selecting the clip in the Canvas also highlights it in the Timeline. The opposite also works. Selecting a clip in the Timeline also highlights that clip in the Canvas.

TIP ▶ This is a good way to select clips that may appear underneath other clips in a multilayered composition, as well as to select multiple clips for simultaneous operations.

So far, you've been individually cropping each side of an image. You can also crop two adjacent sides at once using the corner crop handles.

11   Move the Crop tool to the upper-right corner of the selected clip in the Canvas, and drag down and left to crop the top and right sides at the same time.

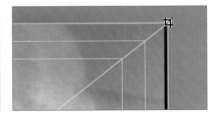

Before   After

12 Using the corner crop handles, crop all four sides of **Surf_Shot_03** to isolate and center the surfer within a smaller region.

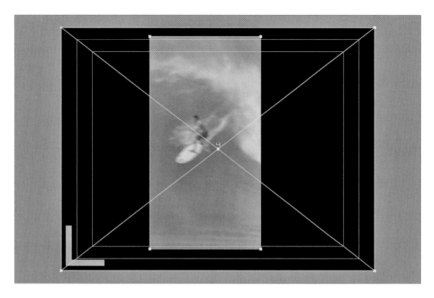

Because the **Surf_Background** clip is also hidden, you can clearly see the background of the sequence, which defaults to black.

> **TIP** Sometimes, to more clearly see what you're doing, it helps to choose a different background, strictly for display purposes.

13 In the View pop-up menu in the Canvas, choose Checkerboard 1.

14 Option click the Visible button for track V3 to solo that track.

15 In the Canvas, click **Surf_Shot_02** to display the wireframe, and crop the four sides to similarly isolate the surfer's movement within a smaller frame. (This time, crop the top and bottom a little closer.)

As you make this adjustment, you can see the clip image against a checkered background.

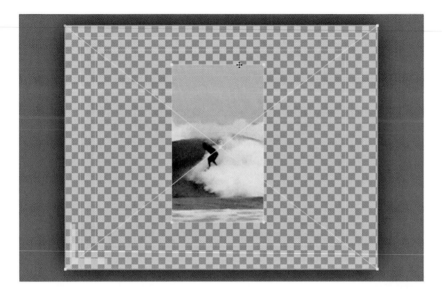

As with the resizing operations you performed, there are also keyboard shortcuts you can use to alter the behavior of the Crop tool.

16 Option-click the Track visibility control for track V3 to return all tracks to visibility.

> Another way to isolate a clip is to use the solo command.

17 Select the clip on track V2 and press Control-S to solo it.

18 In the Canvas, click the isolated clip to display its wireframe, and then hold down Command while you drag the left side of the image to crop both sides evenly.

> **TIP** You can also hold down Command and Shift while dragging an edge with the Crop tool to crop all four sides proportionally to the clip's aspect ratio.

19 Hold down Command and drag down the top edge of the clip to crop the top and bottom of the clip by the same amount.

20 Press Control-S to unsolo the clip, re-enabling all of the clips in the Timeline.

Resizing and Repositioning Clips

Now that you've cropped each of the superimposed clips, it's time to arrange them horizontally in the Canvas. You'll control the selection of clips using onscreen controls in the Canvas and items in the Timeline.

1   Press Home to return the playhead to the beginning of the sequence.

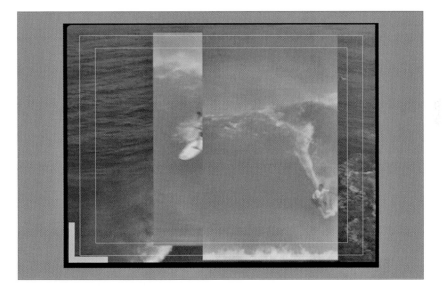

As you can see, the topmost clip is **Surf_Shot_04**.

TIP ▶ Clip ordering in the Canvas depends on the track order in the Timeline— clips in higher-numbered video tracks appear in front of clips in lower-numbered video tracks.

2   Double-click **Surf_Shot_04** to open it into the Viewer, and click the Motion tab, if necessary, to view the clip's motion parameters.

TIP ▶ It's not necessary to open a clip into the Viewer to transform it in the Canvas, but looking at its settings in the Motion tab while you make adjustments lets you see the numeric value of the changes you're making.

3   Press the A key to switch to the default Selection tool, and drag one of the four resize handles (the outer corners, not the inner crop handles) toward the center of the clip until the value of the Scale parameter is approximately 56.

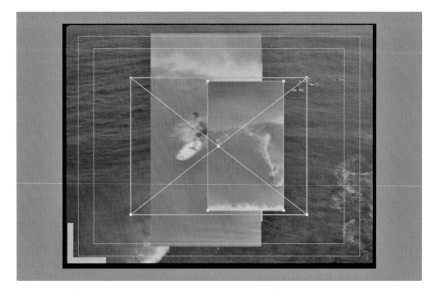

4   Double-click **Surf_Shot_03** to open it into the Viewer, and drag one of its resize handles toward the center of the clip until the value of the Scale parameter is around 70. It's not necessary to be exact.

> **TIP** When you open a clip into the Viewer, whichever tab was open for the previous clip remains open, but it's updated to reflect the settings of the newly opened clip.

At this point, the clips underneath the top two clips in the Timeline are getting obscured. It's time to move the top two clips into position.

5   Open **Surf_Shot_04** in the Viewer, and then Shift-drag the clip to the left until the first value in the Center parameter is about –147.

> **TIP** Release the mouse button periodically to let the Center parameter in the Motion tab update to its current position.

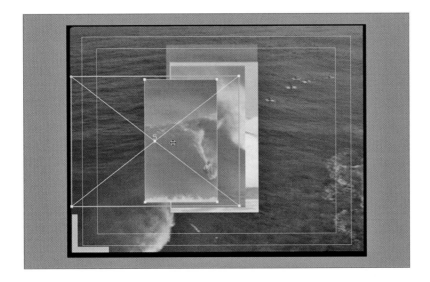

6   Select **Surf_Shot_03** in either the Timeline or Canvas, and Shift-drag it to the right to roughly match this position:

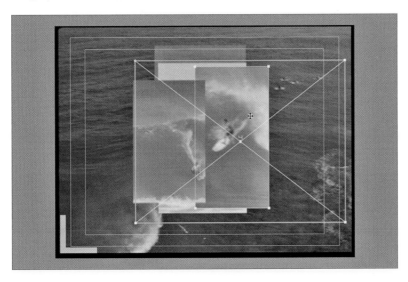

Double-click **Surf_Shot_03** to open its settings in the Viewer. If you look at the Motion tab, you'll see that the Center parameter's value is about 85.

At this point, the onscreen controls of the two front clips are obscuring those of the clips below them. Fortunately, you can still select any clip in the Canvas by selecting it in the Timeline.

7 Move and resize the remaining two clips until your composition in the Canvas resembles this:

TIP ▶ Refer to the *Surf Intro - Finished* sequence to see how your version compares at this point to the finished project.

Positioning Clips Precisely in the Canvas

From time to time, you'll find yourself wanting to nudge a clip's position in the Canvas one pixel at a time. Other compositing applications typically use the arrow keys for this function. In Final Cut Pro, the arrow keys are used to navigate and position clips temporally in the Timeline. However, selecting a clip and then pressing Option with an arrow key lets you nudge a clip spatially in the Canvas.

1 Select Surf_Shot_03 in the Canvas.

2 With the Canvas active, press Option–Down Arrow repeatedly to more closely align the top and bottom of this clip with the superimposed clip appearing all the way to the left.

TIP ▶ This step will only work with the Canvas selected.

Distorting Images

The settings in the Distort parameter group of the Motion tab are useful for many purposes. By adjusting the Aspect Ratio slider, you can mix 4:3 and 16:9 material in the same sequence. By using the corner parameters or the Distort tool in the Tool palette, you can warp an image by its corner handles to create artificial perspective, to make an image fit into a design, or to fit the clip into a composite (such as making a graphic look like a sign on a wall by matching the perspective of the wall).

In this exercise, you'll use the Distort tool to add some angles to your design.

1   In the Tool palette, click the Crop icon and hold down the mouse button. When the related tools appear, select the Distort tool and release the mouse button.

> **TIP** You can also press the D key once, or the C key twice, to change to the Distort tool.

2   Select **Surf_Shot_04**, and then drag each of the four corner handles (not the inner crop handles) to warp the image so that it looks like this:

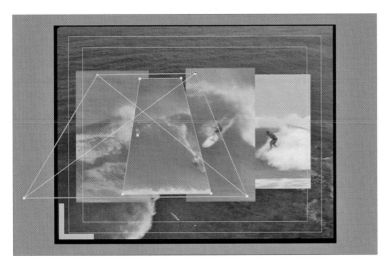

Using the Distort tool, you can independently drag each corner handle to create a wide range of effects.

3 Select **Surf_Shot_03**, and Shift-drag the upper-left corner to the left using the Distort tool.

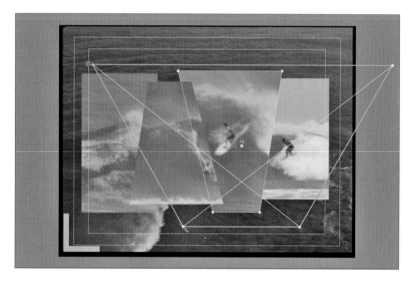

The top corners move outward simultaneously as the bottom corners move inward, simulating a perspective shift, as if the clip were tilting.

4 Use the Distort tool to warp **Surf_Shot_02** and **Surf_Shot_01** to look like this:

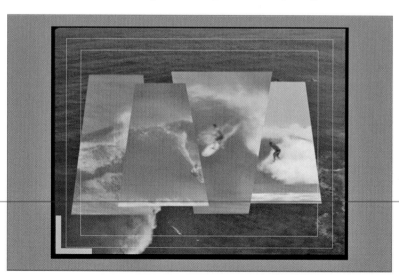

Changing Clip Timing

At this point, the layout is starting to take shape, but it's a little static. An easy way to add some life to the composition is to stagger the introduction of each of the clips so they appear one at a time. You can then take advantage of their pre-edited durations to have them fade out, one at a time, making room for the title graphic to be added later.

1 Drag to select all of the superimposed clips above the **Surf_Background** clip in the Timeline.

![Timeline showing clips Surf_Shot_04, Surf_Shot_03, Surf_Shot_02, Surf_Shot_01 on tracks V5-V2, and Surf_Background on V1]

2 Type *+1.* (1 followed by a period) so that a special indicator appears at the top of the Timeline. Press Return.

TIP The period is a placeholder for two zeros, so you've specified that the selected clips should move 1 second forward.

![Timeline showing the clips Surf_Shot_04, Surf_Shot_03, Surf_Shot_02, Surf_Shot_01 moved forward on tracks V5-V2, and Surf_Background on V1]

3 Command-click **Surf_Shot_01** to deselect it while leaving the clips above selected. Then type *+15* and press Return to move the selected clips forward 15 frames in the Timeline.

4 Keep moving the clips forward in staggered fashion, deselecting the bottom clip by Command-clicking it, and shifting the remaining selected clips forward by 15 frames until the sequence looks like this:

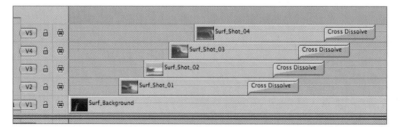

5 Control-click the end point of each clip, and choose Add Transition 'Cross Dissolve' from the shortcut menu.

NOTE ► If your default transition is not set to Cross Dissolve, you can set it to be the default by Control-clicking the Cross Dissolve transition in the Effects tab.

After you've added a dissolve to the end of each clip, your sequence should resemble this:

6 Play the sequence from the beginning.

Each clip should appear 15 frames later than the previous one, dissolving away in the same staggered order.

Experimenting with Composite Modes

Whenever two objects overlap in a video composite, you can mix the images in a variety of ways. The simplest is for one image to completely obscure the other. Another approach is to attenuate the opacity of the top image to create transparency.

Additionally, you can mix the pixels of the two images together in a mathematical equation, such as adding or subtracting the values. The results of such combinations can be significantly different from how either of the images looked originally. Such operations are called composite modes, and Final Cut Pro has several to choose from.

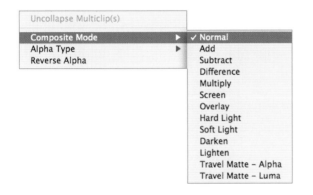

Some composite modes have an overall darkening effect, and some have an overall lightening effect. Some invert color values, and others do a combination of things. Composite mode effects tend to have seemingly unpredictable results, and in most cases the best procedure is to experiment and try different ones.

The composite modes that behave the most predictably are Multiply and Screen. A Multiply effect will only combine the dark portions of the clip, leaving the lighter areas unaffected. Drop shadows are traditionally applied using a Multiply mode, so that the shadow appears to darken the background, without having any impact on the lighter areas.

Conversely, the Screen mode adds only the lightest areas of the clip. Typically, effects like lightning bolts or explosions are combined using a Screen effect so that the background clip is illuminated without affecting the darker areas of the clip.

Overlay does a sort of combination of Multiply and Screen, affecting the darkest and lightest areas of an image without affecting the midrange values.

Composite modes are easy to apply and fun to experiment with.

1   Select **Surf_Shot_01** in the Timeline.

2   Choose Modify > Composite Mode > Add.

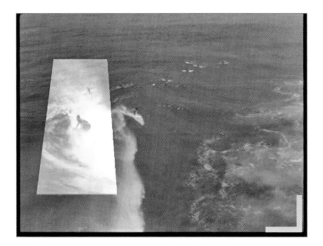

The Add composite mode tends to make the composition brighter.

TIP You can moderate the effect by changing the top clip's opacity.

3   In the Timeline, click the Clip Overlays control to display the opacity overlays.

4   Adjust the overlay for **Surf_Shot_01** to about 50%.

5   Control-click **Surf_Shot_02** and choose Composite Mode > Difference from the shortcut menu.

Difference is one of the most unpredictable composite modes.

6 Control-click **Surf_Shot_03** and choose Composite Mode > Screen from the shortcut menu.

As you can see, each of the modes has a unique and interesting effect. Experiment with the different modes yourself, and don't forget to see how opacity changes moderate the effect.

Adding Graphics from a Layered Photoshop File

Now it's time to add the title graphics. In this project, the title graphics have been created as a layered Adobe Photoshop file. Final Cut Pro can import files from any version of Photoshop. However, Final Cut Pro supports a limited set of Photoshop features. Opacity settings, some composite modes, layer order, and layer names are imported; but features such as layer effects, adjustment layers, and editable text are not supported.

Layered Photoshop files are imported like any other media file, but the way they appear inside your project is quite different.

1   Choose File > Import > Files, and select **Surf_Title.psd** from the Media > Surf Video folder.

> **TIP** ▶ If you have trouble finding the **Surf_Title.psd** file, it's also inside the Clips bin in the Browser.

As you can see, instead of being imported as a clip, the layered Photoshop file has been imported as a sequence.

2   In the Browser, double-click **Surf_Title.psd**.

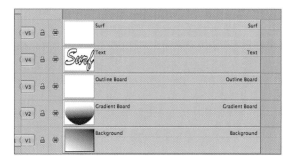

Like any sequence, it opens in the Timeline. There, each layer of the Photoshop file has been translated into a still image on an individual video track.

3   From the Zoom pop-up menu at the top of the Canvas, choose Fit All.

You can see that the graphic itself is quite large.

TIP It's fairly typical for motion graphics artists to provide artwork at a larger size than will eventually be used. That way, you don't have to risk softening the image if you later decide to zoom in on the graphic.

4   Turn off the Track Visibility control for track V1, which contains the background clip.

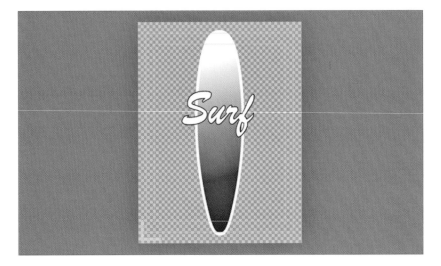

You can tell from the checkerboard background that the top four layers have a built-in *alpha channel*.

TIP An alpha channel is a fourth image channel—in addition to the red, green, and blue channels—that defines regions of transparency in an image.

5   From the Canvas View pop-up menu, choose Alpha.

This sets the Canvas to display the alpha channel as a grayscale image.

White areas of the alpha channel are 100 percent solid; black areas are 100 percent transparent. Gray areas of an alpha channel (if there are any) represent the semi-translucent values in between, with dark-gray areas being more translucent than light-gray areas.

6   From the View pop-up menu, choose RGB to display the image and change back to Black.

Adding the Logo to the Composition

In your composition, you need only the top four images, so you'll copy and paste these into the sequence you've been working on.

1   Drag to select the clips in tracks V2 through V5, and then press Command-C to copy them.

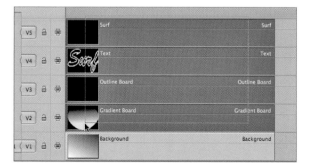

2   At the top of the Timeline, click the Surf Intro tab.

If you simply pasted these clips into your Timeline, the default behavior would be to paste them into the same tracks from which they originated, starting at the position of the playhead. Unfortunately, this would overwrite the existing clips in your sequence.

TIP ▶ You can override this behavior by using the Auto Select controls in the Timeline header.

The Auto Select controls let you determine which tracks in the Timeline are affected by operations such as filters, edits, and copying and pasting.

3   Control-click the gray area above the top video track in the Timeline and choose Add Track from the shortcut menu.

4   Option-click the Auto Select control for track V6.

TIP ▶ Option-clicking an Auto Select control turns on that control and turns off all the other Auto Select controls, effectively "soloing" it. Option-clicking a soloed Auto Select control turns back on all the other Auto Select controls.

5   Move the playhead to 01:00:03:00, and press Command-V to paste the copied clips to track V6 (and above).

All of the superimposed graphics you copied are pasted into your composition sequence, with the bottommost graphic layer appearing in the Auto Select–enabled track, and all the other superimposed graphics clips appearing above it, automatically making new video tracks.

In the Canvas, the graphics now appear superimposed over all of the other clips you've just placed.

NOTE ▶ You may need to scale the text object to match the image above.

Rotating the Surfboard

Next, you'll want to rotate the surfboard so that it's horizontal.

1   Press Command-Shift-A to deselect all the clips in the Timeline, and then select the clip in track V6 so that you're selecting only the surfboard graphic (not the text).

2   Press A to switch to the Selection tool, and then move the pointer to any edge of the wireframe.

> **TIP** ▶ Don't move too close to a corner or you'll get the Resize pointer instead of the Rotate pointer.

3   When the arrow becomes the Rotate pointer, drag in a circular motion to rotate the clip in the Canvas.

You can freely rotate any clip about its anchor point, but there's a keyboard shortcut that's really handy when you want to rotate a clip in 45-degree increments.

4   Hold down the Shift key and drag the edge of the wireframe. Notice how the graphic snaps vertically, diagonally, and horizontally. Drag the surfboard logo's gradient layer so that it's horizontal.

5   On track V7, select the surfboard outline and hold down the Shift key while rotating it to match the orientation of the surfboard logo gradient layer you rotated in step 4.

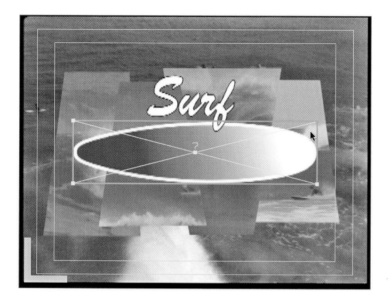

Creating Transparency

Now that the surfboard is correctly oriented, you need to make the center semitransparent to let some of the surfing action show through. Although opacity has no onscreen controls in the Canvas, there are still two ways to adjust it.

1   On track V6, double-click the clip to open it into the Viewer. Click the Motion tab, and click the disclosure triangle next to Opacity.

This is the Opacity slider, which lets you make uniform opacity changes to an entire clip. Opacity is measured as a percentage, from 0 (transparent) to 100 (solid).

TIP If the clip already has an alpha channel, the Opacity slider affects only the visible areas.

2   Drag the Opacity slider to the left until the value field reads 30.

As you drag the slider, you can see the middle of the surfboard become increasingly transparent.

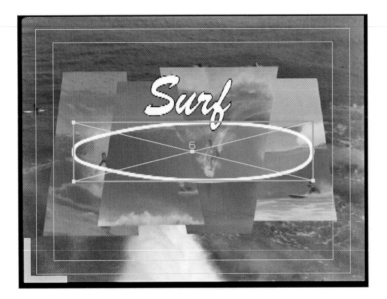

3 Check that the Clip Overlays control is active.

The Clip Overlays control toggles the visibility of the opacity and audio level overlays that appear over the clips in the Timeline. The opacity overlay provides another means of controlling clip opacity.

If you look at the opacity overlay for the clip in track V6, you can see that it's lower than the other clips, because you've already made an opacity adjustment in the Motion tab.

4 Move the pointer directly over the opacity overlay for the clip in track V6. When the pointer turns into the Resize pointer, drag up until the tooltip that appears shows a value between 45 and 50.

When you release the mouse button, the Canvas updates to show the new opacity setting. Unlike the Opacity slider in the Motion tab, the opacity overlays do not allow interactive adjustments to the image in the Canvas.

TIP The overlays are generally more useful for creating dynamic opacity changes using keyframes, which you'll learn in a later lesson, or when you simply need to make a quick opacity change and you don't want to open the clip in the Viewer.

Copying Attributes

The last task to complete the title is to move and resize the text component of the title graphic and add drop shadows to the four superimposed video clips. For both of these exercises, you'll be applying the same settings to multiple clips. To make this process faster, you'll use the Paste Attributes command.

Adjusting the Text Layers

Now that you've moved the surfboard, you need to transform the text of the title graphic to fit the new layout.

1   Select the clip in track V9, and in the Canvas, drag it so that it fits at the center of the surfboard graphic.

2   Resize it so that it's approximately as large as this:

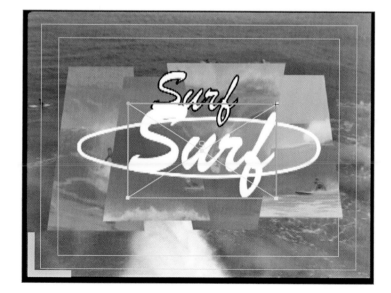

When you move the top clip, you can see that the black outline remains because it was actually created with a second layer in Photoshop.

You could copy and paste the values from the top clip's Motion tab to the corresponding parameters in the bottom clip, or you could manually drag the bottom clip in the Canvas to approximate the size and position of the top clip. But there's an easier way.

3   Select the clip in track V9, and press Command-C to copy it.

4   Control-click the clip in track V8, and choose Paste Attributes from the shortcut menu.

5   In the Paste Attributes dialog, select Basic Motion, and then click OK.

The clip in track V8 is transformed to match the scale and position of the clip you copied.

TIP   Paste Attributes is the opposite of the Remove Attributes command you learned earlier. It allows you to paste the attributes from any copied clip into the Motion parameter settings of another.

Adding Drop Shadows

Now you'll finish off the composition by adding drop shadows to the superimposed video clips and adding transitions to the In points of all the graphics layers in tracks V6 through V9.

1   Move the playhead to the beginning of **Surf_Shot_04**.

2 Double-click **Surf_Shot_04** to open it into the Viewer. Click the Motion tab, and click the disclosure triangle next to the Drop Shadow parameter group.

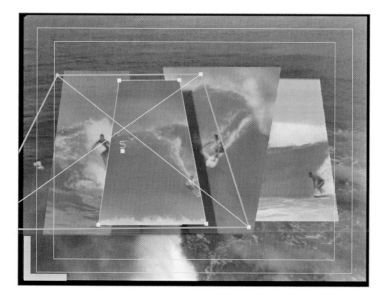

The Drop Shadow parameter group can be turned on and off as a whole, because all the settings within this group adjust the same effect.

3 In the parameter group header, select the Drop Shadow checkbox.

A drop shadow appears on the selected clip.

> **TIP** ▶ Drop shadows are mathematically complex. When creating a composite, delay adding drop shadows until the end of the process.

> **TIP** ▶ Drop shadows give the illusion of depth to objects within a composition.

4   To lighten the drop shadow a bit, drag the Softness slider to 50 and the Opacity slider to 30.

Now that you've customized the settings of one drop shadow, you don't have to go through all of these steps for the drop shadows in the remaining three clips. You can use Paste Attributes just once.

5   Make sure that **Surf_Shot_04** is selected in the Timeline and press Command-C to copy it.

6   Select **Surf_Shot_03**, **Surf_Shot_02**, and **Surf_Shot_01**. Control-click them and choose Paste Attributes from the shortcut menu.

7   In the Paste Attributes dialog, select the Drop Shadow checkbox and click OK. (Don't select any other parameters.)

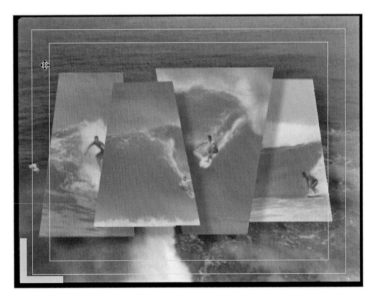

The drop shadow parameters are automatically copied to every selected clip in the Timeline.

8   In the Browser, click the Effects tab. Open the Video Transitions > Iris bin, and drag the Oval Iris transition to the beginning of every clip on tracks V6 through V9.

9   Press Home to move the playhead to the beginning of the sequence. Then play the sequence to see how you've done.

Creating a Travel Matte

A common effect is to use the shape of one image to serve as a matte for another—for example, having the video of the surfers visible inside the letters of the text.

This effect is called a traveling matte (or "travel matte" in FCP parlance).

> **TIP** ▶ It's called traveling because the matte shape can change or move, allowing the video to potentially "travel" across the screen.

The matte doesn't have to move to be considered a travel matte; to qualify, one image must be used to limit which portion of another image is displayed.

In Final Cut Pro, travel mattes are considered a composite mode, because essentially they're just another way of combining two images that overlap in time and space.

1   Double-click the *Travel Matte* sequence to open it into the Canvas and Timeline.

    Track 1 contains a modified version of the Surf title, and Track 2 is disabled.

2   Click the Track Visibility control on Track 2 to turn on track visibility.

The **Surf_Shot_04** clip obscures the Surf title.

3   Control-click **Surf_Shot_04** and choose Composite Mode > Travel Matte - Alpha.

The Surf title now acts as a matte, defining which areas of the other clip are visible.

There is one tricky aspect to creating travel matte effects in Final Cut Pro: Rather than applying the matte to a background image, you must apply the background image to the matte, which may seem counterintuitive.

The clip acting as the matte must be on the track *below* the clip that is to show through the matte, and it is the upper clip that must be set to the Travel Matte composite mode. Read that sentence again: Travel Matte composite mode on top; matte, below.

In the previous example, the Surf title's alpha channel is acting as the matte. Alternatively, you could matte a shot with another image's *luminance* (the levels of brightness or darkness). The affected clip will show through the light areas of the shot on the track below it. Every clip has some luminance values, so any clip can be used in this way. Depending on the clip you use, this can create some really bizarre effects. One great way to use this feature is to use one of the Final Cut Pro generators as the matte.

1   In the Timeline, skip to the second copy of **Surf_Shot_04**.

2   Position your playhead anywhere over the clip and press X to set In and Out points
     around the clip.

3   In the Viewer, click the Generators pop-up and choose Render > Cellular.

The Cellular generator is loaded into the Viewer.

4   Switch to the Controls tab and drag the Size slider to 64 (the maximum value).

5   Click the Gradient Reverse button as shown in the following figure to swap the black
     and white areas.

6   Click the Overwrite button or press F10 to edit the generator into the sequence.

7   In the Timeline, Control-click **Surf_Shot_04** and choose Composite Mode > Travel Matte - Luma from the shortcut menu.

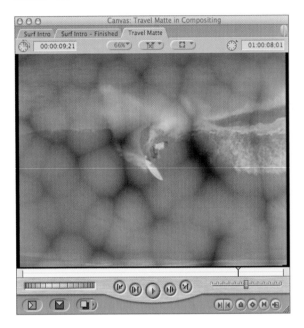

8   Play across the clip to see how the luminance value of the Cellular clip mattes the **Surf_Shot_04** clip.

NOTE ▶ You may need to render the clip (Option-R) to play it back in real time.

Lesson Review

1. Where are each clip's motion parameters located?

2. What motion parameters can you manipulate with the Selection tool using the onscreen controls in the Canvas?

3. What two motion parameters can you manipulate in the Canvas using separate tools?

4. How can you copy the motion effects settings from one clip to another?

5. How do you create a drop shadow for a clip?

6. What is a composite mode?

7. What kind of clips can have a composite mode applied?

8. How do you import a multilayered Photoshop file, and how does it appear within Final Cut Pro?

9. What is a travel matte effect?

10. In a travel matte effect composite, is the matte placed above or below the clip to be matted?

Answers

1. In the Motion tab, whenever that clip is open in the Viewer.

2. Scale, Rotation, and Center.

3. Crop and Distort each have separate tools.

4. Copy the clip with the settings you want to copy, and then use the Paste Attributes command on the clip you want to paste these settings into.

5. In the Motion tab, select the Drop Shadow checkbox, and adjust the Offset, Angle, Color, Softness, and Opacity settings to create the desired shadow effect.

6. Composite modes determine how two clips that overlap in time and space are displayed. Various mathematical equations are used.

7. Every clip can have a composite mode applied.

8. Photoshop files are imported using the File > Import > Files command. They appear within Final Cut Pro as sequences, with each layer of the Photoshop file superimposed on its own video track.

9. A travel matte effect uses one clip to determine which areas of another clip are visible.

10. The matte goes below the clip to be matted, and the upper clip gets the travel matte composite mode applied.

8

Mastering Video Filters

Filters are an easy way to create myriad effects, ranging from the subtle to the sublime. Many filters serve strictly utilitarian functions such as correcting color or screen-direction errors made during production. Others can stylize an image with painterly effects or glows; distort an image with blurs or pond ripples; overlay timecode numbers, borders, or other data; turn areas of an image transparent; and create a wide range of other effects.

The Final Cut Pro video filter system is a flexible and versatile architecture allowing for third-party plug-ins and even scripting directly in the program. Best of all, using filters is simple, easy, and quick to do.

This lesson deals exclusively with video filters. Final Cut Pro also has audio filters designed to create effects with your sound. Those are covered in Lesson 5, "Audio Sweetening."

Applying Filters

Filters can be applied to clips in a wide variety of ways to accommodate diverse work-flows and editing styles. Most editors employ different methods in different situations—dragging and dropping in one case, using the menus in another, and copying and pasting in a third.

One important distinction is whether you're applying the filter to a clip in the Browser or to a clip in a sequence. Modifying a clip in the Browser means that every occurrence of that clip used (from that point forward) will have the filter applied. Applying the filter to a clip in a sequence will modify only that one instance.

Applying Filters to a Browser Clip

If you want every instance of a clip to be filtered, apply the effect to the master clip in the Browser.

1   Open Lesson Files > Lesson_08 > **Filters.fcp**.

2   Double-click **Surf_Background** to open it into the Viewer.

3   Choose Effects > Video Filters > Image Control > Desaturate.

The clip turns black and white.

4 Drag the clip from the Viewer to the Canvas to overwrite it into the open *Applying Filters* sequence.

The clip in the sequence has the Desaturate filter applied.

> **TIP** ▶ If you later use any portion of this same clip, the filter will be applied in that instance as well. However, any changes you make to the master clip, such as deleting the filter or modifying the filter's parameters, will not propagate to the affiliate clips in the sequence. Similarly, changes made to any of the instances in the sequence will not affect any other instance or the master clip in the Browser.

Applying a Filter to a Clip in a Sequence

If you want a filter to be applied to only one use of a clip, after it's been edited into a sequence, all you have to do is park the sequence playhead anywhere over the clip and choose the filter from the Effects menu.

1 In the Browser, double-click the *Surf Clips* sequence.

2 Make sure the playhead is parked on the second clip (**Surf_Shot_02**).

3 Choose Effects > Video Filters > Distort > Ripple.

The filter is applied to the clip under the playhead. This works because of the Timeline's Auto Select feature.

Auto Select on   Auto Select off

However, if a clip is selected in the Timeline, Auto Select is overridden and the filter is applied to the selected clip.

4 Select the fourth clip (**Surf_Shot_04**).

5 Choose Effects > Video Filters > Perspective > Mirror.

The filter is applied to the selected clip, rather than the one under the playhead in the auto-selected track. You won't be able to tell until you play the sequence or move the playhead to the fourth clip.

6 Play the sequence until you can see the Mirror effect.

> **TIP** It's very easy to get confused in a situation like this, where a filter is successfully applied, but is applied to the wrong clip. If you ever apply a filter and don't notice any effect, always check which window is active and which clips are selected.

Using Auto Select with Multiple Tracks

If there is more than one clip under the playhead, the filter will be applied to any clip under the playhead, on a track where Auto Select is active.

1 Click outside the track area, or press Command-Shift-A, to deselect all.

2 Position the playhead over the three stacked clips near the end of the Timeline.

3 Turn off Auto Select for track V2. Make sure Auto Select is on for tracks V1 and V3.

4 Choose Effects > Video Filters > Channel > Invert.

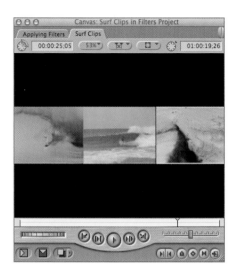

The filter is applied to the clips on the tracks where Auto Select is enabled.

You can also double-click a clip in the Timeline to open it into the Viewer. If the Viewer is the active window, choosing a filter from the Effects menu will apply the filter to that clip.

> **TIP** Always double-check whether the Viewer contains the version of the clip in the Browser or the version of the clip from the sequence.

Clip from Browser   Clip from sequence

> **TIP** The sprocket holes visible in the scrubber bar are the clearest indication that the clip in the Viewer is active in a sequence.

Applying a Filter with Drag and Drop

In most cases, using the Effects menu is the quickest, most efficient method of applying filters, but there is another way, which allows you to see more precisely what is happening.

> **TIP** The Effects tab in the Browser is an exact mirror of the contents of the Effects menu.

Objects in the Effects tab can be dragged directly to clips in any of the other windows.

TIP You can't drag a filter onto a clip in the Browser, but if you open the clip, you can drag a filter from the Effects tab directly to the Viewer.

Applying a Filter to Multiple Clips

Often, you'll use a particular effect on more than one clip in your sequence. If you plan ahead, you can do this in one simple step.

1 Select the third, fourth, and fifth clips in the *Surf Clips* sequence.

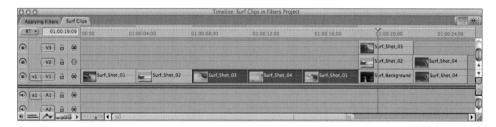

2 From the Effects tab, open the Image Control bin (inside the Video Filters bin) and drag the Desaturate filter to the selected clips in the Timeline.

> **NOTE ▸** Remember to move the playhead so you can see the effect of the filter.

The filter is applied to all of the clips. Unfortunately, if you don't like the default parameters, you'll need to open up each of the three clips and modify their settings individually, undermining the time saved by applying the filter simultaneously. However, if you adjust the settings first, you can apply the modified version of the filter to the clips and be done quickly.

3 Click the Effects tab. Click the disclosure triangles to open the Video Filters bin and the Border bin.

4 Double-click the Basic Border filter.

The filter opens into the Viewer, exposing its parameters.

5   Click the Color picker and change the color to red.

Now the filter is modified and ready to be applied to the clips in the sequence.

NOTE ▸ Changing this version of the filter affects all future uses of the filter.

6   Make sure the same three clips are still selected in the Timeline.

7   In the Viewer, drag the name of the filter onto the selected clips.

The Border filter is applied on top of the Desaturate filter on all three clips.

NOTE ▸ Additional changes made to the filter in the Viewer will not affect the clips in the Timeline.

Copying and Pasting Filters

Although applying a filter to multiple clips works in some instances, it's often difficult to set a filter's parameters without seeing how they look when applied to a clip. For that reason, if you want to apply one filter to multiple clips, it's often more prudent to apply the filter to one of the clips, tweak the settings, and then paste the filter onto the remaining clips.

1   Double-click the *Bike Jumps* sequence.

The playhead should be parked over the first clip.

2   Choose Effects > Video Filters > Stylize > Add Noise.

3   Press Return to open the clip into the Viewer.

TIP   Notice the sprocket holes in the scrubber bar, which indicate that the clip is active in a sequence.

4   In the Viewer, click the Filters tab.

5   Set the following parameters (leave the others at their defaults):

Amount: 0.75

Type: Pink Noise (TV static)

Blend Mode: Add

TIP You should see the effect of the changes in the Canvas. If you aren't seeing the effect, check that the sequence playhead is over the first clip.

6   To see exactly how the filter is affecting the clip, select and deselect the checkbox next to the filter name a few times. Make sure to leave it selected when you're done.

Now that the filter is adjusted, you can apply it to the other clips in the sequence.

7   Select the second and third clips in the Timeline.

8   In the Viewer, click the title bar of the filter (the name) and drag it onto the selected clips.

The filter will be applied.

TIP   Remember that changes made in the Viewer at this point will affect only the clip in the Viewer. Alternatively, you can copy the clip with the filter applied and paste just the filter effect onto other clips.

9   Select the first clip in the sequence.

10   Choose Edit > Copy, or press Command-C.

The clip is copied to the clipboard.

11   Select the last two clips in the sequence.

12 Choose Edit > Paste Attributes, or press Option-V.

The Paste Attributes window opens.

13 Select the Filters checkbox under Video Attributes and leave all the other checkboxes deselected. Click OK.

The filter is applied to the selected clips.

TIP The Paste Attributes window will show only active checkboxes for attributes modified in the copied clip. You can select multiple checkboxes to paste multiple attributes.

Modifying Filter Settings for All Clips in a Sequence

Although this process will save you plenty of time, it does have one significant drawback: If you change your mind about the filter settings, you'll need to open each of these clips and modify the parameters individually.

There are two solutions to this problem. The first is to *nest* the clips into a subsequence and apply the filter just once, so that any changes you make will automatically affect all the clips. (For more information on nesting, see Lesson 10 "Nesting Sequences.")

The other solution is more clunky but also more flexible.

1 Double-click the last clip in the sequence.

2   In the Viewer, click the Filters tab (if it's not already visible).

3   Change the Type to Gaussian Noise (Film Grain), and lower the Amount to .3 (period 3).

TIP ▶ If you aren't seeing the change in the sequence, make sure the playhead is parked on the clip you're modifying.

4   In the Timeline, select the last clip and press Command-C to copy it to the clipboard.

5   Press Command-A to select all of the clips in the sequence.

6   Choose Edit > Remove Attributes.

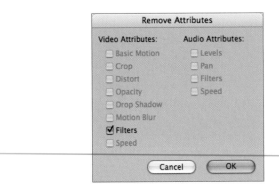

The Remove Attributes dialog appears. The only setting that should be active is the Filters in the Video Attributes, because none of these clips have any other attributes applied.

7   Click OK.

This action removes the filter from all of the clips in the sequence, including the last one, but because you previously copied the clip with the new settings to the clipboard, you're prepared to reapply that filter to all of the clips in one step.

8   If all of the clips haven't remained selected, press Command-A to select all of the clips again.

9   Choose Edit > Paste Attributes, or press Option-V.

The Paste Attributes window appears.

10   Select Filters and make sure that none of the other settings are selected.

> **TIP**   Scale Attribute Times doesn't apply in this case, so it doesn't matter whether it's selected or not.

The Add Noise filter (with the new settings) is reapplied to all of the clips in the sequence.

Applying a Filter to a Portion of a Clip

You can also apply a filter to a section of a clip, rather than to the entire clip. This can be helpful if you have a clip that includes multiple elements, and you want to filter only one portion.

1   Deselect all the clips by clicking in the inactive area of the Timeline or by pressing Command-Shift-A.

2   In the Toolbar, select the Range Selection tool (or press G three times).

3 In the Timeline, click the second clip (**SERIES_JUMPS**) at approximately 02:15, where the first biker just clears the hilltop, and drag to the right until the two-up display in the Canvas shows the first biker just landing (at approximately 01:26:30;15).

TIP The Canvas displays the Start and End points of the selection as you drag.

4 Choose Effects > Video Filters > Time > Echo.

The filter is applied only to the selected range.

TIP You may need to render the sequence (Option-R) to see the effect play in real time.

Using In and Out Points

Instead of using the Range Select tool, you can also use In and Out points and the Auto Select feature to specify which part of the clip you want to apply the filter to.

1 Find the place in the third clip (**WS Guys at mountains riding_2-1**) where the biker's shadow completely passes the rock on the left edge (at around 05:00) and set an In point there.

2   Set an Out point approximately 1 second later when the rock on the left has completely left the frame.

3   Make sure that nothing is selected and that Auto Select is enabled for track V1.

4   Choose Effects > Video Filters > Glow > Bloom.

The filter is applied only to the area between the In and Out points and only on the Auto Select–enabled tracks.

TIP   You can also limit a filter's effect using keyframes. With this technique, you can create gradual changes to individual filter parameters, which results in much more complex and dynamic effects. For more information on keyframing, see Lesson 9, "Creating Dynamic Effects."

Modifying Filters

Nearly 180 filters are available to create a breathtaking variety of effects (and scores more third-party filters are available as plug-ins). What's more, each of those filters has multiple parameters that can dramatically vary its result.

Changing Parameters

In order to modify any filter, you must open it into the Viewer window, but as you learned in the last example, it's usually important to monitor the filter's effect as you adjust. For this reason, it's generally easiest to apply a filter to a clip that's already in a sequence, and then immediately double-click the clip to open it into the Viewer.

1 Double-click the clip to which you applied the Bloom filter.

2 In the Viewer, click the Filters tab.

3 Make sure that the Canvas is displaying a frame in the area affected by the filter.

4 Disable the Add Noise filter, and click its disclosure triangle to hide the parameters.

5 In the Bloom filter, lower the Amount slider to 3, and lower the Threshold setting to about 65.

6   Adjust the Mix slider to reduce the visibility of the effect to your liking.

7   Toggle the Bloom filter on and off to clearly see how it's affecting the image.

Adjusting a Filter's In and Out Points

Remember that this filter is applied only to a portion of the clip because you set an In and Out point in the sequence when applying it. You can modify which section of the clip the filter is applied to in the area to the right of the filter parameters in the Filters tab.

1   Choose Window Arrange > Two Up or simply expand your Viewer window so you can see the controls to the right of the parameter sliders.

This area is another view of the Timeline in which the clip is currently active. Keyframe graphs can be created and manipulated here for instances when you want to modify a filter's parameters over time. (Keyframing effects are discussed in Lesson 9, "Creating Dynamic Effects.")

TIP ▶ The In and Out points correspond directly to the marks in the Timeline and Canvas. Also, the timecode in the ruler is the sequence timecode, and the playhead is the sequence playhead. If you drag the playhead around you'll see it move in the Timeline and Canvas, too.

White vertical lines in each of the keyframe graphs indicate the clip's In and Out points in the sequence.

TIP ▶ You can use the same zoom tools you use in the Timeline to zoom in and out on this mini-Timeline area.

2   Press Shift-Z to make sure the clip is zoomed to fit the window.

3   Clear the In and Out points by pressing Option-X or by Control-clicking the ruler area and choosing "Clear In and Out points" from the shortcut menu.

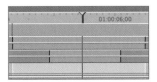

You'll see that there are still two black vertical lines in the area below the ruler and above the keyframe graphs. These lines indicate the boundaries where the filter takes effect.

4   Drag the left line for the Bloom filter to the left to start the filter effect earlier in the clip.

TIP ▶ You can also move the filter's start and end time together, effectively slipping the filter within the clip.

5 Move the pointer anywhere over the area between the filter Start and End points.

The pointer turns into a Slip pointer.

6 Drag to the right, moving both Start and End points later in the clip.

Resetting Parameters

As you get more comfortable experimenting with filters, you may occasionally get to the point when you want to start over and restore the filter to its default settings. Fortunately, this is just one click away.

1 To the right of the filter name, click the Reset button.

2 Readjust the filter's settings to create a unique look.

Deleting Filters

Because filters require so much experimentation, it's also very common to audition several filters before finding the exact look you're seeking.

You can temporarily disable a filter by deselecting the checkbox next to the filter's name in the Filters tab.

> **TIP** Selecting and deselecting this checkbox is a great way to examine the effect of a filter.

You can also easily remove a filter altogether.

1   In the Filters tab, select the Bloom filter by clicking the name.

2   Press Delete.

The filter is removed from the clip.

TIP ▶ You can also use Edit > Cut, Edit > Copy, or Edit > Clear to remove or move filters. As long as another clip's Filters tab is active, you can paste whatever effects are currently stored on the clipboard.

Controlling Filter Order

One thing you'll quickly realize is that the real fun and magic of filters comes from combining different effects to create unique looks. However, it's very important to control the order in which the filters appear.

Filters are applied to each clip in the order in which they appear in the Filters tab, from top to bottom. In some cases, the order will have no effect, but in other cases, the order will dramatically change the look of the clip.

1   In the Timeline, click the Surf Clips tab to make that sequence active.

2   Position the playhead over the third clip (**Surf_Shot_03**) so it's visible in the Canvas, and then double-click it to open it into the Viewer.

TIP ▶ When the Filters tab is active in the Viewer, Final Cut Pro will keep that tab visible, even when opening a new clip into the Viewer. This can be helpful if you're modifying filters on different clips, but it can also confuse you, especially if you have two clips with the same filter applied. Always check the name of the clip in the Viewer title bar to ensure that you're modifying the correct clip.

This clip has two filters applied. A Desaturate filter removes the color from the shot, and then a red border is applied. If the Basic Border filter was applied before the Desaturate filter, the red color would be reduced to gray.

3   Click the name area of the Basic Border filter and drag it to the top of the window, above the Desaturate filter.

Now the red border is being desaturated.

4   Choose Effects > Video Filters > Distort > Whirlpool.

Because the distortion is happening after the border effect, the border itself is distorted. If you want the distorted image to have a border around it, you must change the filter order.

5 Drag the Basic Border filter to the end of the filter list in the Filters tab.

The entire window becomes highlighted, indicating that the effect will be added to the end of the list.

The whirlpool effect is now contained within the border effect.

Moderating Filter Effects

You may have noticed that some filters (such as the Bloom filter used earlier in this lesson) have a Mix slider below the other attributes.

This slider controls how much of the overall effect to apply or, to put it another way, how much of the filtered clip should be *mixed* with the original. This is an enormously helpful way to temper the effect of the filter without having to decrease the actual parameter values.

Controlling Filter Effect Amount

For filters that don't have a Mix slider, there's still a way to accomplish a similar effect.

1 Select the second clip (**Surf_Shot_02**).

2 Choose Edit > Remove Attributes, or press Command-Option-V.

The Remove Attributes dialog appears.

3 Ensure that the Filters checkbox is selected and click OK.

Now the clip has no filters applied to it.

4 Shift-Option-drag the clip onto track V2 to create a duplicate.

5 Be sure that only the top version of the clip is selected, and choose Effects > Video Filters > Stylize > Posterize.

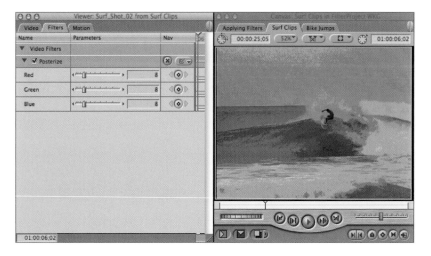

This filter limits the number of colors available and is a great tool for creating stylized high-contrast looks.

TIP The Posterize filter is most effective when you severely limit the number of available colors.

6 Double-click the filtered clip to open it into the Viewer.

7 Click the Filters tab and set the value for all three settings (Red, Green, and Blue) to 3.

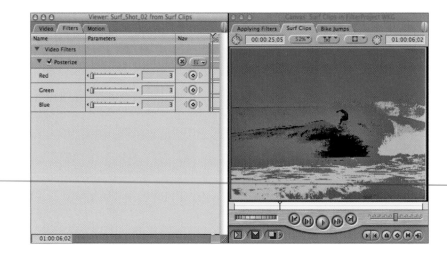

This creates a very interesting look but also makes the overall image a bit too illegible. A Mix slider would come in handy, but alas, no such slider exists in this filter.

8   In the Viewer, click the Motion tab and expand the Opacity controls.

9   Lower the Opacity to about 40.

This reduces the visibility of the filtered image, revealing the unaffected version beneath it and providing the equivalent of the Mix slider.

Masking Filter Effects

You can use a similar procedure to limit an effect to a specific area of the clip. In this case, rather than adjusting the upper clip's opacity, you use a matte filter on the V2 clip to mask certain areas of the image.

For example, rather than applying this posterize effect to the entire clip, you could choose to limit it, so that just the surfer is posterized, and the rest of the shot appears unfiltered.

1   Raise the Opacity to about 75.

2   In the Viewer, click the Filters tab.

3 Choose Effects > Video Filters > Matte > Mask Shape.

A rectangular matte is applied, limiting the posterize effect.

4 Set the Shape to Oval.

5 Click the Center point control, and then click the surfer's foot in the Canvas.

TIP ▶ For best results, you may want to shuttle through the clip to set the center point on a frame that approximates the middle of the surfer's movement throughout the shot. In this example, the sequence playhead is at 01:00:06:02.

6 Lower the Horizontal Scale slider to about 35.

7 Choose Effects > Video Filters > Matte > Mask Feather.

8 Set the Soft slider to about 75.

9 Press \ (backslash) to play around the clip and see the results of your work.

> **TIP** When using filters, you should set your sequence to Unlimited RT, although you may still need to render the clip (Command-R) to play the clip in real time.

You can also invert the filter's effect, so that the entire image is posterized except for the circle around the surfer.

10 In the Mask Shape filter, select the Invert checkbox.

The effect is inverted.

This masking technique can work on any set of filters, but the Final Cut Pro masking features are somewhat limited. The Four-Point and Eight-Point Garbage Mattes give more precise control than the Mask Shape filter does, allowing you to create a custom-shaped mask, but there are no Bezier or B-spline controls built into Final Cut Pro.

There are third-party filters that provide such functionality and allow much more fine control over the shapes of your mattes. Motion also has robust masking tools that can be used in conjunction with Final Cut to apply the same effects.

Furthermore, in this example, the surfer mainly stays in the same small area of the frame; but in many cases the subject will move around, creating an additional challenge. You can manually keyframe the mask to accommodate such movement. However, Final Cut Pro doesn't contain any motion tracking features to automate the process. Shake, Motion, and third-party plug-ins all offer such functionality. For more information on motion tracking, refer to *Apple Pro Training Series: Motion 4.*

Managing Filters

Now that you know how to make good use of the Final Cut Pro filters, take a step back and learn how to manage and organize your filters to maximize your productivity.

Final Cut Pro can access filters from a variety of sources. There are built-in filters, filters provided by QuickTime, FxPlug filters such as those included in Motion, third-party filters created for Final Cut Pro, and even some third-party filters created for After Effects.

Given all these sources of effects, there can be quite a bit of overlap, with multiple filters that create near-identical effects, and even multiple filters with the same names.

Final Cut Pro tries to eliminate any confusion by providing a set of recommended effects, which hides any FxPlug filters if an identically named built-in filter exists.

1   Choose Effects > Effect Availability > All Effects.

Every effect is now displayed in the Effects tab and in the Effects menu. FxPlug filters are labeled as such in the Effect Class column and also have a text description of the filter's effect in the Description column.

With so many duplicates, it may seem wise to just choose Only Recommended Effects and forget about the others, but this prevents you from taking advantage of many benefits available only in the FxPlug versions of the duplicate filters. In many cases, the FxPlug versions are newer filters and have additional or different parameters.

For example, look at the parameters available in a filter as simple as Gaussian Blur.

Built-in version   FxPlug version

For one thing, all of the FxPlug filters contain the Mix setting, described earlier in this lesson. Plus, in the Gaussian Blur filter, the FxPlug version allows you to separately control horizontal and vertical blurring, greatly increasing the versatility of the effect.

But not all FxPlug filters are superior. For example, the built-in Invert filter allows you to invert individual color and alpha channels; the FxPlug version can only invert the entire image.

Built-in version   FxPlug version

Preferred Effects

So what are you to do? Fortunately, Final Cut Pro also provides a way to customize which filters are displayed, allowing you to designate some effects as preferred, and then limit the display so only preferred effects are shown. The downside to this is that you need to walk through every single effect and choose whether or not it should be preferred—and thus displayed—which can be quite a time-consuming process.

1   In the Effects tab, click in the Preferred column—a checkmark notes the selected effects—for each of the effects you want to display.

2   When you've marked all the effects you want to include, Control-click any empty space in the Name column of the Effects tab and choose Show My Preferred Effects from the shortcut menu.

If you do not want to go through the process of selecting preferred effects for every category, you may want to choose Show Recommended Effects.

TIP ▶ Although this section has focused exclusively on video filters, the recommended and preferred effects settings also affect all other classes of effects found in the Effects tab.

Creating Favorite Filters

As you work on more and more projects, you'll discover interesting ways to use filters to create unique effects. If you have a particular filter with specific settings you really like, use often, or need to reuse frequently for a specific client or project, you can save it as a favorite.

Favorite filters are stored in the Favorites bin in the Effects tab, and are then available in the Favorites submenu of the Effects menu.

You can create a favorite filter in a number of ways.

1   Click the Effects tab.

2   Expand the Video Filters and the Border bins.

3   Drag the Basic Border filter to the Favorites bin at the top of the window.

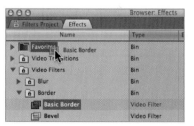

4   Expand the Favorites bin and rename the effect *Blue Border 25*.

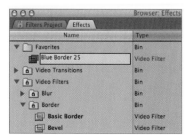

5 Double-click the filter to open it into the Viewer and set the Border to *25* and the color to your favorite hue of blue.

That filter is now ready to use with those preset attributes.

Applying a Favorite Filter to a Clip

However, you often won't realize you want to save a favorite filter until after you've applied it to a clip in a sequence.

1 Open the *Bike Jumps* sequence.

2 Position the playhead over the first clip (**WS Guys at mountains riding_2**), which should have the Add Noise filter that you customized earlier.

3 Make sure no clips are selected and that Auto Select is active for track V1, and then choose Effects > Make Favorite Effect (or press Option-F).

4 Look in the Favorites bin in the Effects tab.

The Add Noise filter is there.

5 Rename the filter *Custom Noise* or something similar that will help you remember what makes this effect special.

> **TIP** Effects saved in the Favorites bin will stick around between projects. You can even move them from one Final Cut Pro system to another as described in "Moving and Preserving Favorites" later in this lesson.

Creating Filter Packs

Often, an effect is composed of several different filters, and if you create a custom effect this way, you can save that too. These saved filters will retain their settings and the order in which they were applied.

1 Click the Surf Clips sequence tab.

2 Position the playhead over the last two clips in the sequence.

The upper clip has been scaled down and feathered using controls in the Motion tab, but has no filters applied. The bottom clip has three filters applied: HSV Adjust, Light Rays, and Replicate.

3 Make sure that nothing is selected and that Auto Select is disabled for track V2 and enabled for track V1.

4 Choose Effects > Make Favorite Effect, or press Option-F.

A sub-bin has been added to the Favorites bin, and inside that sub-bin are the three filters that created the glowing replicated effect used in that composition. This is commonly called a *filter pack*.

TIP ▶ Do not double-click to open the filter pack into its own window. Doing so will alphabetize the filters and change the order in which the filters are listed, rather than preserving the order in which they were originally applied.

5   Rename the Surf Clips (Filters) bin *Glowing Replicated*, or some other descriptive name.

To apply this filter pack to another clip, drag it from the Effects tab of the Browser onto one or more selected clips in the Timeline.

TIP ▶ Filter packs are easiest to apply by dragging them from the Effects tab of the Browser. When using the Effects menu, you can select only one favorite filter at a time from the filter pack, so you need to click into the menu several times to apply multiple filters.

Organizing the Favorites Bin

When you rely on a lot of custom favorites, you may want to spend some time organizing the contents of your Favorites bin so that you can quickly and easily locate what you need. For example, if you regularly work with four different clients on recurring shows, and specific filters are used for each show, you can create a hierarchy of sub-bins, one for each client.

1   In the Effects tab of the Browser, Option-double-click the Favorites bin icon to open the bin as another tab in the Browser.

2   Press Command-B, or Control-click the bin and choose New Bin from the shortcut menu, to add new bins as needed.

Once you've created a hierarchy of bins in the Favorites bin, you can organize the contents however you like. In particular, because there are so many other types of effects that you can store in the Favorites bin (transitions and motion effects, for example), you may want to create sub-bins for each.

NOTE ▶ Although you can store favorite filters, transitions, and motion effects in the same bin, filters are the only type of favorite settings you can apply to a clip as a group. When the effects in a given bin are of different types (filter, transition, or motion), you must apply each effect individually.

3   Close the Favorites tab.

Moving and Preserving Favorites

As you build up a collection of favorites, you'll need to take special steps to preserve them, in case you need to reinstall the software on your computer or move your setup to a new computer.

TIP ▶ When you save a filter, motion, or transition effect to the Favorites bin, that information is stored in the Final Cut Pro preferences file. If you reinstall your system, move to a new system, or delete the preferences file as a part of regular system maintenance or troubleshooting, you'll lose all your favorites!

It's very easy to save all of your favorite filters and effects in a project file that can be moved around and opened on different computers.

1   Create a new project by pressing Command-Shift-N.

2   Select the tab for the new project and drag it out of the Browser so it appears in its own window. This enables you to see it and the Effects tab side by side.

3   Drag the Favorites bin from the Effects tab into the new project.

4   Save and close the new project, naming it *Favorite Effects* or something similar.

You can then copy this project onto a portable drive or even email it to yourself so you can open it on another Final Cut Pro system, When you do, all of your favorite effects will be available on the new system.

Using Specific Filter Categories

Throughout this lesson you've been learning how to apply, modify, and manage filters, but no time has been spent discussing the specific filters and when they might be employed. Although most filters are very flexible and can be used in a wide variety of circumstances, it may be helpful to mentally group the filters into a few basic categories.

Not all of the groupings listed here correspond directly with the way filters are grouped in the Final Cut Pro Effects tab. In some cases, the groupings in the program are simply wrong, and in others they might serve more than one purpose. Either way, as long as you understand how to use the various filters, finding them won't be too much of a problem.

Understanding Corrective Filters

Many filters are designed specifically to solve mistakes made during production or to improve the look of an image to create a desired result. Such corrective filters are generally used in situations when you want to hide the fact that a filter is in use at all.

Blur and Sharpen

Blur filters are commonly employed to help control the point of focus in a scene. By blurring a portion of a shot or certain elements within a composition, you subtly guide the viewers' focus to the area that is in focus. Some specific blur filters, such as Defocus, Zoom Blur, Prism, and Soft Focus, are designed to simulate similarly named effects that can be created photographically.

Sharpening filters can be used to improve the visibility of edges in an image that lacks sharp focus.

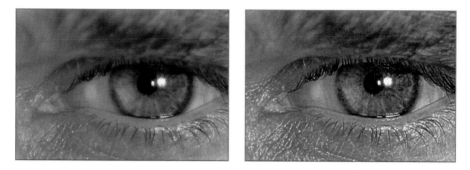

TIP Some of the stylize edge detection filters can be helpful as sharpening tools, although for a subtle effect they must be mixed back in with the original.

Noise Filters

Blurs can also be used to reduce unwanted noise in an image. The Channel and Compound Blur filters affect individual color or luminance channels of an image, which may be especially useful if the noise you're trying to eliminate resides primarily in one of these channels. Anti-Alias (found in the Stylize category) can also be effective at reducing noise.

In other cases, adding noise can be helpful in matching shots that were shot in different environments or with different equipment. Adding noise can also help when seamlessly mixing a computer-generated image into other shots that were created photographically.

The Reduce Banding filter (found in the Image Control section) adds a tiny bit of noise to your image to help mask color banding that can result from inadequate digital sampling.

Image Control and Color Correction Filters

Another category of corrective effects comes in the form of filters designed to overcome exposure, white balance, color, or lighting problems in otherwise useful shots. These filters can generally be divided as follows:

Filters that affect the luminance:

► Brightness

► Brightness & Contrast

► Contrast

► Gamma

► Gamma Correction

Filters that affect the color:

▶   Channel Mixer

▶   Channel Offset

▶   Color Balance

▶   Color Reduce

▶   Desaturate

▶   Desaturate Highlights

▶   Desaturate Lows

▶   Sepia

▶   Tint

Filters that do a combination of these things:

▶   Color Corrector

▶   Color Corrector 3-way

▶   Levels

▶   Proc Amp

▶   HSV, YIQ, and YUV Adjust filters

All of these filters provide subtly different tools to control the same basic aspects. Some are more inclined toward subtle results, and some create more exaggerated effects. In general, you can correct an image only so far before noise is introduced in dark areas, clipping occurs in bright areas, and color becomes unnatural.

For more information on such filters, see *Apple Pro Training Series: Color Correction in Final Cut Studio.*

Flop Filters

Screen direction mistakes are very common and, in many cases, can be easily solved editorially. Screen direction refers to the left-to-right or right-to-left movement or the eye-line of the subjects within a scene. If a car chase shows three shots of the car moving from right to left, and then suddenly there's a shot where the car is going from left to right, it will appear that they're heading back where they came from.

The Flop filter can easily address this problem.

1   Double-click the *Screen Direction* sequence and play it.

Notice that in the first, third, and fourth shots, the bikers are moving from right to left, but in the second shot, they're moving from left to right. Although this scene is not part of a narrative in which such a screen direction would significantly confuse the audience, it still disrupts the flow of action. If this were part of a race sequence, it could be very confusing if some of the shots showed movement in the wrong direction.

2   Select the second clip and choose Effects > Video Filters > Perspective > Flop.

The orientation of the shot is reversed and the bikers are now moving in the same direction in all of the shots.

TIP Be aware that this filter won't work in situations where written words appear in the shot (the words will appear backward) or in situations when the geography of the scene is clearly established (if someone is leaning against a wall, the wall will suddenly be on the wrong side, and so on).

De-Interlacing and Flicker Reduction Filters

Another problem that occurs with regularity is that scan lines in NTSC, PAL, and interlaced HD footage become visible, creating comb-like artifacts in your images.

This can occur for a number of reasons, ranging from mismatched field order settings to creating a freeze-frame effect on an image that contains significant horizontal movement.

In such cases, the De-Interlace filter will eliminate the fields in the offending shot, either by duplication or interpolation.

In some cases, usually due to transcoding one format to another, the scanline order can become inverted or offset. The Shift Fields filter can switch between odd and even interlacing by moving the entire image up or down by a single line.

Lastly, in some cases, interlacing and frame rate conversions can introduce an apparent flicker that is invisible when the playhead is parked, but becomes apparent when the clip is played. The Flicker filter can reduce this effect by blurring together adjacent scan lines.

Image Shake Filters

Camera shake is a fact of life with handheld camera work and, to some degree, it has become a signature style of certain genres. However, there are times when you just wish a shaky shot was a bit less bumpy.

The SmoothCam filter can remove some of that unwanted camera shake. In order to do this, it must first perform an analysis of the clip to be smoothed.

1   In the Browser, double-click **Driving_02** and play it.

2   Choose Effects > Video Filters > Video > SmoothCam.

The Viewer is outlined with a red warning border and the Background Processes window appears. This window indicates the progress of the SmoothCam analysis and provides controls to abort or pause the process.

> **TIP** ▸ As the window's name implies, this process goes on in the background, which means that while it works, you can continue working on other things, including marking and playing the clip that's being analyzed. However, you can't see the results of the filter until the analysis is complete.

3   While you're waiting for the analysis to complete, Control-click the Duration column header in the Browser and choose Show SmoothCam from the shortcut menu.

The SmoothCam column appears and indicates the status of the clip being analyzed.

4   Once the analysis is complete, tear out the Viewer's Filters tab so you can see both the Filters tab and the Video tab simultaneously.

5   Set Auto Scale to 0.

6   Play the clip.

You can see that the car and the cable car remain perfectly steady in the middle of the frame, but the edges of the frame jump around like crazy, as the filter compensates for the camera movement in the shot.

Unfortunately, with a clip that has as much camera shake as this clip does, you would have to zoom in quite far to avoid seeing the shake.

NOTE ▸ Once a clip analysis has been performed, changes made to the clip, including changes to the filter settings, will not require re-analysis.

7   You can adjust the Translation, Rotation, and Zoom settings depending on how much movement your clip has.

TIP ▸ The higher the values, the more Final Cut Pro will compensate for them. The lower the values, the more shake will remain in your clip, but the less you'll have to zoom in to keep the frame full.

Using Utility Filters

Another class of filters is typically used for special situations or in combination with other effects. This category of filters includes mattes, which enable you to mask out part of an image; keying filters, which allow you to identify a portion of the shot (usually by color) and make that section transparent; and timecode display filters, which print a timecode window on top of your video image.

Matte Filters

You already used a simple matting technique to limit the effect of a filter earlier in this lesson. Mattes are also commonly used to mask out equipment or unwanted elements of a frame (hence the name "garbage matte"—a matte used to hide the visual garbage).

Because mattes make part of the frame transparent, they're frequently used in compositing scenarios, where other elements are used to fill in the missing spaces.

However, one of the most commonly used mattes is not used for compositing at all: the widescreen matte masks off the top and bottom of an image to create a more cinematic aspect ratio (though sometimes it's used just to hide a boom microphone that keeps dipping into the frame).

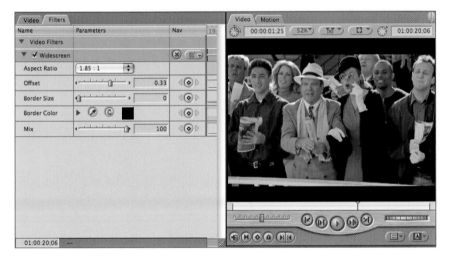

Keying Filters

One of the most common special effects techniques is to shoot a subject against an all-green or all-blue backdrop in order to isolate the subject and later put him or her in a different environment. *Keying* is the act of removing those blue or green sections of the frame and turning them transparent. Final Cut Pro has several robust keying filters, and there are widely respected third-party plug-in keying filters available as well.

TIP ▶ Keying is a very specialized task, and successful results require that the footage is lit properly and that the shooting format contains adequate color information.

Timecode Display Filters

There are times when you need to see timecode numbers burned right into your video image.

Typically, this approach is used when passing files between people to ensure that everyone is perfectly clear about specifically when various elements begin and end. For example, when exporting audio to go to a sound mixing facility, it's customary to also send along a *window dub* of the edited show (a copy of the video with the timecode visible in a window onscreen), so that the sound mixer can ensure that his audio mix is always in perfect sync with the video.

To some degree, this is a legacy technique, carried over from days of yore, before all video files had timecode data embedded in them. Still, there's nothing like seeing the numbers right there in front of you to ensure that they're accurate.

TIP ▶ Final Cut Pro has both a Timecode Generator filter (which displays numbers that the filter generates based on your input settings) and a Timecode Reader filter (which displays the exact timecode numbers from the embedded timecode values in each clip).

Using Non-Corrective Filters

Most of the video filters in Final Cut Pro fall into the category of non-corrective. These are filters that modify the image in ways that are not subtle or realistic. There are several subcategories for such effects.

NOTE ▶ For this section, you can examine many of the examples described in the Filter Examples sequence. Track V2 contains the filtered clip and Track V1 shows the raw clip. Toggle visibility for track V2 to quickly see a before-and-after effect.

Distortion Filters

These filters displace pixels to simulate the effect of the image flowing like water, or the image being projected onto an uneven surface.

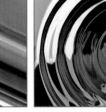  

Distort > Scrape Filter   Distort > Pond Ripple Filter   Distort > Cylinder Filter

Several distortion filters (Bump Map, Displace, and Refraction) require an input image or video clip, which is applied as a texture or projection surface.

To use one of these filters, just drag a still image, video clip, or generator onto the Map Image target.

Stylization Filters

The next most common types of effects are created using stylization filters. These filters modify the pixels of a clip to simulate a painterly effect, or group pixels together based on color value or luminance. Common effects such as Diffuse, Posterize, Find Edges, and Solarize fall into this category.

Stylize > Solarize Filter Stylize > Diffuse Filter Stylize > Line Art Filter

At low settings, these filters can be quite subtle, but very quickly they can become highly abstract. Filters such as Slit Scan, Slit Tunnel, Stripes, and Target (the last two are found in the Distort category) are particularly extreme, turning your image into an abstract mess but providing hours of entertainment.

Stylize > Slit Scan Filter

Tiling and Perspective Filters

Two more filter categories that are undeniably fun are the Tiling and Perspective filters. Tiling takes part of your image and repeats it. This includes such filters as Mirror (found in the Perspective group), Replicate (found in the Stylize category), and Kaleidoscope.

Perspective > Mirror Filter Stylize > Replicate Filter Tiling > Kaleidoscope Filter

Similar to these are the Perspective filters, which allow you to move the imaginary screen upon which your clip is projected. These include Rotate, Curl (similar to a page peel), and the versatile Basic 3D.

TIP ▶ Although Final Cut Pro doesn't have any actual 3D capability (you have to use Motion for that), the Basic 3D filter can do a pretty good job of simulating the most common 3D effects.

Perspective > Basic 3D Filter

NOTE ▶ The drop shadow in the figure is not part of the Basic 3D filter, but rather a setting in the Motion tab.

Glow Filters

Used in small quantities, these popular filters can simulate the subtle bloom of overexposed film, but a more generous helping quickly transforms an image into a burst of light.

Glow > Dazzle Filter

Time Adjustment Filters

Most of the filters previously described work by modifying the pixels of the image in geo-graphic space, but one category of filters works by mixing the surrounding frames in time.

You used one of these, the Echo filter, earlier in the lesson. Other time-based filters include Strobe, Trails, and Scrub, which allow you to mix your video in time the way a DJ scratches a record.

Using Other Filters

There are many other filters that don't neatly fit into the categories described in the pre-ceding sections. Some have multiple uses, and others do very specific and unique things, such as Camcorder (which overlays a blinking Record light to simulate the viewfinder of a consumer video camera).

The best advice is to get in there and experiment. And remember, each filter can yield widely different results depending on the settings used, and the combination of various filters can often surpass the sum of the individual effects.

Lesson Review

1. Does Auto Select override a manual selection?
2. Does pasting attributes on a clip that already has the same filter applied modify the existing filter settings or does it apply an additional copy of the filter?
3. How can you remove filters from multiple clips?
4. Does it matter what order you use to apply filters?
5. How can you apply a filter to a portion of a clip's duration?
6. How can you apply a filter to a portion of a clip's image?
7. Which are superior: built-in filters or FxPlug filters?
8. What is a "filter pack?"
9. What is the SmoothCam filter used for?
10. What is the sacrifice SmoothCam requires?

Answers

1. No. Manual selections in the Timeline override Auto Select.

2. Pasting attributes will add an additional filter to the recipient clip.

3. Use Remove Attributes.

4. Yes, filters affect a clip in the order in which they're applied.

5. Use the Range Select tool (GGG) or set In and Out points before you apply the filter.

6. Create a duplicate copy of the clip and apply a matte filter to the top clip.

7. Neither type of filter is inherently superior. Each case is different.

8. A group of filters saved as a single favorite, which appears in the Favorites bin as a subfolder and can be applied, *en masse*, to another clip.

9. For reducing camera shake.

10. You must zoom in on the clip to accommodate for the smoothing effect.

9

Lesson Files	Lesson Files > Lesson_09 > Animating_Effects.fcp
Media	Surf Video
Time	This lesson takes approximately 60 minutes to complete.
Goals	Animate objects and parameters over time
	Keyframe motion parameters in the Canvas
	Keyframe motion and filters in the Viewer
	Modify and manipulate keyframes in the Timeline
	Save and reapply keyframed effects

Creating Dynamic Effects

The video medium is engaging because it moves. If you want your effects to be compelling, they need to be dynamic. Whether you want an object to move across the screen, or a title to appear or disappear over time, or if you want an effect to occur gradually, Final Cut Pro can facilitate it.

The mechanism for these effects is called animation, or *keyframing*. A keyframe is simply an indicator that says, "Make this effect happen at this point in time." When you set two keyframes, Final Cut Pro interpolates the changes between them. For example, to create a common one-second fade-in, you set two opacity keyframes. On frame 1, set the opacity to 0%, and 24 frames later, set it to 100%. Final Cut Pro automatically makes each of the 22 frames in between increasingly opaque, resulting in the familiar fade effect.

Keyframing Basics

Keyframing can seem complicated at first because it requires you to think about two things at the same time. Whenever you set a keyframe you must always answer two questions: What is the parameter value, and when does it occur in time?

You'll be surprised at how easily you can forget to answer one of these questions; if you do forget, your clever and exciting effect won't work. Furthermore, it's critical to understand that setting one keyframe doesn't actually create a change over time. It's not until you add a second keyframe (at a different value elsewhere in time) that the animation will occur.

Keyframes are easiest to understand and manipulate when you picture them on a graph, so Final Cut Pro generates such graphs in no less than six different places:

▶   You can keyframe opacity and audio levels in the Timeline.

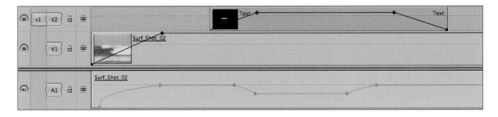

▶   You can keyframe audio levels and pan settings in the Audio tab of the Viewer.

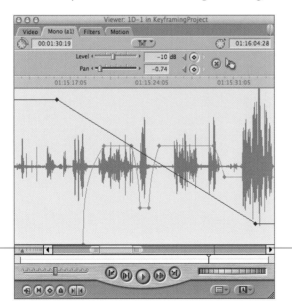

▶ You can keyframe filter parameters in the Filters tab.

▶ You can keyframe motion parameters in the Motion tab.

▶ You can animate a clip's position in the Canvas or the Video tab of the Viewer.

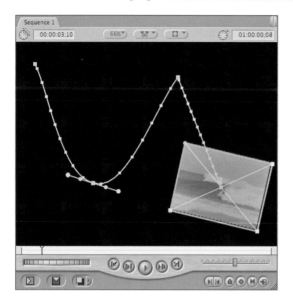

▶ And you can display any single filter or motion parameter in a special optional keyframe graph in the Timeline.

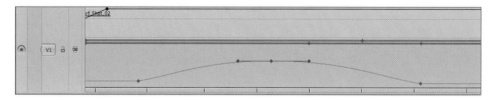

Fortunately, keyframes work exactly the same in all of these places, so once you grasp the basics, you'll quickly become comfortable creating dynamic effects of all types.

Keyframing in the Canvas

Although animating objects in the Canvas is one of the more difficult methods of keyframing, it's a good place to start because moving objects around the screen is such a common effect, and the keyframe graph in the Canvas is the most intuitive.

1 Open **Animating_Effects.fcp**.

The **Surf Intro - 1** sequence automatically opens into the Canvas and Timeline.

This is a slightly modified version of the sequence you built in Lesson 7. In that lesson you animated the four surf clips using a transition effect. In this lesson, you'll make them appear in a different way, using keyframes.

2   Choose Window > Arrange > Two Up.

This arranges your interface to enlarge the Canvas window, making it easier to animate the items there.

3   In the View pop-up menu, ensure that Image+Wireframe is selected.

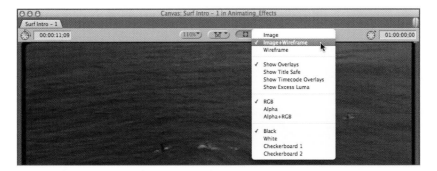

4   Set the Zoom level to 50%.

This will ensure that some pasteboard area (in gray) surrounds the visible frame.

5 Type *3.00* and press Return to move the sequence playhead to exactly 3 seconds.

6 Option-click the Track Visibility control for Track V3.

> **TIP** Option-clicking a track's Visibility control effectively *solos* it by hiding all the other tracks. Option-click again to *unsolo* it.

7 In the Canvas, drag the clip so the lower-right corner of the cropped area lines up precisely with the action safe boundary, and the upper edge of the clip (not the cropped area) lines up with the title safe area on the top.

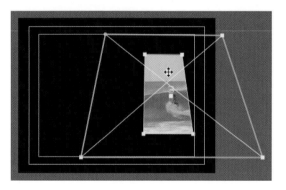

This is the position where the clip will land at the end of the animation.

> **TIP** Display of the action safe and title safe boundaries is controlled by choosing Show Title Safe in the View pop-up menu in the Canvas.

8 In the Canvas, click the Add Motion Keyframe button.

The clip's wireframe turns green and the cropped area turns blue.

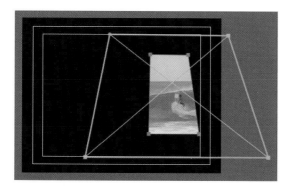

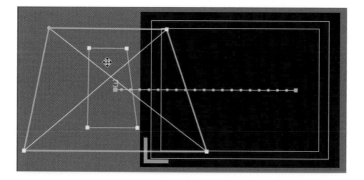 The colored wireframe indicates that the playhead is parked on a keyframe for the selected clip.

Remember, setting the first keyframe doesn't create an animation; rather, it's as if you've pinned the clip to that part of the screen at that point in time.

9 Press the Up Arrow key to move the playhead to the beginning of the clip.

Although the clip hasn't moved, the wireframe is no longer green. You're now ready to set your second keyframe.

10 Drag the clip to the left until the cropped portion is just past the frame boundary. Hold down Shift to constrain the movement to a straight line.

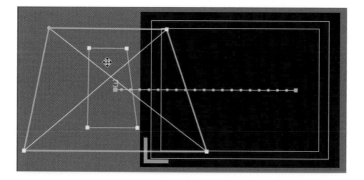

You'll notice that several things happen automatically. First of all, the clip's center point turns green. This indicates that a keyframe for the clip's Center Point parameter has automatically been added.

TIP The edges, corners, and cropped edges remain white because keyframes have not been added for the rotation, scale, and crop parameters.

You don't need to add a second keyframe. Because you told Final Cut Pro that the clip must be on the right side of the frame at 3 seconds in, putting it somewhere else at a different point in time forces Final Cut Pro to create an animation.

Additionally, you'll see a dotted line indicating the motion path that the clip will follow. This is the clearest indication that you've successfully created an animation.

11 Play the sequence to see your animated effect.

> **TIP** Although it may seem strange to set the end before the beginning, it's actually a very smart way to work. The object will be at its starting position for only one frame, but the ending composition is what your viewer will see for the duration of the scene. Furthermore, in this example (and in many real-world scenarios), the object begins offscreen. If you began by setting the first keyframe when the object is out of sight, locating the object to drag it to the final position would be difficult.

Modifying the Path

The dotted line provides a clear indication of the animation you created. If you modify that path, you'll change the clip's movement.

1 Press Option-K to move the playhead to the first keyframe.

> **TIP** Option-K will navigate the playhead to the previous keyframe for any selected objects. Shift-K will navigate to the next keyframe.

2 Click the middle of the path and drag it upward.

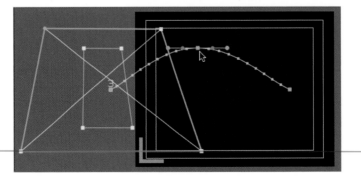

This adds a new keyframe, and forces the clip to move along a new path. It also automatically curves the path (which may or may not be desirable).

3 Play the sequence again.

The blue dots along the path indicate how fast or slow the object will move. The closer together the dots are, the slower the clip moves. This is where it becomes very important to track both aspects of a keyframe: the parameter value, and when it occurs in time.

4 Press Command-Z to undo the change you made to the clip's path.

5 Position the playhead somewhere about 1/4 of the way through the clip's duration (at approximately sequence time 1:20).

6 Drag the clip toward the lower center of the canvas.

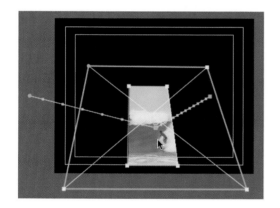

You'll see that there are several differences this time. The path is not automatically curved. (Don't worry. You can curve it later, if you want.) Additionally, the speed indicators are now closer together after the new keyframe, and farther apart before it.

7 Play the sequence.

The clip moves at a brisk pace between the starting position and the second keyframe and then moves more slowly to its final resting place.

In the first example (when you grabbed the path), you defined the parameter value, identifying where the clip should be located, but you hadn't planned when you wanted it to be there. In the second case, you first picked a point in time, and then decided where the object should be.

Both are valid ways of working, depending on whether the position or the time is your priority.

Smoothing Your Path

One other difference between those two methods was that in the first case, the path defaulted to a curve; in the second, it defaulted to create a corner point.

You can toggle this setting in the shortcut menu for each keyframe.

1 Make sure the clip is selected, and then right-click (or Control-click) the middle keyframe and choose Linear from the shortcut menu.

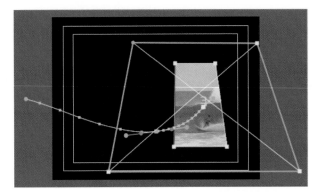

The path becomes curved.

2 Use the Bezier handles to adjust the shape of the curve.

TIP Zoom into the Canvas to better control the curve.

3 Hold down the Command key and drag one of the handles.

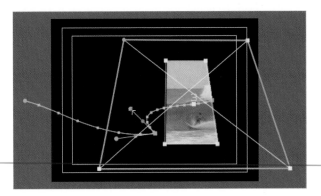

This allows you to modify one side of the curve, but it constrains both handles' lengths to reciprocal movement. If you lengthen or shorten one length, the other changes by the same amount, even though its position doesn't change.

4   Hold down Command and Shift and drag one of the handles.

This allows you to independently control one side of the curve.

> **TIP** ▶ Hold down Shift (but not Command) to modify only the length of the handle independently.

5   Right-click the middle keyframe and choose Make Corner Point from the shortcut menu.

The path is returned to its original shape.

Moving the Path

In some cases, you may create a path that you like but need to move to a different location in the Canvas. You could move each individual keyframe, but that's time-consuming, and it would be very difficult to maintain their relative positions.

For these reasons, there's a way to move the entire path in one step.

1   Press Command-Shift until your pointer becomes the hand tool; then, while still holding down the keys, drag the clip upward.

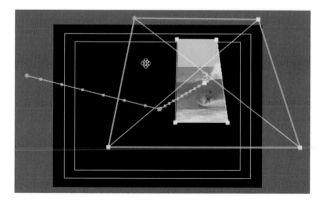

The path is moved as a single entity.

Deleting Keyframes

There are two ways to remove keyframes in the Canvas.

1   Right-click the middle keyframe and choose Delete Point from the shortcut menu.

The keyframe is removed.

The other way to delete a keyframe offers more flexibility.

2   Press Command-Z to undo step 1 and restore the middle keyframe.

3   Press Shift-K or Option-K until the playhead is parked on the middle keyframe.

4   In the Canvas, right-click the Add Motion Keyframe button.

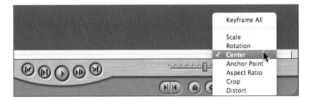

The shortcut menu shows all of the parameters currently keyframed at that point in time. In this frame, only the center point is keyframed.

5   Click Center to remove the checkmark and delete the keyframe.

Controlling Acceleration

In addition to setting a path's shape, you can control how fast or slow the clip will move as it moves to and from each keyframe. First, you'll return the clip to its intended location.

1   Command-Shift-drag the clip until its top edge aligns with the action safe boundary.

2   Right-click the first keyframe (the one in the gray pasteboard area) and choose Ease In/Ease Out from the shortcut menu.

3   Right-click the second keyframe and choose Ease In/Ease Out from the short-cut menu.

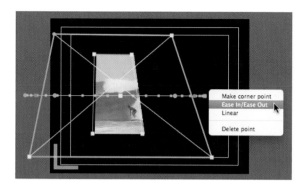

Notice that this affects the relative spacing of the dots along the path.

4   Play the sequence.

The clip slowly leaves its starting position, reaches a cruising speed, and then slows down as it settles into the second position.

This enables you to simulate the real-world phenomena of inertia and momentum, or to put it more simply, it makes your movement feel more organic.

> **TIP** ▸ You can also drag the inner blue dots on the Bezier handles to control a clip's acceleration as it approaches and leaves that point. However, it's not possible to achieve precise results this way.

Keyframing in the Viewer

Although keyframing in the Canvas can be quick and easy, the more complex your animations become, the more you'll find yourself wishing for more precise control and for more specific feedback on each parameter. The Canvas lets you achieve approximate settings, but if you want to guarantee specific numeric values, you'll have to use the Viewer.

For example, when dragging those clips to their positions, how do you know if they're accurately lined up? In the Viewer, you can see the precise numerical value of each setting.

1   In the Timeline, Option-click the Track Visibility control for track V2.

In this exercise, you'll animate the scaling, distortion, and cropping effects similar to the ones you created in Lesson 7.

2   Navigate the playhead to 4:00, click **Surf_Shot_03** in the canvas to select it, and press Control-K to add a motion keyframe.

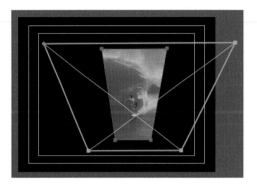

TIP Pressing Control-K has the same effect as clicking the Add Keyframe button in the Canvas—adding keyframes to all motion parameters on the active frame.

The Clip's handles and boundaries turn green and blue indicating that keyframes have been added for the various motion parameters.

3   In the Canvas or the Timeline, double-click the clip.

The shot opens into the Viewer. Notice the sprocket holes, which indicate that you're editing the version from the sequence (and not the master clip from the Browser).

4   Switch to the Motion tab.

Here, you can see the numerical values for each of the parameters you manipulated, and once keyframes have been added, a graph appears showing how the values change over time.

5 Press the Up Arrow key to move the playhead to the first frame of the clip.

6 In the Motion tab of the Viewer, drag the Scale slider to the right until it reaches 100.

> **TIP** ▶ Hold down Command while dragging any slider to constrain it to moving by whole integers. Hold Shift to adjust the slider by values smaller than whole integers.

A keyframe is automatically added for the current frame. Because the change from 70% to 100% is rather subtle, the graph shows only a mild adjustment. However, you can expand the graphs to see more resolution.

7 Drag the line beneath the Scale graph downward.

> **TIP** ▶ For more effective animating, zoom in or out on the keyframed area of the clip. Press Command-+ (plus) or Command-− (minus) to zoom in or out on the ruler area.

Each parameter has its own Add Keyframe button, and if you're parked on a keyframe, the corresponding button is colored green. Furthermore, the Previous Keyframe and Next Keyframe buttons (on either side of the Add Keyframe button) will dim if there are no more keyframes in the relevant direction.

8 With the playhead still on the clip's first frame, expand the Crop section in the Motion tab. Then type *0* in each of the four crop fields, and *50* in the Edge Feather field.

9 Play the sequence to see the effect of the animation you've created thus far.

The effect is starting to come together but there's much more to do.

10 Make sure the playhead is back on the first frame of the clip, and in the Viewer, expand the Distort parameter group.

> **TIP** Parameters that correspond to exact coordinates in the canvas don't display graphs in the Motion viewer. You can type numbers into the fields or manipulate the object directly in the canvas.

11 Press D to select the Distort tool and drag the lower-left and right corners of the clip until they're outside the visible area in the Canvas.

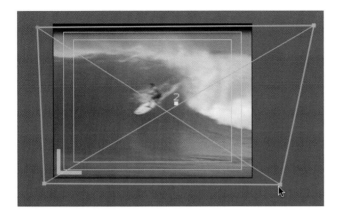

12 Play the sequence again to see how the animation looks so far.

Each group of parameters has an overview bar showing the keyframes for the parameters within each group.

13 Click the Keyframe Overview pop-up menu for Crop to select which parameters to display in that overview graph.

14 Select Hide All, and then open the menu again and select just Edge Feather.

Now only the Edge Feather keyframes are displayed in the overview graph.

The overview graph is visible even when the parameter group is collapsed, which allows you to simplify your view and see only information vital to the current operation.

15 Click the disclosure triangle to hide the Crop parameters.

TIP You can restore all default values and delete all keyframes for every parameter within each group by clicking the Reset button.

Smoothing Keyframes

When manipulating keyframes in the Canvas, you used Ease In/Ease Out to create organic, smooth motion. You can apply similar smoothing to the keyframes here.

1   Right-click the second keyframe in the Scale parameter graph.

2   Choose Smooth from the shortcut menu.

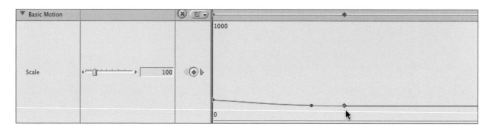

A Bezier handle appears, and the keyframe path automatically becomes curved. If you don't modify the Bezier handle, this should approximate a smooth "ease" effect in which the parameter reaches the value gradually.

TIP ▸ Although you can manipulate the Bezier handles directly to create custom acceleration curves, it can be difficult to achieve precise results this way.

Animating Filters

Filter parameters can be animated using exactly the same method as the motion effects you've been manipulating throughout this lesson.

1   With the Viewer window active, choose Effects > Video Filters > Blur > Gaussian Blur to apply that filter to the clip.

2   Click the Filters tab.

Remember, whenever you keyframe you need to not only set the value of the parameter you want to animate, but also choose the frame in which you want to apply it.

3   Move the playhead to the first frame of the clip.

4   Click the Add Keyframe button for the Radius parameter, and set the slider to 20.

5   Move the playhead approximately halfway through the clip and drag the Radius slider to 0.

6   Play the sequence.

The amount of blur is animated so the clip starts out very blurry and then comes into sharp focus.

TIP ▶ You could create a more gradual focusing effect by smoothing the keyframes as you did with the Scale parameter earlier.

Keyframing in the Timeline

In addition to keyframing in the other windows, you can view, create, and modify keyframes directly in the Timeline. Clip opacity levels and audio volume settings are both adjusted so frequently that Final Cut Pro can display keyframe graphs for these parameters right on top of the clip objects in the Timeline tracks.

Clip Overlays (Option-W)

To display these overlays, you must turn them on in the Timeline.

1 Open the **Surf Intro - 2** sequence.

This is another copy of the *Surf Intro* sequence with all of the motion and filter key-frames already applied. The Surf title graphic has been added as well.

2 Press Control-U to return your screen layout to Standard view.

3 Click the Clip Overlays control (or press Option-W) to turn on clip overlays.

A black line appears on each of the video tracks, representing that clip's opacity.

4 Option-click the opacity overlay (black line) for **Surf_Shot_03** four times to add four keyframes as shown in the following figure.

> **TIP** ▶ Clicking keyframes that are very close to the edge of a clip in the Timeline is often difficult because the Selection tool defaults to selecting the edge of the clip, rather than the keyframe. If you want to ensure that you can select a keyframe, switch to the Pen tool (P).

5 Drag the leftmost keyframe down to the lower-left corner of the **Surf_Shot_03** clip.

This creates a fade-in effect as the opacity transforms from 0% to 100% opaque.

6   Step through the frames where the keyframe graph changes to see the fade-in effect.

7   Right-click the second keyframe and choose Smooth from the shortcut menu.

8   Adjust the Bezier handle to create a slight convex angle to the curve (as shown in the preceding figure), thus creating a more gradual fade-in.

You can employ all the same keyframe manipulations as in the other windows.

9   Repeat steps 4–8 on the second pair of keyframes to create a fade-out effect.

> **TIP** ▶ Just as you adjust video clip opacity, you can also modify audio levels by adding and changing keyframes directly in the Timeline tracks once the clip keyframes are turned on. For more information on setting audio levels, please see Lesson 5, "Sound Editing."

Displaying Keyframe Bars

But wait, there's more! Not only can opacity and audio levels be animated in the Timeline, you can actually view parameters from applied filter or motion effects, although in a limited way.

1   Turn off clip overlays in the Timeline.

2   Click the Clip Keyframes control.

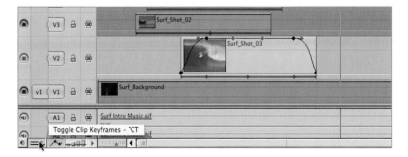

A blue line appears beneath each of the clips in the Timeline.

3   Right-click the Clip Keyframes control.

The Clip Keyframes settings shortcut menu appears.

In the Clip Keyframes shortcut menu, you can customize exactly what happens when you turn on clip keyframes. You can display filter keyframes, motion keyframes, a keyframe graph, and speed indicators for video clips, as well as similar elements for audio clips.

Currently, this sequence is set to display only the motion bar (the blue line). It's an overview of all motion parameters, collapsed into a single bar. The primary advantage to seeing keyframes in the Timeline is that you can evaluate clips to compare when their effects occur. For example, if you wanted one clip to begin fading out on the exact frame where another clip begins scaling down, you could see (and align) all of those keyframes at once.

You can also use the Timeline keyframe bars to compare and align keyframes across different types of parameters such as filters and motion effects.

4   From the shortcut menu on the Clip Keyframes control, choose Video > Filters Bar.

This adds a green bar beneath each clip with filters applied and displays any key-frames for those filters right in the Timeline.

Customizing Keyframe Bars

The trouble is, if you have a lot of keyframes, this simple display can quickly become a mess. So in most cases, rather than displaying all keyframes, it makes sense to limit which parameters are visible for any given clip.

1   Right-click the blue line beneath the **Surf_Shot_03** clip.

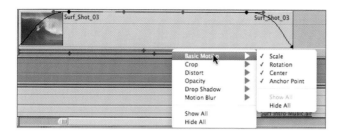

A shortcut menu appears, listing all of the Motion parameters for that clip. If you poke around the menu, you can see which parameters are active (indicated by a checkmark) and which are hidden from view.

TIP ▶ Right-click the green bar to hide and show specific filter parameters in the Timeline filters bar.

By default, just about all the parameters are selected, so the blue bar is showing every single keyframe for every single parameter. If two parameters have keyframes on the exact same frame, you won't know which keyframe you're looking at (or manipulating), which can be problematic.

2   From the shortcut menu, choose Hide All, and then choose Crop > Edge Feather.

Now only that parameter's keyframes are visible.

TIP ▶ The Keyframe Overview menu for each parameter set in the Motion tab is live-linked to this shortcut menu. Turning a parameter on or off in either place will change the other.

In this example, the goal is to align the end of the edge feather effect with the second keyframe from the Gaussian Blur filter.

3   Drag the blue keyframe to the left to align it with the second keyframe in the green bar.

4   Render and play the sequence to see the result of the effect.

The blur and edge feather animations now correspond precisely.

TIP ▶ These keyframe bars can also be used to compare and coordinate keyframes across multiple clips in the Timeline.

Editing Keyframe Graphs in the Timeline

The keyframe bars allow you to compare the timing of keyframes across effects and across clips, but you can change only a keyframe's position in time; you can't change its value. If you need to see an entire parameter graph in the Timeline, you can do so, but for only one parameter (per clip) at a time.

1   Right-click the Clip Keyframes control and choose Video > Keyframe Editor from the shortcut menu.

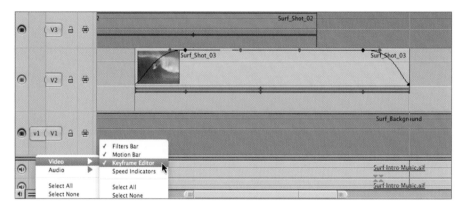

More space is added beneath each of the clips (so each track takes up quite a bit of space), but no keyframe graph will be visible until you specify which parameter graph you want to see.

2   Right-click the area beneath the blue and green keyframe bars for **Surf_Shot_03** and choose Basic Motion > Scale from the shortcut menu.

The scale graph is displayed for that clip. Only one graph can be displayed at a time, so if you choose another parameter, its graph will replace this one.

You can increase the size allocated for the graph on a track-by-track basis.

3   Drag the rightmost edge of the track header area for track V2 upward.

As you increase the size of the graph, the entire track area gets larger.

This graph is identical to the one in the Motion (or Filters) tab except that it's larger, giving you more flexibility and precision control. Changing values in one place automatically affects the other. You can do all of the same keyframing operations here as in the other graphs (except parameters with coordinate values such as center or anchor point).

The main advantage of accessing a keyframe graph here is to compare this graph with a graph on another clip. You can compare the relative slopes of various parameter animations and adjust them to make them more or less similar.

4   Click the Clip Keyframes control to hide the keyframe controls.

5   Option-click the Track Visibility control for track V2 to turn on all the tracks and play the sequence.

Bonus Exercise

This lesson leaves the Surf Intro sequence incomplete; however, you're encouraged to finish it yourself by using the various animation techniques you learned in this lesson.

Watch the finished movie, **Surf_Intro_Finished**, and see how accurately you can recreate it on your own. If you get stuck, or want to cheat, you can see all of the keyframes required by examining the **Surf Intro - 3** sequence.

Lesson Review

1. What is a keyframe?

2. Which windows permit keyframing?

3. How do you change a corner point to a smooth point?

4. What is Ease In/Out?

5. How do you delete a keyframe?

6. How do you navigate to a keyframe?

7. How are filters animated?

8. What parameters' keyframe graphs can be viewed in the Timeline?

9. How do you grab a keyframe that's positioned too close to a clip's In or Out point?

10. How can a clip's motion or filter keyframes be viewed in the Timeline?

Answers

1. A mark to indicate that a parameter must be at a specific value on a specific frame.

2. The Canvas, the Timeline, and all of the tabs in the Viewer window.

3. Right-click a keyframe and choose Smooth from the shortcut menu.

4. Ease In/Out automatically sets the acceleration of an animation to slow down as it approaches and ramp up as it leaves a keyframe.

5. Right-click the keyframe and choose Delete or Clear from the shortcut menu, or in some cases, just drag it off the graph. In the Canvas, you can also park on the keyframe and deselect it from the Add Motion Keyframe shortcut menu.

6. Shift-K and Option-K will take you to the next or previous keyframe for the selected objects. In the Viewer, you can also use the Previous Keyframe and Next Keyframe buttons.

7. Animate filters by opening the Filters tab and using the keyframe controls to the right of the parameter settings.

8. Any parameter can be viewed in the Timeline using the Clip Keyframes' keyframe editor (albeit only one at a time, per clip). Clip opacity and audio levels can be viewed directly on top of the clips in the Timeline by turning on clip overlays.

9. The Pen tool can be used to select keyframes in the Timeline when the Selection tool is erroneously selecting the clip edge.

10. Keyframe bars for both motion and filters can be displayed in the Timeline by activating the Clip Keyframes control.

10

Nesting Sequences

When working with complex sequences involving multiple tracks, you may want to treat a group of clips as a single object. For example, you may wish to apply a single filter to multiple items, or to scale or rotate several clips at once. Final Cut Pro's nesting features can efficiently accomplish such complex tasks.

Furthermore, nested sequences also allow you to quickly add effects and perform tasks that would otherwise be time-consuming or impossible any other way. Learning to manage nested sequences will enable you to create powerful effects, as well as improve your overall workflow and flexibility within Final Cut Pro.

Understanding Nested Sequences

You can treat any sequence as a clip and edit it into another sequence by dragging it into the Canvas or Timeline. The embedded sequence is called a *nested* sequence, and the sequence it's embedded into is often referred to as the *parent* sequence.

You can also select a group of clips already in a sequence and turn it into a nested sequence—replacing the group of items with a single item.

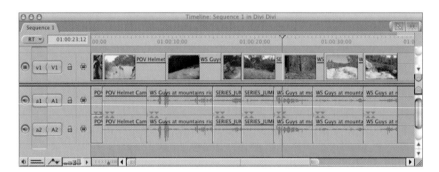

Before nesting

Nested

Basic Nesting

First you'll edit one sequence into another.

1   Open Lesson Files > Lesson_10 > **Nesting.fcp**.

The *Bike Jumps* sequence should be open in the Timeline.

2   Play the sequence to get familiar with it.

The sequence contains three clips on track 1 and a title clip on track 2.

3   In the Browser, double-click *Motocross Sequence*.

It opens as a second tab in the Timeline.

4   Press the Home key to ensure that the sequence playhead is at the beginning of the sequence.

5   In the Browser, select the *Bike Jumps* sequence.

6   Drag it into the Canvas and drop it as an Insert edit.

You've now nested the *Bike Jumps* sequence inside *Motocross Sequence*.

> **TIP**   You can identify a nested sequence by its unique color in the Timeline.

When you play *Motocross Sequence*, clips nested in the *Bike Jumps* sequence will play as they were originally edited—including the title from track V2.

Understanding Live Links

The link between a nested sequence and its parent sequence remains active. Any changes made to clips or other items inside a nested sequence are automatically updated in the parent sequence.

1   In the Timeline, click the Bike Jumps tab.

2   Position your sequence playhead anywhere over the title clip to see the results of changes you make in the Viewer.

3   Double-click the title clip on track V2 to open it into the Viewer.

4   In the Viewer, click the Controls tab. Type *Motocross Madness!* in the text box and press Tab or click anywhere outside the text box to update the Canvas.

The Canvas reflects the change.

> **TIP** ▶ If your playhead isn't over the area of the title, drag it there to confirm that the text has been updated.

5   In the Timeline, click the *Motocross Sequence* tab.

6   Scrub the playhead through *Motocross Sequence* until you see the section where the title should appear.

Notice that the text has been updated here as well.

Whenever you change the title clip from the *Bike Jumps* nested sequence in the Controls tab of the Viewer, the changes continue to update live in *Motocross Sequence*, the parent sequence.

Applying Effects to Multiple Clips

You can use nesting to apply a single effect to multiple items at once. This saves time by eliminating the need to individually apply a filter or transformation to each clip. If you later decide to change the parameters of the effect, the changes will affect all clips simultaneously.

In this example, you'll tint all of the clips inside the nested sequence red.

1   Be sure that *Motocross Sequence* is open in the Timeline.

2   In the Timeline, select the *Bike Jumps* nested sequence.

3   Choose Effects > Video Filters > Image Control > Tint.

The tint effect affects every clip in the *Bike Jumps* nested sequence.

The filter is applied to the nest and not the individual clips contained in the nest. Open the nested sequence in the Viewer to modify the parameters of the filter.

Ordinarily, double-clicking a clip in the Timeline opens it in the Viewer. But when you double-click a nested sequence, it opens in the Timeline and Canvas as a new tab, just as any sequence does when you double-click it in the Browser.

4   In the Timeline, select the *Bike Jumps* nested sequence (if it's not already selected).

5   Press Enter, or choose View > Sequence.

> **TIP** You can also right-click (or Control-click) a nested sequence and choose Open in Viewer from the shortcut menu.

The *Bike Jumps* sequence is now displayed in the Viewer as if it were an individual clip.

6   In the Viewer, click the Filters tab.

The Tint filter controls should be visible.

7   Set the color of the tint to a pale red by clicking the color picker and adjusting the color settings.

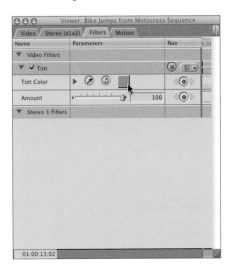

8   Play *Motocross Sequence*. Notice that the new reddish tint affects the entire *Bike Jumps* segment.

You could accomplish the same results by applying the tint filter to each individual clip. However, if your client decided that she preferred a blue tint instead of red, you would then have to open and modify the clips individually. With nested sequences, you can modify filter settings once to affect all the clips at once.

Applying Complex Geometric Settings

Some effects can be achieved only by using nested sequences. For example, by combining multiple clips into a single element in the Timeline, you can apply geometric attributes such as scale, rotation, and movement to all of the clips as a single unit.

1   In the Browser, double-click the *Split Screen* sequence to open it into the Timeline.

The *Split Screen* sequence contains four clips scaled down to 50% and arranged into quadrants in the Canvas so that all four images are visible onscreen at the same time.

> **TIP**   If your system is powerful enough, you may be able to play the sequence without rendering. If the Timeline displays a red line in the render bar area, you might not have selected Unlimited RT in the Real-Time Effects pop-up menu in the Timeline. Selecting Unlimited RT and Dynamic quality, instead of Safe RT, will allow you to play more effects in real time. For more on RT settings, see Lesson 7, "Advanced Compositing and Effects."

2 If necessary, render your sequence by pressing Option-R.

3 Play the sequence.

The four video clips play simultaneously.

Earlier in this lesson, you created a nested sequence by dragging one sequence into another. In the following steps, you'll create a nested sequence in place using the Nest Items command.

4 Select the four clips in the Timeline.

5 Choose Sequence > Nest Item(s) or press Option-C.

The Nest Items dialog appears.

6 In the Name box, type *Quadrant Sequence*. Leave the other settings at their default values and click OK.

Now, instead of four clips on four tracks, the parent sequence contains one item, *Quadrant Sequence*. The image in the Canvas doesn't change.

> **TIP** The Nest Items command automatically puts the new nested sequence on the lowest available track. If a clip already occupies the lowest track, the next available higher track will be used. In some cases, Final Cut Pro will generate a new track to make space for the item. The following figures show an example in which V2 becomes the location of a nested sequence created from clips on V1 through V4.

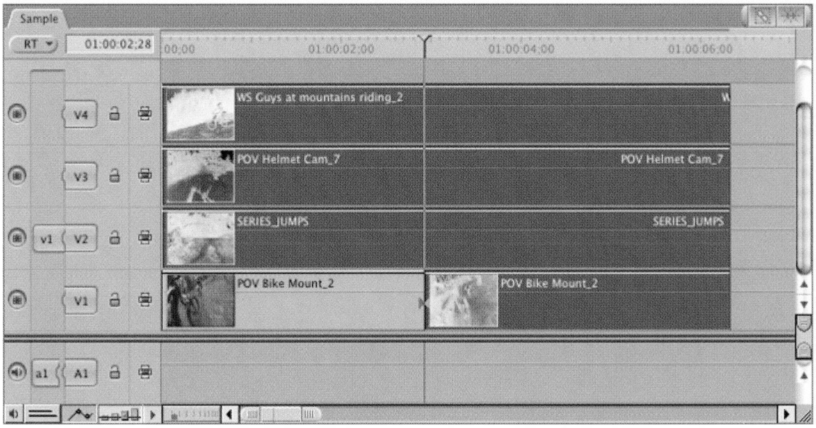

Un-nested

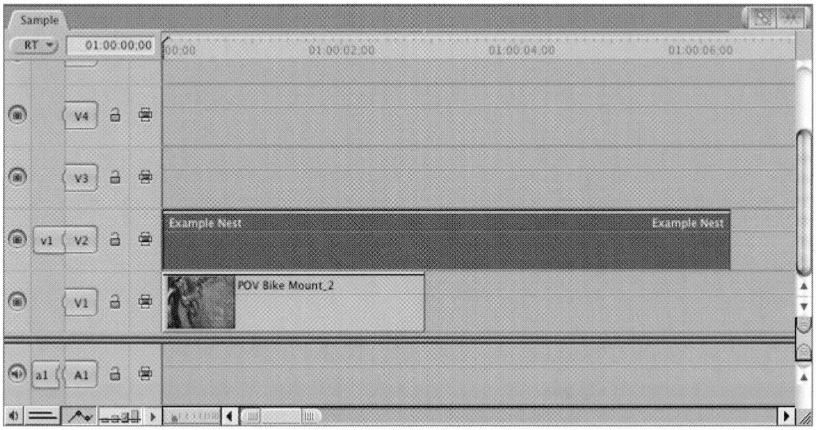

Nested

Nest Items also adds a new sequence in your project. You can use this sequence like any other. Any changes you make to the nested *Quadrant Sequence* will modify the parent *Split Screen* sequence.

Applying Motion Parameters

All four clips are now neatly contained in a nest, so you can modify the Motion parameters of the nest without affecting the individual motion parameters of the clips within.

For example, nesting these clips is particularly useful if you want to rotate all four clips as a group while maintaining their individual X/Y positions and rotation values.

1   Open *Quadrant Sequence* into the Viewer by selecting it in the Timeline and pressing Enter.

2   In the Viewer, click the Motion tab.

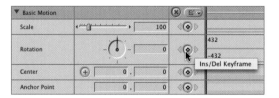

3   Press the Home key to bring your playhead to the beginning of the sequence in the Viewer.

4   Click the Add Keyframe button for the Rotation parameter.

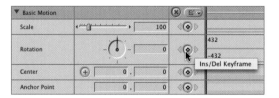

5   Move the playhead 6 seconds into the sequence in the Viewer by typing +600, or by typing 6 and then a single period. Press Enter.

6   Set the Rotation value to *1440* degrees (four rotations) and press Enter.

A second keyframe is automatically added.

When you play this sequence, the four videos will spin in unison around a common center point. Setting similar Rotation parameters for each clip individually would have resulted in each clip spinning around its own center point.

7   With your playhead on the last Rotation keyframe, in the Motion tab of the Viewer, type *–500* and press Enter.

This moves the playhead 5 seconds earlier.

8   Add a keyframe for the Scale parameter (leaving the value at 100).

9   Move the playhead forward 5 seconds again so it lines up precisely with the Rotation keyframe.

10   Set the Scale parameter to *0* and press Enter, which will shrink the nest over time until it's invisible.

11   Play the sequence.

The four clips spin around a single center point and then vanish into the distance.

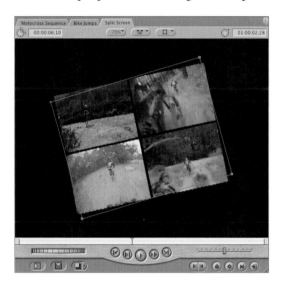

Add a Background Element

At this point, the clips vanish into a black field. You can use this effect as a transition, revealing another clip as the spinning clips disappear.

1   In the Timeline, Shift-drag *Quadrant Sequence* from track V1 onto track V2. Holding down Shift as you drag up or down prevents the clip from moving left or right.

> **TIP** ▶ You can move a selected clip from one track to another in the Timeline by pressing Option–Up Arrow or Option–Down Arrow (this works only if the destination track is empty but will create a new track if none exists).

2   Drag **Blue Background** from the Browser into the Timeline, dropping it on track V1 directly underneath *Quadrant Sequence*.

When the four clips scale down, **Blue Background** will be revealed.

3   Play back the sequence.

Adjusting the Anchor Point

In the **Blue Background** clip, the bike icon is slightly off center. To integrate the four quadrant clips with the background clip, you'll alter the anchor point of the nested sequence so that the clips spin around and vanish into that bike icon.

1   In the Canvas, move the playhead near the end of the sequence and park it on a frame where the background bicycle graphic is visible. Note the approximate position of the bicycle.

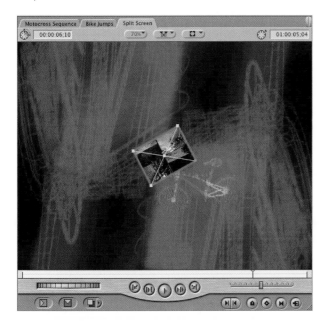

2   Select the Distort tool (D) and press the Home key to bring the playhead to the beginning of the sequence.

3   In the Canvas View menu, choose Image+Wireframe.

4   Make sure the nest is selected and drag the center point of *Quadrant Sequence* to the approximate position of the bicycle.

This modifies the clip's anchor point, the point around which the object rotates and scales.

> **TIP** ▶ Don't be confused by the onscreen feedback. Final Cut Pro displays a representation of the change in the motion path, based on the rotation and scaling keyframes you already set.

5   Render, if necessary (Option-R), and play the sequence.

Now the four rotating clips vanish into the location of the bicycle.

Changing the Render Order

Effects in Final Cut Pro are rendered in a specific order. Filters are applied in the order they're listed in the Filters tab of the Viewer, from top to bottom. Rearranging the render order can change the results. For example, if you apply a Mask Shape filter after applying a Blur, the edge of the matte will be sharp, but the image behind the matte will be blurred. If you apply the matte first and then add the Blur, the edge of the matte will blur along with the rest of the image.

Blur before Mask Shape

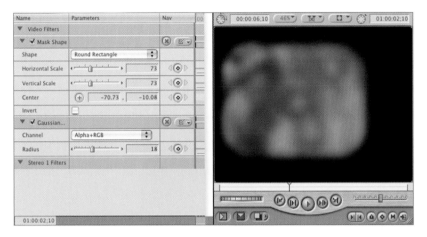

Mask Shape before Blur

Furthermore, filters are rendered before motion parameters. This is easy to remember, because the Filters tab appears to the left of the Motion tab in the Viewer. So if you apply a distort filter, such as Wave or Ripple, and then reduce the size of the image, the filter will be applied before the scale operation. The distortion effect is limited to the clip's original size, so the effect may end abruptly at the edges of the clip.

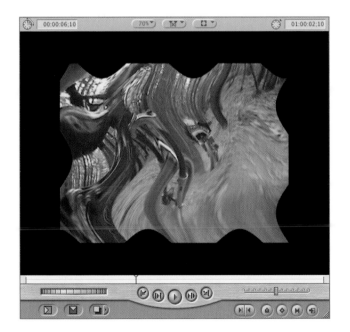

To make the wave effect apply to the scaled image, you're trying to reverse the built-in render order so that the Motion tab is rendered before the Filters tab. The only way to accomplish this is by nesting the scaled clip, and applying the filter to the nested sequence.

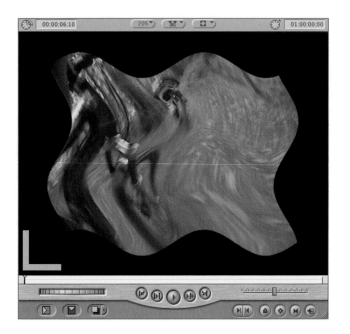

1   Create a new sequence and name it *Render Order*.

2   To make the effect more visible, set the Canvas background color to white using the Canvas View pop-up menu. Be sure the Selection tool is active.

3   Insert the clip **POV Bike Mount_2** into the new *Render Order* sequence.

4   With the Canvas in Image+Wireframe mode, use the Selection tool to drag one of the corner points and scale the clip down to approximately 80 percent of its original size.

5   Double-click **POV Bike Mount_2** and select the Motion tab in the Viewer.

6   Select the checkbox to activate the Drop Shadow.

7   Increase the Offset slider to 10.

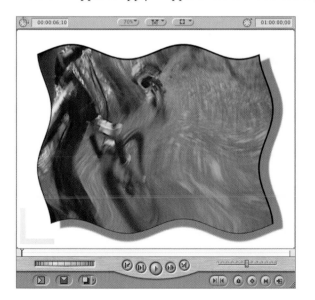

8   Select the clip in the Timeline and choose Sequence > Nest Items, or press Option-C.

TIP ▸ When nesting a single clip, you have the option to keep any currently applied effects with the clip, or move the effects to the nested sequence.

9   Name the new sequence *POV Bike Mount Nested Sequence* and click OK.

10 Select the nested sequence in the Timeline, and then choose Effects > Video Filters > Distort > Ripple to apply a ripple effect to the nested sequence.

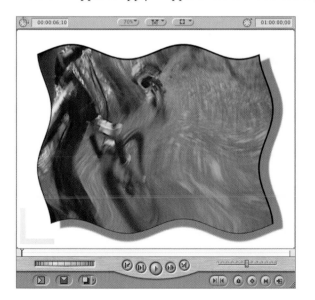

Applying the filter to the nested sequence allows the filtering effect to be processed after the clip's motion parameters are applied. In this case, you can see how the drop shadow is distorted along with the image.

11 Click the View pop-up menu in the Canvas and choose Black to reset the background color.

Reordering Motion Effects

You can also use nesting to reorder effects within the Motion tab. In an earlier exercise, you changed an anchor point that affected both scaling and rotation. Now, you'll change the anchor point for the scaling, but leave rotation alone, by applying a second nesting operation.

1 Open the *Split Screen 2* sequence.

This sequence is just like the *Split Screen* sequence you modified earlier. The rotation has already been applied to *Quadrant Sequence*, but the Scale and Anchor Point settings have not yet been modified.

2 Select *Quadrant Seq* and choose Sequence > Nest Items.

3 In the Nest Items dialog, name the nested sequence *Rotating Quadrant Sequence*
and set its frame size to *1140 x 760*.

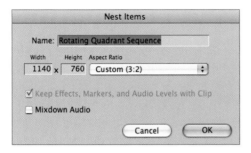

Increasing the nested sequence frame size allows the clips plenty of room to rotate
in virtual space without bumping into the edge of the frame.

4 Click OK.

Although *Quadrant Sequence* is already a nested sequence, you can nest it again.

> **TIP** ▶ There is no limit to the number of times you can nest a sequence.

5 Open *Rotating Quadrant Sequence* into the Viewer and click the Motion tab.

6 Set a keyframe value of *100* in the Scale parameter at 1:00.

7 Set a second keyframe at 6:00 with a value of *0*.

8 Temporarily set the opacity for the nested sequence to 20%, so you can see where to drag the anchor point.

9 Press the Home key or drag the playhead to the beginning of the sequence.

10 Select the Distort tool and drag the center point of *Rotating Quadrant Sequence* to the approximate position of the bicycle.

11 In the Motion tab of the Viewer, set Opacity back to 100%.

12 Render, if necessary, and play back your sequence.

The sequence will rotate around the center point of the four quadrants, but when it scales down, it will vanish into the center of the bike logo observing the modified anchor point.

Mixing Sequence Sizes

In the Nest Items dialog, you can modify the frame size for newly created nested sequences. Changing the frame size further expands the creative possibilities of nesting.

For example, if you want to build a background composed of multiple video images and pan across that background, you can construct a sequence with a large frame size and nest it into a standard, NTSC-sized sequence.

1   Open the *Stacked* sequence from the Browser.

This sequence contains three clips that are stacked one on top of another. All are full-frame, standard DV resolution.

2   Select the three items and choose Sequence > Nest Items.

3   In the Nest Items dialog, set the Aspect Ratio pop-up menu to Custom.

4   Set the frame size to *2160* x *480*.

This frame size is three times the width of a standard NTSC DV frame.

5   Name the new sequence *Wide Sequence* and click OK.

6   Double-click *Wide Sequence*.

A new Timeline tab appears.

> **TIP** The Canvas displays the wide sequence, reduced to fit into the viewable area, so that you can see your nonstandard frame size.

7   Set your Canvas background back to Black and then set the Canvas view to
Image+Wireframe mode.

8   With the Selection tool, select the clip in track V3 in the Timeline. In the Canvas,
drag it to the left.

9   In the Timeline, select the clip in track V2.

10   In the Canvas, drag this selected clip to the right of the frame.

> **TIP** ▶ Hold down the Shift key to constrain the movement to horizontal only.

All three clips now appear side by side in the Canvas window.

11   From the Generator pop-up menu in the Viewer, open a new text generator.

> **TIP** ▶ Notice that the generator defaults to the same size as the currently active
> sequence.

12   Target track V3 and place the Timeline playhead in the center of the clips.

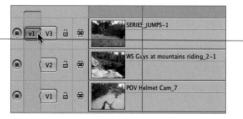

13 Drag the Text clip from the Viewer to the Canvas and drop it as a Superimpose edit.

This action places the text on a new track above the existing clips.

14 In the Timeline, double-click the text from track V4 to open it into the Viewer.

15 In the Controls tab in the Viewer, change the text to *Motocross*.

16 Set the text color to your liking. Set the font Size to *100*.

The Canvas updates to reflect your changes.

17 In the Controls tab in the Viewer, use the Origin control to adjust the text so that it's centered across the three images.

18 In the Canvas, click the Stacked tab.

Currently, the *Wide Sequence* is scaled down to view the entire sequence in the 720x480 frame size.

19 Open the *Wide Sequence* into the Viewer and scale to 100 percent under the Motion tab.

20 Set the Canvas Scale pop-up menu to Fit All.

This allows you to see the entire wireframe boundary box of the nested sequence inside the *Stacked* parent sequence.

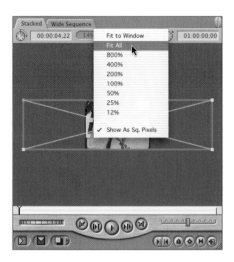

TIP It may help to think of this view as looking through the standard-sized window of the *Stacked* parent sequence into the wider nested sequence within it.

21 In the Canvas, Shift-drag the wireframe for the nested *Wide Sequence* to the right, until its left edge aligns with the visible area of your sequence.

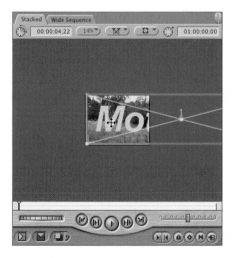

22 Press the Home key to move the playhead to the beginning of the sequence.

23 With the nest still selected, add a keyframe by clicking the Add Motion Keyframe button in the Canvas, or by pressing Control-K.

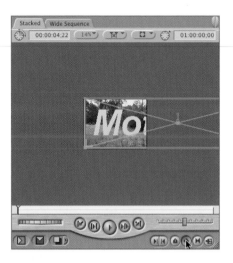

The wireframe for the nest turns green to indicate that a keyframe has been created.

24 Move the playhead to the last frame of the sequence.

25 In the Canvas, Shift-drag the nested sequence to the left until the right edge of the visible image aligns with the right edge of the boundary box.

A new keyframe is automatically added, and a motion path appears in the Canvas.

> **TIP** If you don't see a motion path, it probably means you tried to drag the sequence to its new position before moving the playhead.

26 Set the Canvas back to Fit to Window. Render (Option-R), if necessary, and play the sequence.

Using Nesting as an Editing Tool

Although Final Cut Pro doesn't prevent you from building hours of program material in a single sequence, it's not the most efficient or practical way to work. When editing long-format shows such as TV programming or feature films, most editors break the program into sections (often called scenes, reels, or segments) and edit each one in a separate sequence. When individual segments are complete, they can be edited into a single main sequence for viewing and output.

When editors nest a scene or segment into a longer main sequence, some will call the main sequence a *master* sequence, instead of a *parent* sequence, and sometimes call the nested sequence a *subsequence*.

The differences in terminology are strictly a matter of preference. In Final Cut Pro, a master sequence is identical to a parent sequence, and a subsequence is identical to a nested sequence. The terms are often used interchangeably in everyday industry practice; we will use them interchangeably in this section to help you get used to the terminology.

Nesting allows you to quickly rearrange entire segments to experiment with scene order. You can manipulate the sequences as if they were a series of clips, trim nested sequences using the trimming tools, and add transition effects using In/Out points and Bezier handles.

Nesting facilitates flexibility because you can modify the contents of individual subsequences, and the parent sequence will update to reflect the latest edits.

1   Create a new sequence named *Master Sequence* and open it.

2   Drag the *Stacked* sequence from the Browser directly into the Timeline.

The *Stacked* sequence is now nested in the master sequence.

Marking a Sequence with In and Out Points

By setting an In or Out point in a sequence before you nest it, you define which portion of the sequence will be included in the master sequence. As when editing a single clip, the portions that fall outside the In and Out points become handle frames to accommodate transition effects, such as a cross dissolve, or for trimming of the edit points in the Timeline.

1   Double-click the *Bike Jumps* sequence to open it in the Timeline.

2   Set an Out point at the end of the title on track V2.

3   In the Timeline, click the *Master Sequence* tab to bring it to the foreground.

4   Press the End key to make sure your playhead is at the end of the sequence, one frame past the nested *Stacked* subsequence.

5   Overwrite *Bike Jumps* into *Master Sequence* by dragging it from the Browser to the Canvas or Timeline.

Now the master sequence contains two subsequences: *Stacked* and *Bike Jumps*.

TIP Because subsequences follow all the standard rules of three-point editing when edited into master sequences, the Bike Jumps sequence ends at the Out point you designated earlier.

Editing Within the Nested Sequence

Imagine that these are the first two scenes of the finished program. You can continue to make editorial changes to clips inside the individual subsequences, and the master sequence will be updated automatically.

If you add, delete, or trim individual clips inside a nested subsequence (or even another nested sequence) the master sequence will ripple to accommodate the changes, making the master sequence shorter or longer.

> **TIP** This behavior only applies when the subsequence was first added without In or Out points set.

1   In the Browser, double-click the *Stacked* sequence to open it into its own Timeline tab.

This subsequence was edited into the master sequence without marked In or Out points. Now you're going to change the duration of the nested subsequence by adding a clip.

2   Drag the clip **SERIES_JUMPS** from the Browser and edit it in at the end of *Wide Sequence*.

3   Switch back to *Master Sequence*.

The subsequence appears correspondingly longer, and the whole master sequence has gotten longer too. Observe the new sequence duration is 6:10.

Using Pre-Trimmed Subsequences

If you set an In or Out point in the subsequence *before editing it into the master,* making subsequent edits in the subsequence will *not* cause the master sequence to ripple.

1   In the Browser, double-click the *Bike Jumps* sequence.

2   Drag the **SERIES_JUMPS** shot from the Browser into the Timeline to add it to the end of this sequence.

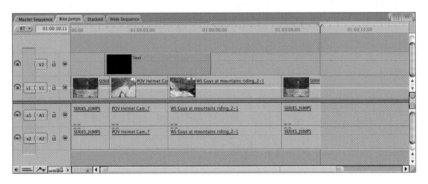

Although this action lengthens this subsequence here, the Out point set earlier still defines the sequence's length within the master sequence.

3   Bring *Master Sequence* to the front.

Notice that nothing in *Master Sequence* has changed. The sequence time remains at 6:10.

Of course, you can manually ripple the nested subsequence in the master, just like any clip, to reveal more of its content.

4   In the master sequence, drag the right edge of the *Bike Jumps* subsequence to make it longer.

The additional content in the subsequence is now visible in *Master Sequence.*

Editing the Content of a Subsequence

In all of the examples so far, you've been nesting multiple clips and treating them as a single item to add effects or edits to a group of clips at one time. Occasionally, you may need to perform the reverse technique to un-nest individual items in a nested sequence.

This is necessary when making an Edit Decision List (EDL), which is a text list of all of the In and Out points for all of the clips in your sequence. If your master sequence contains a nested sequence composed of multiple clips, the EDL will mistakenly represent that nested sequence as a single clip. This may cause serious problems if you're using the EDL to re-create your sequence on another system.

1   Close all of your open sequences by closing the Canvas window.

2   In the Browser, double-click *complex sequence.*

This sequence contains a series of clips, as well as a nested sequence.

The nested sequence *Complex Nest 1* is also located in the Browser. You'll replace *Complex Nest 1* with the clips that it contains in its parent sequence.

3   Make sure snapping is enabled (N).

4   In the Browser, select the *Complex Nest 1* sequence and drag it over the Timeline. Position it directly over the existing instance of the same nest, but do not release the mouse button yet.

5   Hold down the Command key.

The Timeline overlay identifies the individual clips in the sequence.

6   Make sure you're performing an overwrite edit (not an insert edit) by placing the pointer in the lower section of the Timeline track. Release the mouse button first to drop the five clips originally edited into *Complex Nest 1* as an overwrite edit.

The nested sequence has been replaced by its original clip contents. You have un-nested the sequence, and your EDL will accurately reflect all of the individual clips used to build the master sequence.

NOTE ▶ After you complete this operation, there is no live link between the sequence and the individual clips. From this point forward, changes made in the nest will not have an effect on this sequence.

Nesting is incredibly versatile. For audio-intensive projects, you can use nesting to combine groups of sounds to approximate the bussing features of audio-specific tools. For example, you might make a nest of different sound effects tracks and then control the overall volume with a single slider. Or you might use nesting to output a sequence with Timecode Print filters applied to nests so that both sequence and source timecode are burned in when output to tape. As you become more adept at nesting, you'll find countless ways to use it. Nesting is one of the fundamental tools for exploring the true depth and flexibility of Final Cut Pro.

Lesson Review

1. Identify two ways of nesting a sequence.

2. Can you apply filters to a nested sequence?

3. If you adjust the Rotation parameter of a nested sequence with four composited layers, what happens to those layers?

4. If you edit one sequence into another sequence and later change the In and Out points of the nested sequence, what happens to the duration of the master sequence?

5. If you edit one sequence inside another without first setting its In and Out points, what happens if you later change the duration of the subsequence?

6. How do you edit the content of a sequence into the Timeline without nesting it?

Answers

1. Edit a sequence inside of a second sequence, or select one or more clips in the Timeline and choose Sequence > Nest Items.

2. Yes. Filters affect every clip within a nested sequence to which they're applied.

3. The layers all rotate together as if they were a single clip.

4. Nothing. Setting the In and Out points of a nested sequence locks the master sequence's duration.

5. The nested sequence with the changed duration gets longer or shorter, rippling the position of the other items in the master sequence.

6. Command-drag a sequence into the Timeline.

11

Lesson 11
Variable Speed

Speed effects are among the most common and versatile effect types in Final Cut Pro. Basic speed changes such as slow motion can be employed for dramatic effect, and increasing playback speed can simulate time-lapse photography.

The real fun happens when you employ variable speed effects (sometimes called *ramping*) to change a clip's speed *during* playback. For example, a shot can begin playing in slow motion, speed up, and then return to regular speed near the end of the shot. A speed-varied shot can slow to a freeze frame or play in reverse. Final Cut Pro displays clip speed data in several ways. Learning how to read speed keyframe graphs and the Timeline Speed Indicators is essential to mastering the variable speed feature.

Constant Speed Changes

Before delving into variable speed effects, it's important to review how Final Cut Pro handles constant speed changes such as slow motion.

1   Open Lesson Files > Lesson_11 > **Variable_Speed.fcp**. The *1. Bearcats* sequence should be open in the Timeline. Play the sequence.

2   Select **Old and New** (the third clip) and choose Modify > Change Speed.

3   Type *50* in the Rate field and press the Tab key.

The Duration field updates to show the clip's duration at that speed.

TIP ▶ You can also type in a specific duration and let Final Cut Pro figure out the percentage automatically.

4   For now, ignore the Start and End buttons and just make sure the checkboxes are selected for Ripple Sequence, Frame Blending, and Scale Attributes.

Ripple Sequence ensures that the clip's duration change is accounted for in the Timeline.

Frame blending generates new frames by blending the surrounding frames to create a smoother slow-motion effect.

Scale Attributes adjusts the timing of any keyframes applied to the clip, so they maintain their relative position.

5   Click OK.

The clip's speed is changed and the Timeline is rippled accordingly.

6   Play the sequence to see the effect.

NOTE ▶ If you play the sequence using Unlimited RT instead of rendering, you can see a preview version of the effect. However, frame blending will not be applied until you render the sequence.

7   Press Option-R to render the sequence and watch it again.

The effect appears much smoother when the Frame Blending effect is rendered.

Maintaining Sequence Length

If you want to perform a speed change without changing the duration of the sequence, you can deselect the Ripple Sequence checkbox in the Change Speed dialog.

If you speed up the clip (set a value higher than 100%), more frames will be required from the source media to keep the clip at its original duration. This might expose undesired frames that you previously trimmed out.

If you slow a clip down (set a value lower than 100%), fewer frames will be seen and the complete action visible in the original shot may now be cut off.

1   Select the fourth clip, **mid-air cross**.

2   Press Command-J to open the Change Speed dialog.

3   Deselect the Ripple Sequence checkbox.

4   Set the Rate to *200%* and click OK.

The clip's speed is changed, but the duration in the Timeline doesn't change.

> **TIP** Sometimes Final Cut Pro will adjust the actual speed percentage away from the exact number you entered, to ensure that the clip contains only whole frames.

5 Play the sequence.

Now there's a moment of empty sky at the end of the shot.

Scaling Attributes

When you change a clip's speed you may or may not want the keyframes applied to that clip to be adjusted along with the clip length. If you used keyframes to create a fade-in/fade-out effect on a clip, those keyframes could remain fixed to the exact frame number, or they could be tied to the specific content of the frame which would move forward or backward if the clip's speed were altered.

1 Click the Clip Overlays button to turn on Keyframe Overlays.

The second clip, **Bearcat-Hornet formation**, has opacity keyframes applied. These are exactly the type of attributes the Scale Attributes checkbox affects.

2 Press Command-Shift-A to deselect all.

3 Position the playhead anywhere over the second clip.

4 Choose Modify > Change Speed or press Command-J.

> **TIP** When no clip is selected Final Cut Pro uses the playhead location and the Auto-Select track buttons to control selection.

5   Set the Rate to 75%, select the Ripple Sequence checkbox, deselect the Scale Attributes checkbox, and then click OK.

The clip is stretched out but the keyframes remain in their original position. This is almost certainly not what you want.

6   Press Command-Z to undo the last operation.

7   Press Command-J again to reopen the Change Speed dialog.

8   This time, set the Rate to 75% and make sure the Scale Attributes checkbox is selected, and then click OK.

Now the opacity keyframes are scaled to match the duration of the shot.

TIP ▶ If you had only a fade in, and wanted it to remain at exactly 20 frames long no matter how long the speed-affected clip became, you would leave that checkbox deselected.

Before	After

Displaying Speed Indicators

The Timeline can display tick marks to indicate the speed of a clip. These can be helpful for an at-a-glance view of the relative speeds of your clips, and you'll see that it's vital when working with Variable Speed effects.

1   Click the Clip Keyframes control to turn it on.

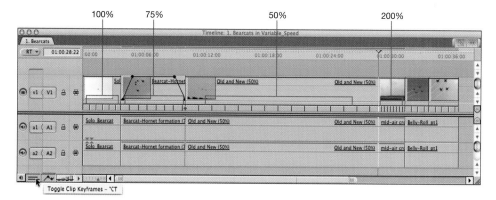

Notice that difference in the spacing between the tick marks on the different clips. The tick marks with the white highlight (on the first, fifth, and sixth clips) indicate speed set at 100%.

When a clip is slowed down, as are the second and third clips, the tick marks are spread farther apart. Notice that the tick marks on the third clip (set to 50%) are more spread out than on the second clip (set to 75%). When a clip is sped up, like the fourth clip, the tick marks appear closer together.

TIP ▶ When a clip is playing in reverse speed, the tick marks appear in red. When a clip is set to freeze on a single frame, no tick marks appear at all.

Variable Speed Changes

Although there are many cases in which a constant speed change is exactly what you want, there are other times when you may want a clip to *ramp* from one playback speed to another while it's playing. This has quickly become an overused effect applied with little rhyme or reason in music videos, commercials, and even in feature films.

NOTE ▶ Variable speed effects can't be applied to audio clips.

Ramping Constant Speed Effects

Before you get into making a crazy complex example where a clip changes from backward to forward playback and at all different speeds, you'll start with a simpler, subtler example.

1   Select the third clip and press Command-J.

The Change Speed dialog opens, showing the current speed settings for the clip.

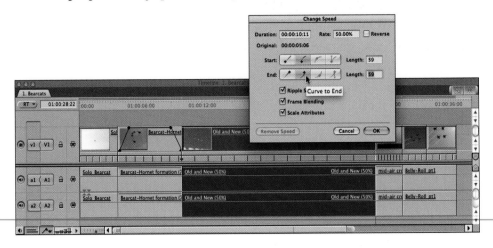

The Start and End controls in the center of the dialog allow you to ramp the speed to the value set in the Rate field. If you change the Start setting, rather than abruptly beginning playback at 50%, the clip will start at 100% and slow down over the number of frames in the Length field. If you adjust the End setting, the clip will ramp from the speed in the Rate field back to normal speed by the end of the clip.

2   Click the Curve from Start and the Curve from End buttons, and then click OK.

3   Play the sequence to see the effect.

> **TIP** ▸ Notice that the tick marks beneath the clip start out closer together and spread out as they get toward the center of the clip, and then they get closer together again as the clip speeds back up to regular speed by the end.

Creating Speed Segments

Although the previous exercise is technically a variable speed effect, most people think of ramp effects as a clip playing at different speeds across the duration of a single shot.

To create this effect in Final Cut Pro, you break a clip into segments and apply a speed value to each segment. Rather than using the Blade tool to create distinct segments, you can apply speed keyframes to create the segment boundaries.

> **TIP** ▸ Although making individual segments using the Blade tool can give a similar result to using speed keyframes, the latter allows you to create smooth transitions from one speed value to another, generating the organic-looking effect most clients desire.

1   Open the *2. Ballet* sequence.

This sequence contains a single shot of a dancer leaping across an empty stage. The Speed Indicators should already be showing.

2   Play the sequence to familiarize yourself with the clip.

This clip was photographed in slow motion, but that doesn't mean you can't modify the speed of the playback now.

TIP By shooting slow motion in-camera (only some cameras allow this) you record more frames per second than at regular speed. Those extra frames come in handy when modifying the speed in Final Cut Pro. You can always speed it up to look "normal," but the additional frames allow you to maintain a sharper, clearer image when slowing the clip down.

Similarly, shooting at a higher frame rate (such as 60i or 60p instead of 24p or 30p) will typically yield smoother slow-motion results in Final Cut Pro.

3 Find the frame just before the dancer leaps into the air (around 2:07).

4 Click the Speed Indicators at that frame to add a speed keyframe.

Simply adding a keyframe doesn't change the speed of the clip, but it designates a boundary between two *speed segments* for the clip.

Notice that keyframes are automatically added to the beginning and end of the clip. Each segment is defined as the area between two speed keyframes.

5 Find the frame where the dancer lands after her jump (around 3:08) and add a second keyframe by clicking the Speed Indicators.

> **TIP** In older versions of Final Cut Pro you had to use the Time Remap tool to create speed keyframes. In Final Cut Pro 7.0 you can create them by clicking the Speed Indicators with the Arrow pointer.

Now the clip has been divided into three speed segments: before the jump, the jump itself, and after the jump.

6 Right-click (or Control-click) the area between the middle two keyframes. From the shortcut menu, choose Change Speed Segment.

TIP Be careful not to choose Change Speed, which would affect the speed of the entire clip and will require you to remove existing speed segments.

The Change Speed Segment dialog opens.

Although it looks nearly identical to the Change Speed dialog, the Change Speed Segment dialog affects only the area between the keyframes.

7   Set the Rate to 50% and leave the rest of the settings at their default, and then click OK.

The speed indicators change to show that the segment of the clip has been slowed down. That segment now takes up more of the clip's duration.

NOTE ▸ Variable speed effects never ripple the Final Cut Pro sequence.

8 Play the sequence to see the results of your work.

TIP ▸ Hover your pointer over a speed segment and a help tag will appear indicating the speed currently applied to that segment.

9 Right-click the speed segment between the first two keyframes (before the dancer jumps), and from the shortcut menu, choose Change Speed Segment.

10 Set the rate to 150% and click OK.

11 Play the sequence.

Now the dancer moves at a natural speed (compensating for the slow-motion way the shot was photographed) until the jump begins, then she moves into slow motion, and then after she lands, she returns to the original rate of the shot.

Smoothing Speed Segments

The clip is now clearly playing at different speeds at different points in the clip, but the changes are happening abruptly. You can smooth the speed changes by using the Speed to Segment controls.

1 Right-click the Speed Indicators on the segment containing the dancer's jump.

2   From the shortcut menu, choose Speed From Segment Start > Curve From Start.

3   Play the sequence.

This sets the speed to remain constant at 150% until the first keyframe, and then gradually slow down from that point until the next keyframe.

4   Again, right-click the Speed Indicators for the segment containing the dancer's jump. From the shortcut menu, choose Speed From Segment Start > Curve Centered on Start.

5   Play the sequence.

Now the ramping effect begins before the keyframe, making it hard to see where the keyframe actually kicks in.

6 Again, right-click the Speed Indicators for the segment containing the dancer's jump. From the shortcut menu, choose Speed To Segment End > Curve Centered on End.

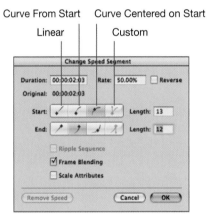

This creates a similar smoothing effect at the end of the speed segment.

7 Play the sequence.

This creates a similar smoothing effect at the end of the speed segment.

TIP You can also set the curve for a speed keyframe by clicking the buttons in the Change Speed Segment dialog.

Here you can also set a duration for the transition from one speed to another using the Length fields.

Custom Speed Keyframe Curves

These default smoothing settings are ideal for most purposes, but if you're trying to do a particularly complex effect, you may want to employ a custom curve shape on the Speed keyframe graph. For that, you must head to the Motion tab in the Viewer.

1 Open the 3. *Ballet Smoothed* sequence from the Browser.

This is a duplicate of the *Ballet* sequence containing all of the settings you should have applied in the previous exercises.

TIP ▶ You can continue working in the original *2. Ballet* sequence if you prefer.

2 Double-click the **SF Ballet** shot to open it into the Viewer, and then click the Motion tab.

3 In the Motion tab, expand the Speed controls and if necessary, stretch the window so you can see the whole keyframe graph.

The Curve to Keyframes setting is what adds the Bezier handles to the keyframes in the Speed graph.

You can further customize the way the speed ramps up or down by adjusting the Bezier handle in this graph.

NOTE ▶ Be careful when manipulating these handles. Small movements can have dramatic effects and may completely alter the subtlety of the speed settings you just established.

▶ Reading a Speed Graph

The speed keyframe graph displays the progression of the frames over time. The X-axis shows sequence time and the Y-axis shows the frame number from the source clip. The following figure shows all the different possible graph states:

▶ A steady upward trajectory indicates forward play at regular speed.

▶ Downward trajectory means backward playback.

▶ The steepness of the line indicates the relative speed (steeper is faster).

▶ A perfectly flat line indicates no movement at all (freeze frame).

4 Press Command-+ (plus sign) to zoom in to the second keyframe in the graph (around 1:13).

5 Adjust the Bezier handle to create different types of smoothing effects.

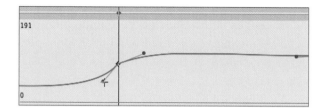

TIP ▶ To manipulate the handles independently, hold down Command, Shift, or Command and Shift together. For more specific information, see Lesson 9, "Creating Dynamic Effects."

Once you touch these handles, Final Cut Pro describes the type of curve applied as Custom.

6 In the Timeline, right-click the middle speed segment and from the shortcut menu, choose Change Speed Segment.

The Start curve is set to the Custom button. You can reset the keyframe here by clicking one of the other buttons (Linear, Curve from Start, or Curve Centered on Start).

7 Click the Curve from Start button and then click OK.

TIP ▶ You can also reset a keyframe to Linear by right-clicking the keyframe in the Motion tab Speed graph and choosing Linear from the pop-up menu.

Dragging Speed Keyframes

In addition to manipulating keyframes using the controls you've already learned, there is another way: dragging the keyframes directly in the Timeline Speed Indicators areas. Although this method is less precise than choosing a specific rate or duration for a speed segment, often it's more important to have a speed effect begin or end on a particular frame in your sequence.

You can move a keyframe's position by dragging it around in the Motion tab, but that wouldn't allow you to coordinate the movement with other elements in your sequence, such as a marker, keyframe in another clip, or sound effect.

Fortunately, you can manipulate speed keyframes directly in the Timeline in two different ways.

1 Open the *4. Ballet Title* sequence.

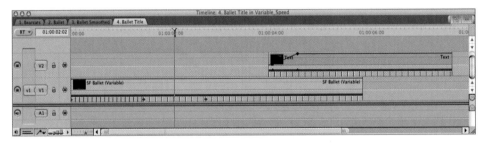

This is a duplicate of the dancer sequence with a title added and some speed keyframes already added where the dancer begins and ends her jump.

2 Play the sequence.

Instead of changing the speed of the jump by opening the Change Speed Segment dialog, you'll change the speed by dragging the keyframe in the Timeline. In this case, rather than setting the speed by a percentage, you'll set it to line up with the appearance of the title on Track 2.

3 Drag the keyframe to the right until it lines up with the end of the fade-in on the title.

TIP ▶ While dragging, a help tag appears to display the new speed for the segment before and after the keyframe being manipulated.

4   Play the sequence.

The speed effect does now end as the title fades in, but the last speed segment is now comically sped up.

TIP ▶ To slow down the speed of the middle segment without automatically speeding up the adjacent segment, Shift-drag.

5   Right-click the last speed segment, and from the pop-up menu that appears, choose Change Speed Segment.

6   In the Change Speed Segment dialog, set the Rate to 100% and click OK.

Although you've now added more frames to the clip (by slowing down that last section from 247% to 100%), you've actually reduced the portion of the source clip that is visible in the sequence. That's because changing a speed segment will never ripple the sequence. If you want the clip to play for a longer duration, you must trim it manually.

7   Drag the right edge of the **SF Ballet** clip to the right as far as it will go.

8   Play the entire sequence to see the results of your work.

> **TIP** ▶ You can also Option-drag a speed keyframe to change the speed of a segment without moving the keyframe's position in the Timeline.

Creating a Temporary Freeze

You may already know how to create a freeze frame using the Modify > Make Freeze Frame command, but sometimes you want to create a freeze frame as part of a variable speed effect. This is sometimes used to introduce characters in title sequences and trailers.

1   Double-click the *5. Freeze Frame* sequence to open it into the Timeline.

This is another copy of the same shot. This time you'll create a freeze frame at the apex of the dancer's leap.

2   Play the sequence and stop playback when the dancer is in mid-leap (at approximately 2:18).

3 Click the Speed Indicators to add a keyframe.

4 Type +2. (plus 2 period) to move your playhead forward 2 seconds.

5   Add a speed keyframe on that frame.

The clip still plays at normal speed, but you've prepared it to create the freeze-frame effect.

6   Press Option-K to navigate your playhead to the keyframe at 2:18.

7   Choose View > Match Frame > Master Clip, or press F.

This loads the source clip into the Viewer, parked on the identical frame. You'll use this as a visual reference for setting the speed keyframe.

8   Press Shift-K to navigate to the next keyframe.

9   Option-drag the keyframe to the left until the frame on the right side of the Canvas matches the frame in the Viewer.

> **TIP** ▶ You may need to hold down the Command key (in addition to the Option key) while dragging to change the value in smaller increments. Zooming in to the Timeline before you begin will also allow you to make finer adjustments.

TIP ▸ You can compare the timecode numbers in the Viewer Current Frame field and in the overlay in the Canvas. In this case: 09:19:09:09.

The help tag will display 0% as the speed value for the Speed Left.

10 Play the sequence.

The freeze frame works as intended, but the remainder of the clip has been sped up to accommodate the change. That can easily be fixed using the Change Speed Segment dialog.

11 Right-click the speed segment to the right of the freeze frame.

12 In the Change Speed Segment dialog set the Rate to 100% and click OK.

13 Play the sequence again.

The speed indicators can also assist you in identifying when you've achieved the freeze frame. They won't contain any tick marks for the duration of the freeze.

TIP ▸ When creating freeze frames, you need to check how the output looks on an interlaced external monitor to be sure that no field artifacts are visible in the frozen frame. If you select a frame that contains fast, horizontal movement, the freeze frame might look good on your computer screen, but it will flicker when displayed on a TV monitor.

If you see flicker in the freeze frame, choose a frame that doesn't contain lateral movement. If you must choose a frame that contains movement, you can eliminate the flickering effect by applying the De-Interlace filter to the range of the clip that includes the freeze frame. Be aware, however, that removing interlacing from a clip can have a negative effect on slow-motion effects, amplifying the strobe or stutter effect mentioned earlier in the lesson.

14 Double-click the clip and open the Motion tab.

15 Expand the Speed section to view the Speed keyframe graph.

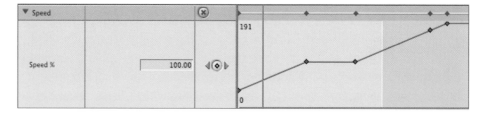

A flat horizontal line indicates the freeze frame.

Using the Speed Tool

There is yet another way to make speed changes in the Timeline, and it's best used when setting a precise rate is not your overriding concern.

1 Open the *6. Bearcats_02* sequence.

2 Move your pointer to the Slip tool in the Tool palette and hold down the mouse button until the additional tools appear, and then select the Speed tool (or press SSS).

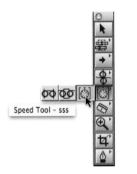

TIP ▶ Prior to Final Cut Pro 7.0, this tool was called the Time Remap tool and had a different function.

3 Drag the right edge of the last clip (**Belly-Roll_pt2**) to the right.

The clip gets longer, but instead of adding frames from the source footage, slow motion is applied.

TIP ▶ Dragging the clip to the left would speed it up.

This tool works slightly differently when applied to an edit point between two existing clips.

4   With the Speed tool, drag the edit between the two clips to the right.

The speed of the first clip is decreased and simultaneously the speed of the second clip is increased. The overall duration of the sequence is never affected.

5   With the Speed tool, drag the edit to the left.

No matter where you put the edit, the timing of the cut (halfway through the planes' roll) remains accurate, just like rolling an edit with the Roll tool.

TIP ▶ You can also use the Speed tool to add speed keyframes by clicking directly on the body of the clip instead of in the Speed Indicators area. Be careful not to accidentally add Speed keyframes when you intend only to select or open a clip. When you're done with the Speed tool, always press A to return to the Arrow pointer.

Removing Speed Effects

At any point you can remove all speed effects and return the clip to its original state. There are myriad ways to accomplish this.

1   Open the *7. Bearcats Final* sequence.

2   Press A to make sure the Arrow pointer is active.

3   Right-click the speed indicators under the first clip and choose Remove Speed.

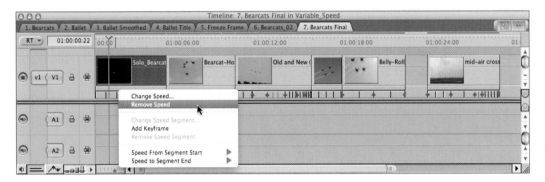

4   Select the second clip and press Command-J to open the Change Speed dialog.

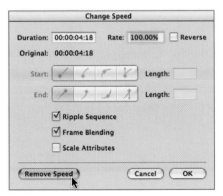

5   Click the Remove Speed button.

The dialog closes and the speed changes are removed.

6   Double-click the third clip and open the Motion tab.

7 Click the Red X for the Speed section.

8 In the Timeline, select the fourth and fifth clips.

9 Choose Edit > Remove Attributes.

Remove Attributes

Video Attributes: Audio Attributes:

☐ Basic Motion   ☐ Levels
☐ Crop   ☐ Pan
☐ Distort   ☐ Filters
☐ Opacity   ☐ Speed
☐ Drop Shadow
☐ Motion Blur
☐ Filters
☑ Speed

Cancel   OK

The Remove Attributes dialog opens.

10 If it's not automatically selected, select the Video Attributes: Speed checkbox and click OK.

The speed effect is removed from both clips.

Copying and Saving Speed Effects

Speed effects are recorded in the Motion tab, so you can copy and save a clip's speed settings just as you can copy and save any motion setting.

1 Select the last clip (**mid-air cross**) and choose Edit > Copy (or press Command-C).

2 Select the first three clips and choose Edit > Paste Attributes (or press Option-V).

The Paste Attributes dialog appears.

Paste Attributes

Attributes from mid-air cross:
☑ Scale Attribute Times

Video Attributes: Audio Attributes:

☐ Content   ☐ Content
☐ Basic Motion   ☐ Levels
☐ Crop   ☐ Pan
☐ Distort   ☐ Speed
☐ Opacity   ☐ Filters
☐ Drop Shadow
☐ Motion Blur
☐ Filters
☑ Speed
☐ Clip Settings (capture)

Cancel   OK

3 Select the Speed checkbox and click OK.

TIP ▶ If you're pasting attributes to a clip of a different length, selecting the Scale Attribute Times box will scale your keyframes to fit the length of the new clip.

You can also save the speed settings so they'll be available to use on other clips.

4 Double-click the first clip and choose Effects > Make Favorite Motion.

Make Favorite Motion stores all motion settings (Scale, Distortion, Drop Shadow, Speed, and so on) that are currently applied to the clip in the Motion tab.

5 In the Browser, click the Effects tab and open the Favorites bin.

The custom effect also appears in the Effects > Motion Favorites submenu.

You can now apply this setting to any clip in any sequence.

Lesson Review

1. How can you make simple, linear changes to the speed of a clip?
2. Can constant speed changes start and end gradually?
3. How do you create Speed Segments?
4. What are three ways to change a Speed Segment's rate?

5. How do you identify a clip's speed using the speed indicators?

6. How do you create gradual changes between Speed Segments?

7. How do you change the rate at which a gradual speed change occurs?

8. When will the Change Speed Segment dialog display the Custom setting?

9. What are two ways to remove speed effects from a clip?

Answers

1. Select the clip, choose Modify > Change Speed, and specify the rate at which you want the clip to play.

2. Yes, but they are then considered variable speed changes.

3. Click the Speed Indicators in the Timeline.

4. Drag (or Option-drag) the keyframe in the Timeline; right-click the segment, and choose Change Speed Segment; or open the clip in the Viewer and manipulate the Speed keyframes in the Motion tab.

5. Tick marks that are farther apart indicate slow motion; tick marks that are closer indicate fast motion; and no tick marks means a freeze frame.

6. Change the segment's Speed to Segment and/or Speed From Segment settings.

7. Modify the Length field in the Change Speed or Change Speed Segment dialog.

8. When you've manually modified the Bezier handles in the Motion tab.

9. Remove Attributes; choose Remove Speed from the Speed Indicators Shortcut menu; click Remove Speed in the Change Speed dialog; or click the Red X button in the Speed section of the Motion tab.

RED Baron—Brian Gonosey

IN THE TNT SERIES *LEVERAGE*, Oscar winner Timothy Hutton leads a team of five high-class, high-tech thieves who scam the wealthy and corrupt in a personal vendetta for justice.

It's a daring plotline, but the show made headlines in the post-production world for entirely different—but equally daring—reasons. The series is tape-less, shot on a RED ONE camera, and created entirely within the walls of Electric Entertainment, a self-contained digital post shop run by *Leverage* Executive Producer Dean Devlin.

The RED source footage comes back from the shoot on hard drives and goes on an Xsan RAID. Then every department pulls off those servers, whether it's for digital effects, sound effects, sound mixing, picture editing, or color correction—all of which is done in Final Cut Studio.

Few people are as intimate with the show's end-to-end Final Cut workflow as editor Brian Gonosey, who has been part of the editorial team since the pilot. We asked him what life is like on the bleeding RED edge.

How has working with RED source footage changed your average workday?

The most significant change has been in the high-quality images that the RED footage source files—and the ProRes dailies—produce. The more detail we can see in the edit room, the more we can make editorial decisions based on footage that we might not have until later in the online process.

RED's 4k source files are far larger than any existing broadcast TV exhibition format. Are there other benefits from working with such high-res originals?

Editorially speaking, knowing that our source image is 4K gives *Leverage* another arrow in the quiver. All of our editors take advantage of being able to scale up shots, which can change the mood and emotion of scenes drastically. It's like having a DI right in the cutting room.

Once you're in the edit suite, does the tapeless workflow have any significant impact on you?

Cutting with the RED source footage is the same as cutting any other high-resolution images. However, if we ever need to go back to the raw negative to check lighting or color for a shot, the footage is one click away, and we can re-transfer the footage with a new color look.

Leverage uses a Final Cut Studio-centric workflow from ingest to delivery. How does this compare to a more traditional broadcast TV workflow?

Our specific in-house workflow is always evolving and becoming more efficient. Currently, the turnaround time for getting the dailies to the editors is roughly the same as traditional film-to-tape dailies, but ours are being done in-house by just one or two people.

However, the time it takes to transfer RED footage into ProRes dailies is continually getting faster, which will allow us to shorten the time is takes to get the footage to our editors.

Leverage is shot in a unique style, with an almost constantly moving camera. Are there creative challenges to cutting such a stylized show?

Not too much. With our show, we shoot a lot of multicam setups and we have a second unit that shoots during production. This means that there is a lot of footage to cover during each episode's seven-day shoot. This all helps with the quicker-cutting style of the show.

Do you expect more TV shows to follow Leverage's *lead?*

I do. Our workflow has made us an extremely efficient post-production studio and has allowed us to produce a high-quality product. I think it just takes a leap of faith for producers to leave the traditional film and tape-based methods of finishing shows and films.

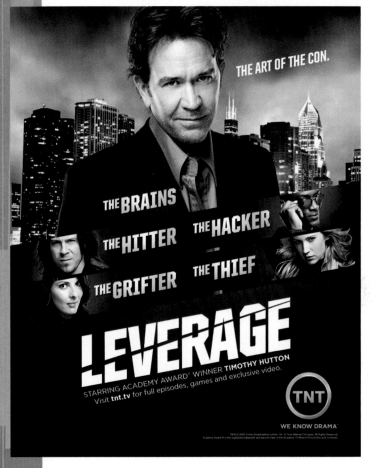

Finishing Techniques

12

Lesson Files	Lesson Files > Lesson_12 > Finishing.fcp
Media	Bearcat, Other Shots
Time	This lesson takes approximately 45 minutes to complete.
Goals	Learn to mix and match 4:3 and 16:9 clips
	Convert 4:3 to 16:9 and vice versa
	Use cropping and filters to letterbox video
	Master the Media Manager
	Consolidate all the media from a project into one folder
	Trim a sequence to eliminate unused media

Lesson 12
The Big Finish

All good things must come to an end, and no end is more satisfying than declaring your project finished and ready for the world. However, there is always a collection of last-minute details and final tweaks you should at least consider to make your show truly shine.

Traditionally there are a whole set of post-production tasks known as *finishing*, which include prepping your sequence for an audio mix (and performing the mix itself); incorporating any special effects shots; prepping for, and performing a color grading pass; and finally, outputting the final files required for whatever distribution method you're employing.

At the professional level, these finishing tasks are complicated, elaborate jobs with many individual details and steps. Correspondingly, the *Apple Pro Training Series* contains volumes specifically dedicated to color grading and sound mixing using Final Cut Studio. But there are a handful of useful tasks done inside Final Cut Pro, as part of the preparation process, or for projects that don't require quite that Hollywood level of polish, and those are described here.

Widescreen Workflows

Over the past few years, video has been moving steadily toward a new form factor. The square-ish shape of traditional television screens has given way to the more rectangular *widescreen* shape similar to movie theater screens. All modern televisions and even many computer monitors are configured this way, and for good reason: It matches the way our eyes work.

Look straight ahead in front of you and you'll observe that your field of view is much greater horizontally than vertically. Perhaps if we had evolved on a planet where predators more frequently came from above and below, our eyes might have been stacked vertically, and then, presumably, so would our TV screens. But here on Earth, peripheral lateral vision has proven to provide an evolutionary advantage. So, in an effort to create an immersive media-viewing experience that simulates the real world, filmmakers have embraced a similarly shaped screen configuration.

Unfortunately, older video equipment is still stuck in the less-engaging, less-immersive near-square shape of NTSC or PAL. In another 5–10 years, standard definition devices will become obsolete, replaced by HD devices. But during these interim years, you may find yourself trying to integrate both square and widescreen footage into one project, or updating older square projects to be exhibited on widescreen devices, and just as frequently, creating square-screen versions of projects acquired using widescreen cameras.

Conveniently, Final Cut Pro can handle all different frame sizes and shapes, and can help you manage all types of media easily and with great versatility.

Planning Ahead

It's important to keep your ultimate exhibition method in mind when changing the aspect ratio of your video. If you're exhibiting on an HD projector or a widescreen computer monitor, or printing your show to film, you should work in a widescreen sequence, and as necessary, convert any 4:3 shots as described in the following section.

If you're planning to primarily show your movie on television sets, and you want to accommodate older, 4:3 screens, edit in a 4:3 sequence and add a letterbox as needed to incorporate your widescreen footage. That black area you add is baked into your video, which ensures that no matter where the video is watched, the aspect ratio will be correct. However, it does eat up some of your screen resolution, effectively lowering your picture quality somewhat.

One compromise between the two options is to create an anamorphic HD version, which can be burned to DVD, and displayed on either 4:3 or widescreen monitors. However, viewers will need to set the correct display settings on their screens.

▶ Anamorphic Widescreen

There's more than one way to display video in a widescreen format. An image can be stored in a rectangular grid of square pixels or alternatively, the pixels themselves can be distorted so that they're squeezed in the camera and then expanded when they're displayed. This is called *anamorphic* display. The native version requires more pixels, and therefore more data, which means larger file sizes.

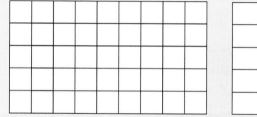
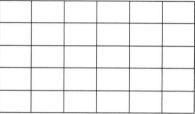

Native widescreen   Anamorphic widescreen

Many DV cameras can be set to record an anamorphic image automatically, and an anamorphic lens can be added to almost any camera. Anytime video is shot anamorphically, the display on which it's played back must "unstretch" the pixels so that it looks correct. If you attempt to play the video back on a monitor that can't perform the unstretch, the video will look tall and skinny, and no letterbox will be present. To show anamorphic video on such a display, most editors convert the widescreen footage to 4:3 by adding a letterbox (as described below).

Any Final Cut Pro sequence can be displayed anamorphically by selecting the Anamorphic 16:9 checkbox in the Sequence Settings dialog, and the image will be stretched horizontally, but this setting is only intended to be used for sequences using a traditional 4:3 pixel size such as 720x480 or 720x540 (and of course, with footage shot anamorphically). Putting a square pixel image into an anamorphic sequence will stretch it unnaturally. Similarly, putting an anamorphic shot into a square sequence will display a squeezed image.

There are actually many types of "anamorphic" distortions employed by different cameras and compression formats; for example, the HDV and DVCPRO HD formats use custom pixel shapes that enable them to reproduce widescreen HD images using far fewer pixels (1440x1080 for HDV or 960x720 for DVCPRO HD). In order for these images to be displayed properly, the pixel aspect ratio setting in Final Cut Pro must be set properly.

Converting 4:3 Footage to Widescreen

The most common task regarding widescreen footage is the need to prepare traditionally shot footage for a widescreen viewing environment.

> **TIP** This would be the same workflow you would use regardless of whether your widescreen sequence was native or anamorphic.

This might simply be adding a piece of archive footage to an otherwise widescreen project, or it might be taking a whole, edited 4:3 sequence and converting it to a widescreen version for showing on the web, DVD, or another widescreen-friendly venue.

You have two basic choices in this situation: Either you can chop off some of the picture, or you can add a *pillar-box*, which consists of vertical black bars on the left and right of the image. The decision of which way to go will probably be determined by the original framing and whether you can trim the image without compromising the intended content of the shot.

> **TIP** You could also stretch the image to fill the wider screen size, but this is very rarely a desirable option as it modifies the content of the shot in a very inorganic way.

1   Open Lesson Files > Lesson_12 > **Finishing.fcp.**

2   Press Command-Option-N to create a new sequence from a preset.

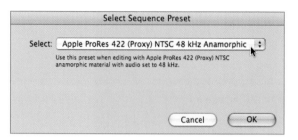

The Select Sequence Preset dialog opens.

3   From the pop-up list, choose Apple ProRes 422 (Proxy) NTSC 48k Hz Anamorphic and click OK.

A new sequence is added to the project.

4   In the Browser, rename the new sequence *Widescreen Sequence* and double-click it to open it into the Canvas and Timeline.

5   Drag **Blue_Angels_01** from the Browser into the Canvas to add it to the sequence.

The Change Sequence Settings warning appears.

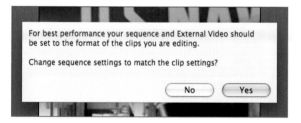

6   Click No.

TIP ▶ This is one of those rare occasions when you don't want to match the sequence settings to the clip settings. Otherwise the widescreen sequence would be converted to 4:3, undermining your whole intention. However, that means you must manually make sure the frame rate, compression type, and other settings match your intended output.

The clip is added to the sequence, and a pillar box is automatically created. Moreover, Final Cut Pro automatically modifies the clip to fit it to the sequence. This might mean changing the scale and/or Aspect Ratio parameters in the Motion tab.

7 Double-click the clip in the Timeline to open it into the Viewer, and then click the Motion tab.

The scale has been automatically adjusted so that the clip fills the sequence frame on at least one axis.

TIP If the clip already had some motion parameters, such as scale or Center point, adjusted prior to adding it to the sequence, Final Cut Pro will not automatically scale it to fit the sequence.

This is all you need to do if you want to ensure that the entire 4:3 frame is visible in the widescreen sequence. If, however, it's more important to fill the frame with video, you can scale the clip up, but this means cutting off the top and/or bottom of the source clip and lowering the resolution significantly.

TIP Zooming in on video will significantly degrade the visible image quality. This is especially true for DV footage. Uncompressed or ProRes compressed footage (even at low resolutions) will scale with somewhat less degradation.

8 Increase the Scale parameter to *135*.

The clip is enlarged to fill the frame. By adjusting the scale slider, the image remains centered in the frame, but there's no reason you have to leave it this way.

In this clip, there's plenty of room to adjust the positioning of the clip as long as you restrict the movement to vertical movement only.

TIP Zoom out in the Canvas to see the area around the visible area.

9 With the Canvas window active, press W to turn on Image+Wireframe display.

10 Drag the clip in the Canvas to lower it in the frame to center the letters.

TIP Shift-drag the clip to restrict the movement to vertical only.

Converting Widescreen Footage to 4:3

There are also instances when you need to prepare widescreen footage to be displayed in a square viewing environment. This is how you can permanently unsqueeze footage shot anamorphically.

Just as in the above example, you have two choices in this situation: You can add a letter-box (black bars above and below the image), or you can cut off the left and/or right edges of the picture (sometimes called *pan and scan*).

When the latter choice is done, you may also need to move the image to ensure that the important elements of the shot are visible in the new, smaller frame.

> **TIP** You can "pan and scan" the position of the image within the frame to ensure the subject is always visible using keyframes as described in Lesson 9.

1   Press Command-Option-N to create a new sequence from a preset.

The Select Sequence Preset dialog opens.

2   From the pop-up list, choose Apple ProRes 422 (Proxy) NTSC 48 kHz and click OK.

A new sequence is added to the project.

3   In the Browser, rename the new sequence *4:3 Sequence* and double-click it to open it into the Canvas and Timeline.

4   Drag **Blue_Angels_02** from the Browser into the Canvas to add it to the sequence.

The Change Sequence Settings warning appears.

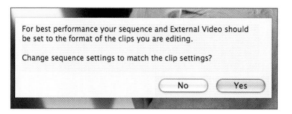

5   Click No.

TIP ▶ Again, you don't want to match the sequence settings to the clip settings. Otherwise the widescreen sequence would be converted to 16:9, undermining your whole intention.

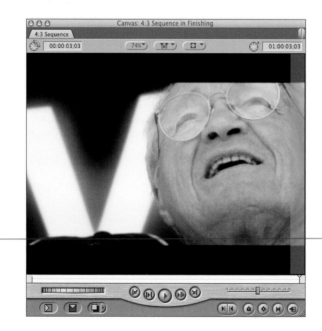

The clip is added to the sequence, and a letterbox is automatically created.

This is all you need to do if you want to ensure that the entire 16:9 frame is visible in the widescreen sequence.

6   Double-click the clip in the Timeline to open it into the Viewer, and then click the Motion tab.

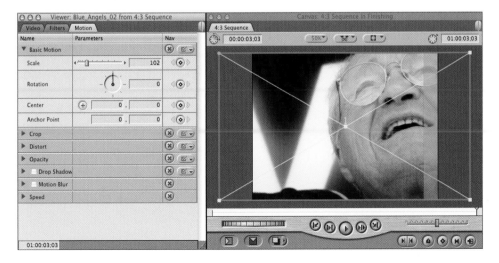

The scale has been automatically adjusted so that the clip fills the sequence frame on at least one axis. In this case, this is an HD clip being added to an SD sequence, so the scale has been reduced to make it fit.

7   Increase the Scale parameter to *102*.

The clip is enlarged to fill the frame, again remaining centered.

In this clip, the man's face, which is presumably the subject of the shot, is getting cut off on the right edge.

8   If necessary, with the Canvas window active, press W to turn on Image+Wireframe display.

9   Drag the clip in the Canvas to the left, until the right edge of the clip aligns with the right edge of the Canvas.

Now the shot is properly framed for the smaller screen.

More Letterboxing Techniques

Another similar workflow can be employed when you have 4:3 source footage, but you want to create a letterboxed version within a 4:3 sequence. This can be done in one of two ways, by cropping the clip or by using the Letterbox video filter.

1   Drag **Blue_Angels_01** from the Browser into the *4:3* sequence after the **Blue_Angels_02** clip.

2   Make the Canvas window active, press C to select the Crop tool, then press Command and drag the top or the bottom edge of the clip to create a widescreen effect.

Although this technique is quick and easy, it can make it difficult to be precise.

TIP You can approximate the standard 16:9 letterbox by turning on the Title Safe overlay in the Canvas and cropping to just inside the title safe boundary.

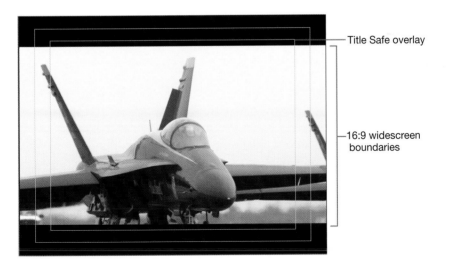

To be more precise, you can apply the Letterbox filter, where you can set not just a 16:9 letterbox (used in HD video) but also other settings commonly used for different types of film.

3 Undo the cropping you performed in step 2.

4 Select the **Blue_Angels_01** clip in the Timeline and choose Effects > Video Filters > Matte > Widescreen.

The filter defaults to 1.66:1, but you can easily choose a different-sized matte to simulate HD or 35mm film.

5 Double-click the clip to open it into the Viewer, and then click the Filters tab.

6 In the Type pop-up menu, choose 1.78:1.

This setting is the ratio equivalent to standard HD (16:9) video.

TIP The Widescreen filter doesn't add black to the letterbox area; it makes it transparent, so if you put the clip on track V2 or higher, video on lower tracks will show through the matte.

The Offset slider allows you to shift the vertical position of the clip within the matte, so you can better center the main action of the shot.

Letterboxing an Entire Sequence

Any of these methods could be used on an entire sequence just as easily as on a single clip. Simply nest one sequence inside of another and treat the sequence as if it were the single clip in the previous exercises.

TIP Alternatively you could select everything in a sequence and choose Sequence > Nest Items.

One advantage of this approach is that you can apply a single filter (or crop setting) to the entire sequence at once, and it can easily be modified or removed. The main disadvantage is that it becomes much more difficult to make individual adjustments to the vertical off-set of each clip (either by moving the cropped clip, or by adjusting the Offset slider in the Widescreen filter).

For more on nesting sequences, see Lesson 10.

Managing Your Media

At the end of every project you must decide what to do with all the source files you used while creating your show. Typically, you'll have much more source footage than the por-tions that wind up in your finished movie, so there's likely to be a lot of stuff that you don't really need. This footage can take up quite a lot of disk space, so you might decide to throw out the pieces you don't need, or back up just the source clips you wound up using. You might need to collect clips that are spread out across multiple folders and multiple drives.

All of these tasks fall into the category of managing your media, and in Final Cut Pro, they're all handled using the Media Manager tool.

Whether you're moving your project from one computer to another, trying to eliminate clips and files you're not using, preparing a sequence for output, or even recompressing a group of files from one codec to another, the Media Manager is your one-stop shop.

Consolidating Media

When you need to move a project from one computer to another, you may not know where all of your media resides. Although most files are probably in your Capture Scratch folder, a graphic or still image may be in another location. Sound effects files may be stored in yet another location. Rather than manually scouring your disk for related files, you can use the Media Manager tool to be sure you won't miss anything (and to avoid grabbing files you don't need).

1   Activate the Browser and press Command-A to select everything.

2   Choose File > Media Manager.

3   In the Media section, choose Copy from the pop-up menu.

This will duplicate all the media associated with the selected items (in this case, the entire project) and place it in a new location.

4   Select the "Include render files" checkbox.

5   In the Media Destination section, click the Browse button and select a disk location for the copied files. Create a new folder for the copied media.

TIP ▶ To move your files from one computer to another, you typically would want to set this destination to a removable or external hard disk that you could move to a new edit station.

6   In the Media section, select "Delete unused media from duplicated items."

This setting usually has a dramatic impact on the green bars in the Summary section.

In this example, you want the project on the new computer to be identical to the previous version, so you don't want to delete anything.

7   Deselect "Delete unused media from duplicated items."

NOTE ▶ The summary at the top of the window details your operation. The size of the bars indicates the relative amount of disk space your media is occupying. The top bar is the current state, and the bottom bar shows what will happen after you complete the Media Manager operation. Because in this example you aren't deleting anything, the two bars are identical.

8   Leave the "Base media file names on" pop-up menu set to "existing file names."

9   In the Project section, be sure that "Duplicate selected items and place into a new project" is selected.

This last setting creates a new project on your destination volume that points to the new versions of the media files. Although this step isn't required (you could manually copy your existing project file in the Finder), it ensures that the new project won't have any offline files, and you won't have to reconnect media when the project gets to the new workstation.

10   Click OK.

Immediately, you're prompted with a Save dialog, asking you to name and save the new project file. You'll save it on the same disk as the new media.

11   Give the project a name, then click Save.

The program performs the Media Manager operation and opens the new project in the Browser.

12   In the new project, open the sequences and clips to confirm that the new project is an identical copy of the old project. Then close the new project.

Moving Media

If you have limited disk space, or you're consolidating media onto a single disk (as you might do when preparing a project for backup to DVD), you can choose Move instead of Copy in the Media Manager.

With this setting, all the files used in your project will be copied to a new location, and the originals will be deleted. You won't wind up with duplicate copies of your files.

Trimming Sequences in Media Manager

This type of trimming has nothing to do with adjusting edit points; rather, it's a way to eliminate excess media after your sequence has been completed. Usually, you shouldn't do this until you've completely finished making major editorial changes.

1   Select sequences *Bearcats_02* and *Bearcats_03*.

The operation will be applied only to the media referenced in these two sequences.

2   Control-click the selected items and choose Media Manager from the shortcut menu.

3   In the Media pop-up menu, choose Copy.

> **TIP▶** Although Final Cut Pro won't prevent you from choosing Move or Use Existing, doing so when trimming clips is extremely dangerous. If a power failure or crash occurs during the operation, your files could be left in an unusable state, requiring you to recapture all of your media. When trimming, always create new files. After the operation is complete, you can delete the original media manually.

4   Select "Delete unused media from duplicated items."

When you select this option, the summary section at the top of the dialog changes dramatically. Now, the Modified media bar is much smaller than the Original. This difference reflects the media outside the In and Out points of the clips used in the two selected sequences.

5   Select Use Handles and set the value to *1:00*.

Although presumably you're completely done editing, there could be an emergency or problem that might require a tiny adjustment to your edit. Adding a little bit of wiggle room is a good way to accommodate such an unforeseen issue if one should arise after this operation is completed.

6   Deselect "Include affiliate clips outside selection."

If this option is selected, the Media Manager will scan the rest of your project for any other uses of the clips contained in the selected sequences. If such clips exist, and they have In or Out points set, the Media Manager will include that section in the newly created clips. This means that you won't save as much space as you would by ignoring those clips.

NOTE ▶ Because you specified Copy for this operation, there's no harm in ignoring this additional media. If you had specified Move or Use Existing (instead of Copy), then you'd be permanently deleting the media that you might be planning to use in another sequence.

7   Select "Duplicate selected items and place into a new project."

This will create a new project containing only the selected sequences and pointing to the new, trimmed media.

8   Set your destination and click OK.

9   Name the new project and click Save.

After the files are processed, the new project is automatically opened. If you don't plan to make any additional changes or use any of the media from the old project, you can select all the items in the old project and use the Make Offline command to delete the media files from your disk.

Lesson Review

1. Why would you want to convert 4:3 footage to 16:9?

2. Name three ways to convert 4:3 footage to 16:9.

3. What is the setting in the Widescreen matte filter to create a 16:9 letterbox?

4. What does it mean to consolidate a sequence or a project?

5. How do you consolidate media?

6. What does it mean to trim a sequence?

7. Why would you want to trim a sequence?

8. When would you trim a sequence?

9. How do you trim a sequence?

Answers

1. To display it full screen on modern HDTVs and monitors.

2. Edit a 4:3 clip into a 16:9 sequence and don't change the sequence settings to match the clip; use the crop tool on the top and/or bottom edge; apply a Widescreen matte filter.

3. 1.78:1.

4. To collect all of the media associated with the selection and copy or move it to a single folder.

5. Use the Media Manager and select Copy or Move from the Type pop-up menu, and specify a location where the files should be saved.

6. Creating a copy of the sequence where only the media between the clips' In and Out points is kept, and the excess media is discarded.

7. Generally, to save disk space or to create a streamlined backup of your sequence for later recapture.

8. Only after editing is completely finished.

9. Use the Media Manager and select the "Delete unused media from duplicated items" setting.

13

Lesson Files	Lesson Files > Lesson_13 > Outputting.fcp
Media	Bearcat
Time	This lesson takes approximately 60 minutes to complete.
Goals	Understand the Final Cut Pro Share window
	Export a finished sequence for playback on Apple Devices
	Create DVDs, Blu-ray Discs, and AVCHD discs directly from Final Cut Pro
	Customize a DVD menu from the Share window
	Output video to YouTube or MobileMe
	Create a custom web video using presets from Compressor
	Export audio in a variety of different formats
	Create a self-contained QuickTime version of your sequence
	Generate EDLs and XMLs of your project data

Sharing Your Work

Final Cut Pro makes it almost too easy to output your project in a variety of formats, media, and venues, even publishing it right to You Tube or MobileMe with a single click. This lesson covers a wide range of outputting options, applicable to amateur and professional editors alike. Just be sure that your movie really is ready to go before you begin. No one wants to get that email after 100,000 hits that you misspelled someone's name in the credits!

Regardless of what format you shot or edited in, presenting it to the world invariably requires converting it into an *exhibition* format, which will almost certainly be of a lower quality than your original. And, because there are so many exhibition formats, there are many different technical variables you must manage in order to make sure your show looks its best in each environment. Laying your show off to tape involves one set of concerns, and burning optical media such as DVDs and Blu-ray Discs involves a totally different set. Displaying your movie on the web or as a standalone digital file opens a whole different can of worms, and should you be printing your project out to film, you'll be presented with yet another set of concerns and requirements.

Frame sizes, bit rates, and quality settings change depending on your intended format. Compression (used to make your movie small enough to distribute electronically or on optical media) can be performed in an almost unlimited number of ways; misapplied, it can turn your pristine HD images into a smeary blurry mess. This has long been a very difficult and complicated realm—often jokingly referred to as a "black art." Final Cut Pro even comes with a dedicated tool for preparing files for DVD, the web, and various Apple devices (iPod, iPhone, and AppleTV), called Compressor.

But many users don't have the time or inclination to learn a whole new software program just to get their movies out into the world, and fortunately they don't have to. You can take advantage of the Compressor engine without ever launching that software, by using the Share window right inside Final Cut Pro. Although this doesn't offer access to all of the optimizations and adjustments available in the full program, it's versatile and robust enough to satisfy the vast majority of users.

In addition to discussing those sharing options, this lesson also covers outputting QuickTime movies, sound files, and project data from within Final Cut Pro.

Sharing to Apple Devices

Given the ubiquity of iPods, iPhones, and other Apple devices, and because Final Cut Pro is itself an Apple product, it only makes sense that you would expect to be able to effortlessly output your show to play on those devices. And you'd be right. Creating a version of your movie tailored for the different Apple devices is simple, even though each device does have its own preset.

1   Open Lesson Files > Lesson_13 > **Outputting.fcp**.

2   In the Browser, select the *Finished* sequence.

> **TIP** Whenever you're outputting, pay special attention to what's selected. Individual clips can be outputted as well as finished sequences.

> **TIP** If the Canvas or Timeline is active when choosing an output option, the frontmost tab will be used as the output source.

3   Choose File > Share or press Command-Shift-E.

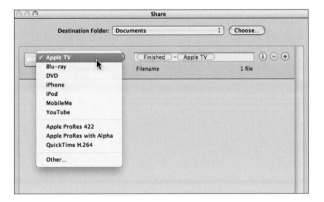

The Share window opens.

4   If the output type isn't already set to Apple TV, click the Output Type pop-up menu and choose Apple TV.

At this point, you could just click Export and a copy of your movie (optimized to play in iTunes and on an Apple TV) would be saved to the folder listed in the destination pop-up menu at the top of the window. It's that easy.

But if you want to know more about what's being exported, or if you want to change the name of the file or the folder in which it's saved, follow the next few steps.

5 Click the Show Info button.

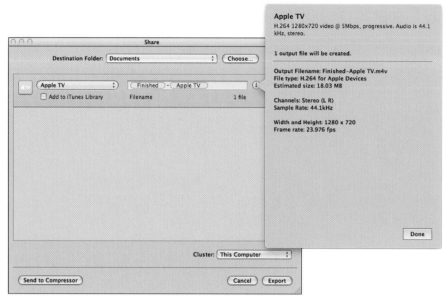

An Info window appears containing a detailed description of the file to be created, including its format, estimated file size and so on.

6 Click Done to close the Info window.

The clip's filename is automatically generated based on the name of the selection (in this case, the sequence named *Finished*) and the name of the Preset type (in this case, Apple TV), but both components are customizable.

7 Click the Finished bubble in the Output Filename field.

The text is selected.

8 Type *Finished* and add today's date.

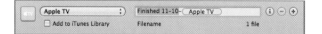

This will become the name of the file that's created.

One of the most powerful aspects of the Share window is that you can output many versions of your sequence in a batch. In addition to making the Apple TV version, you can also create a version optimized for the iPhone.

9 Click the Add Output button.

A new output is added to the list.

NOTE ▸ By default, the Share window will set the next output type in the list.

10 Choose iPhone from the Output Type pop-up menu.

11 Change the filename for this output so that it is similar to the Apple TV version.

TIP ▸ Although it's not required that multiple outputs have similar names, be careful to name your outputs clearly. It's very easy to wind up with many similarly named files that may be difficult to differentiate once they're just a list of files in the Finder.

12 Click the Show Info button to see how this file will be different from the Apple TV version.

Both files will be .m4v files, but the estimated file size for the iPhone version is only 5.4 MB, whereas the Apple TV version is estimated to be more than 18 MB! This makes sense because the iPhone is a smaller screen (640x360) than the Apple TV (1280x720).

13 Click Done to close the Info window.

14 Select the Add to iTunes Library checkbox for the Apple TV version.

The Action drawer opens, allowing you to select a playlist from your iTunes library into which the newly exported movie can be automatically added.

15 Click the Destination Folder pop-up menu and select Movies to save the files to the Movies folder in your user's Home folder.

> **TIP** Feel free to save these files to a different location. Click the Choose button to select any folder available on your computer or local network.

16 Click the Export button to begin the export operation.

The Transcoding Progress window appears, showing how long the operation will take. The speed of the operation will depend on the power of your processor.

TIP ▶ Exporting is a background task, so you can continue working in your project while the export process operates.

The files will be saved to the destination folder you chose, and the Apple TV version will appear in the Movies category of your iTunes library.

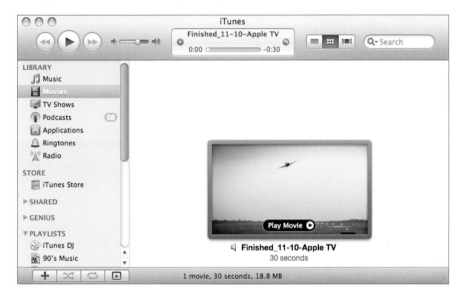

These presets are optimized for playback on specific devices, but the files they create are just QuickTime movie files that can be shared, distributed manually, or even streamed on the web (though there are other web-specific presets that will be discussed in the following exercises).

Sharing to Optical Media

As you've probably already noticed, the Share Output Type pop-up menu also includes options to output to DVD and Blu-ray Disc. These presets represent a huge step forward in simplifying the process of getting your movie directly onto a disc. You don't need to know what format is required, and you don't need to use iDVD or DVD Studio Pro (though both of those programs do offer far more versatility for creating custom menus and additional features).

Creating a DVD

First, you'll create a standard definition DVD that can be played on just about any DVD player.

1 In the Browser, make sure *Finished* is still selected, and choose File > Share.

2 Select the iPhone output and press Delete.

3 On the remaining output, set the output type to DVD.

4 Click the Show Info button.

DVDs require separate audio and video files, but this preset makes both automatically. Per the DVD specification, the audio is stored in the .ac3 format and the video is stored in MPEG-2 (using the .m2v extension).

In the Info window you can see the details for both files by choosing from the "Show info for" pop-up menu.

TIP ▸ Standard DVDs can be displayed in either standard 4:3 or anamorphic 16:9. When using the Share window, this setting is automatically determined by the selected item's settings.

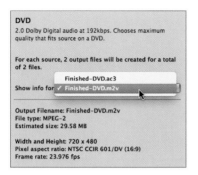

5   Click Done to close the Info window.

By default, exporting the DVD preset will make the two files needed to go on a DVD, but you'd still have to bring them into another program to actually create the disc. However, Final Cut Pro can go ahead and do that for you too.

6   Select the Create DVD checkbox.

The Create DVD Action drawer opens. Here you can choose which attached DVD burner to use, select from one of two presets (black or white), name the DVD, and even determine the starting action when a DVD is inserted.

You can customize the menu by choosing your own background image.

7   Click the Background: Add button and navigate to Book Files > Media > DVD Menu Art and select **Blue_Angels_DVD_Background.tif**.

The graphic is added to the preview area and will be included as the background for your DVD menu.

8   In the Title field, type *Blue_Angels_Bearcats*.

9   Click Export to begin the exporting and DVD burning process.

The audio and video files are compressed and saved in the folder chosen in the Destination Folder field at the top of the Share window. When the DVD is ready to be built, Final Cut Pro will ask you to insert a disc.

10   Insert a blank DVD.

TIP ▶ The Please Insert dialog may not be dismissed right away. Be patient and your disc burning should begin.

The Transcoding Progress window will show the progress of the disc building.

TIP ▶ Although most DVD media is reliable, errors are not infrequent. Always check your DVD on more than one DVD player to ensure it plays without audio or video glitches before replicating or distributing it.

When the disc is complete, a Burn Complete message will appear, and provide the opportunity to make additional copies of the disc.

Burn Complete.

Burn Again   OK

NOTE ▶ The export status dialog in Final Cut Pro will remain open until this Burn Complete dialog is dismissed, but fear not—you can continue working in Final Cut Pro while the disc is being burned.

Creating an HD Disc

Regular DVDs are, by definition, standard def, so if you've got an HD sequence, when you burn it to a DVD you're throwing away a large portion of your resolution and image quality.

For those projects, you might consider making a Blu-ray Disc or an AVCHD disc, which won't play on as wide a variety of disc players, but will retain the highest possible quality.

The highest quality option is to create a true Blu-ray Disc, which requires having a Blu-ray Disc recorder attached to your Mac. However, even without a Blu-ray Disc recorder, you can create an HD disc, either as a Blu-ray disc image that can be moved to another system (with a Blu-ray recorder) and laid off there; or, alternatively, you can create a red-laser HD disc, called an AVCHD disc.

AVCHD discs can be burned by any regular DVD burner (and recorded on regular DVD media) and will play back (in true HD) on many Blu-ray Disc players. The big drawback is that a standard DVD holds far less data than a Blu-ray Disc, so there's much less room to store your video. That means that the quality of the video won't be as high as on a regular Blu-ray Disc, especially if you're outputting a very long program.

1   In the Browser, Select the *Finished* sequence and choose File > Share.

2   In the Share window, set the output type to Blu-ray.

3   Click the Show Info button to see the details about the files to be created.

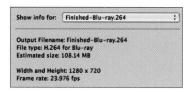

Blu-ray Discs (like regular DVDs) keep audio in a separate file, so Final Cut Pro outputs two separate files, an .ac3 (containing the audio) and an H.264 (containing the HD-quality video).

4   Click Done to close the Info window.

Just like when you burn a regular DVD, Final Cut Pro allows you to burn the HD disc straight from the Share window.

5 Select the Create Blu-ray disc checkbox.

> Output Device: MATSHITA DVD-R UJ-868 (AVCHD) ⬍
> Disc Template: Black ⬍
> Title: Finished-Blu-ray
>
> **Customize Your Disc**
>
> When Disc Loads: Show Menu ⬍
> Markers: ☐ Use Chapter Marker Text as Subtitles
> Loop: ☐ Include Loop Movie Button
> Background: (Add...)
> Logo Graphic: (Add...)
> Title Graphic: (Add...)
>
> [Main Menu Chapter Menu]

The Create Blu-ray action drawer opens. Although very similar to the regular Create DVD action drawer, this one has additional options. The Output device pop-up menu allows you to select the drive to use.

If you have a Blu-ray Disc burner attached, it will appear in this list. If you have a regular DVD burner attached, it will appear in the list appended with the characters (AVCHD).

Alternatively, you can select Hard Drive (Blu-ray) to create a Blu-ray-compatible disc image, saved to the location specified in the Destination Folder pop-up menu at the top of the Share window.

There are additional disc templates available to choose from in the Disc Template menu. Third-party templates are also widely available to further expand your menu options.

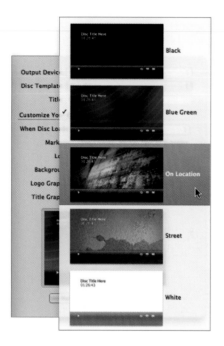

6 Select the Disc Template of your choice.

The display area shows an animated preview of the menu.

Once you select the settings you prefer, you can click Export and follow a process identical to the steps described above for regular DVDs.

TIP ▸ Files created for AVCHD discs are approximately half the size of those created for Blu-ray Discs. If you open the Show Info window after setting the Output Device to an AVCHD drive, the estimated file size for the H.264 file will reflect the adjusted size.

7 Rather than going through with the disc burning, click Cancel to close the Share window.

Sharing to the Web

Perhaps the most common way videos are being shared these days is via the Internet. Just like the one-click options to create optical discs, Final Cut Pro can compress and upload your file directly to YouTube and to a MobileMe account, automatically adding the video to your gallery if you desire.

Automatic uploading requires that you have a live Internet connection and that you enter your account information, so that Final Cut Pro can access your online account and post the videos there.

If you set the output type to MobileMe, Final Cut Pro creates three versions of your movie: Mobile, Medium, and Large. That way viewers looking at your MobileMe page can watch the version best suited to their bandwidth limitations.

The steps for outputting such movies using Final Cut Pro's Share window are nearly identical to the steps described above for Apple devices or optical discs. Just make sure to fill in the forms in the Action drawer for either MobileMe or YouTube completely.

Both versions allow you to set the movie's view options to private so that you can control who'll be able to see the video once it's uploaded.

Creating a Custom Web Movie

If you want to create a QuickTime file to upload onto your own privately hosted website, you can still do that directly from Final Cut Pro. The Share window can access all the presets from Compressor, which include a wide range of file types intended for web distribution.

1   If the Share window isn't already open, select the Finished sequence and choose File > Share.

2   From the Output Type pop-up menu, choose Other.

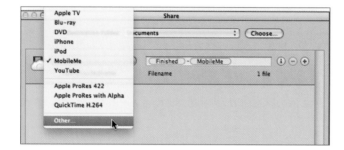

The settings window from Compressor opens.

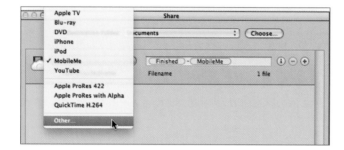

This allows you to choose any preset from Compressor and add it to the item in the Share window. Compressor contains dozens of handy presets for a wide range of uses, and you can even create and save your own custom settings.

In this exercise, you're going to create a version of the movie intended for medium-bandwidth web connections.

3   In the "Select a setting" field in the upper right, type *h.264*.

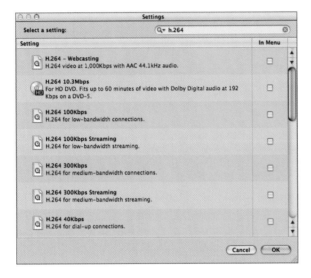

The list is filtered to show only presets that include that phrase in the name. This includes the built-in presets intended for web use.

4   Select the H.264 300Kbps preset.

If there are presets you intend to use frequently, you can add them to the Final Cut Pro Share Output Type pop-up menu.

5   Select the checkbox in the In Menu column for the H.264 300Kbps preset.

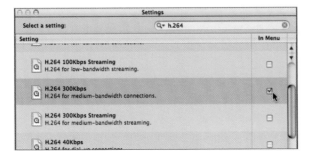

Now that preset will always appear in the Output Type pop-up menu.

6   With the H.264 300Kbps preset selected, click OK.

The preset is applied to the output in the Share window.

7   Click the Show Info button to see the details for the preset you selected.

TIP ▶ Remember that the Share window can stack up many outputs and batch process them all together. If you're not sure exactly which preset to use, try making several of them, and then after they're all made, watch the videos to see which one provides adequate quality for the given file size.

8   Click Done to close the Info window and click Export.

The file is compressed and saved to the location specified in the Destination Folder pop-up menu at the top of the Share window.

TIP ▶ Optimizing your compression settings to get the highest-quality video at the lowest file size is a painstaking process that often requires much trial and error. To learn more about the varied compression options, see the *Compressor User Manual* or the *Apple Pro Training Series: Compressor Quick Reference Guide* by Brian Gary.

▶ **A Note about Web Video**

There are countless video formats currently in use on the web. Final Cut Pro Studio includes presets for two popular formats: MPEG-4, a high-quality, low-bandwidth, widely compatible codec; and H.264, which produces excellent results at low-bandwidth settings but requires QuickTime 7 or higher for playback. Technically, H.264 is a variant of the MPEG-4 codec, but it's not playable on some older devices that can play MPEG-4 video, such as cell phones.

After choosing which codec you want to use (H.264 in this example), you must additionally choose whether your file should use streaming or progressive download. Typically, shows shorter than 10 minutes are ideal for progressive download, whereas streaming is appropriate for longer shows. However, streaming files require special streaming software on your web server, whereas progressive download files can be embedded into any web page without requiring additional software.

Exporting Audio

Final Cut Pro can export audio in a wide variety of formats, each tailored to a specific workflow. Final Cut Pro can accommodate your workflow whether you're finishing your audio mix in Soundtrack Pro, Pro Tools, or another dedicated audio tool; recording multiple channels directly to a multichannel recorder (using special audio I/O hardware); or outputting tracks to be encoded for multichannel surround sound.

Creating a Stereo Mix

The simplest type of audio output is a simple stereo mix. This will generate a two-channel AIFF file that can be played back in any stereo-capable software or hardware.

1   In Final Cut Pro, select the *Finished* sequence.

2   Choose File > Export > Audio to AIFF(s).

The Save dialog appears.

3   Name the file *StereoOutputTest* and set Where (the destination) to Desktop.

4   Set the Rate pop-up menu to 48 kHz, Depth to 16-bit, and Config to Stereo Mix.

> **TIP** ▶ Final Cut Pro can output audio up to 24-bit and 96 kHz for maximum quality; however, there's no advantage to exporting to a quality setting higher than the source audio.

5   Click Save.

The stereo audio file is saved to your desktop.

Exporting Channel Groups

In addition to exporting a stereo mix, Final Cut Pro can also export audio as channel groups. This option exports multiple mono or stereo AIFFs based on the audio channel settings in your sequence. This can be useful if you plan to modify the individual channels in another program and re-import them back into Final Cut Pro.

1   Double-click the *Finished-6-channel* sequence to open it.

2   Choose Sequence > Settings to open the Sequence Settings window.

3   Click the Audio Outputs tab.

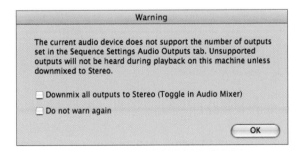

This sequence has six outputs: four mono channels and one stereo pair.

4   Click OK to close the Sequence Settings window.

> **NOTE ▶** You'll probably see a warning dialog indicating that the current audio device doesn't have enough outputs to play the sequence correctly. This sequence requires special audio hardware. To complete this exercise, don't select the Downmix check-box. Click OK to close the Warning message.

5   Choose File > Export > Audio as AIFF(s).

The AIFF Save dialog opens.

6   From the Config pop-up menu, choose Channel Grouped.

7 Set the desired destination for your output files and click Save.

NOTE ▶ Because the Channel Grouped setting will create as many files as you have audio outputs, each file will be based on the name you enter in the AIFF Export dialog with an incrementing digit appended to the end (such as xxx-1, xxx-2, xxx-3, and so on).

Making a Multichannel QuickTime Movie

It's also possible to export a single QuickTime file with as many audio channels as you have set in your Final Cut Pro sequence. This would be used in similar situations as the channel group export, but all the audio is stored in a single file, making it extremely portable and convenient. Importing such a clip back into Final Cut Pro would result in a clip with many audio tabs.

1 Choose Sequence > Settings or press Command-0.

The Sequence Settings window opens.

2 In the General tab, make sure the Audio Settings: Config pop-up menu is set to Discrete Channels.

TIP ▶ The other two choices in this menu are identical to the Stereo Mix and Channel Grouped options discussed earlier in this exercise.

3   Click OK to close the Sequence Settings window.

   If the Audio Output warning dialog appears again, click OK to close it.

4   Choose File > Export > QuickTime Movie.

   The QuickTime Movie Save dialog appears.

5   From the Include pop-up menu, choose Audio Only, and select the Make Movie Self-Contained checkbox.

6   Set a destination for your output and click Save.

   A single QuickTime movie will be created with six audio tracks, corresponding to the six tracks in your Final Cut Pro sequence.

Exporting Audio to OMF

Many filmmakers prefer to perform their final audio mix using Pro Tools or another dedicated audio workstation. You can export audio from a Final Cut Pro sequence to an interchange format called Open Media Format (OMF) that can be imported into Pro Tools and other software. An OMF file contains all of the audio data from all of the tracks in a Final Cut Pro sequence. It also maintains the arrangement of individual clips and tracks, so when the OMF file is opened in another program, the audio portion of your Final Cut Pro sequence is faithfully reproduced. Be aware, however, that audio filters and effects will not be included in the OMF file.

1   Choose File > Export > Audio to OMF.

The OMF Audio Export dialog opens.

Although you can modify the sample rate and bit depth, it's usually best to leave those settings unaltered so that they match the audio in your sequence and source footage.

2   Set Handle Length to 5 seconds (00:00:05:00).

Adding handles is especially important for audio clips. The engineer who will import your OMF will likely be adding fades to the beginning and end of every single audio element in your show. The more extra footage you provide, the more flexibility the audio editor will have.

3   Leave the Include Crossfade Transitions checkbox selected and the Include Levels and Include Pan checkboxes deselected. Click OK.

> **TIP** ▶ Most audio editors prefer to set their own audio levels rather than import the level you set during your rough cut. Always check with your audio mixer about the settings they prefer.

The OMF Save dialog appears.

4 In the lower-left corner of the window, deselect the Hide Extension checkbox.

> **NOTE** ▸ You may need to expand the window to see the Hide Extension checkbox.

The .omf extension is added to the filename. Because the file may be going to a Windows-based workstation, it's best to leave the .omf extension visible.

5 Choose a destination for your OMF file and click Save.

Delivering Corresponding Video

If you're creating your audio mix in a separate application, it's very important to lock your picture before exporting an OMF. If you make editorial changes in Final Cut Pro after handing off the audio to a sound editor, you could create sync problems that will be difficult to fix.

Typically, in addition to the OMF, you'll also deliver to your sound editor a QuickTime movie of the corresponding picture with BITC (burned-in timecode) that matches the timecode in the OMF (which is based on the timecode in the exported sequence).

It's essential that the picture and sound are exactly the same length. It's also a good habit to provide a sync beep at the head and tail of your show.

> **TIP** ▸ A one-frame clip of Bars and Tone serves as an effective sync beep; or, if you want to get fancy, you can replace the video with one frame of a circle shape generator.

You can see an example of sync beeps at the head and tail of the *Finished* sequence (note that the audio appears in every track).

Exporting QuickTime Movies

A QuickTime movie is a good archive of a finished project (along with your precious project file, of course). You can save a single file that contains your whole movie in its native resolution, so you can archive or delete the bulky media files referenced by your project. You can use that file in Compressor or any other QuickTime-compatible program to create more MPEG or H.264 files, or files in any other formats.

You can output that file to tape, just as you'd output directly from your edited sequence. Effects will never become unrendered, and you'll enjoy the convenience of having all the data in one safe place rather than in a reference movie that links to myriad files all over your disk(s).

You might also want to deliver a full-resolution copy of your show to another editor or use it yourself in a new project. For example, you might want to generate a trailer or promo spot based on the finished show, or you might want to include a section in a show reel.

1   In the Browser, select the *Finished* sequence.

2   Choose File > Export > QuickTime Movie.

The QuickTime movie export Save dialog appears.

3   Name the new file *Blue_Angels_Bearcats.mov* and navigate to your desired destination.

By default, the Setting pop-up menu is set to Current Settings, which means the exported movie will have the same frame size, frame rate, audio, and compression settings as the sequence. The source footage that matches those sequence settings is displayed in gray in the Timeline render bar, and it won't be recompressed, thus pre-serving the highest possible quality.

In nearly all cases, you'll leave the Setting pop-up menu unchanged. However, if you ever want to transcode your sequence into a different sequence preset, you could do that by changing this setting. In most cases, there is a better way to transcode: edit-ing the clips into a sequence with the desired settings within Final Cut Pro, or using Compressor.

4 From the Include pop-up menu, choose Audio and Video. From the Markers pop-up menu, choose All Markers.

The Markers pop-up menu allows you to control which types of markers are included in the QuickTime movie. Many of the marker types are readable by other software, such as DVD Studio Pro or Soundtrack Pro.

5 Select the Make Movie Self-Contained checkbox and click Save.

TIP You almost never need to select the Recompress All Frames checkbox. Final Cut Pro will automatically recompress any frames that have changed.

Creating Reference Movies

The Make Movie Self-Contained checkbox is a very powerful setting. It determines whether your exported movie is a huge file containing a copy of all of the video and audio clips used in your sequence, or whether you get a tiny *reference movie* that is merely a pointer to all of those files, wherever they may exist on your computer.

Reference movies are great. They're much quicker to make than regular movies, they're very small, and you can use them in Compressor just like a regular QuickTime movie or any other QuickTime-compatible program. However, if you move, modify, or delete any of the video files that were used in the sequence from which you exported, the reference movie will no longer work. If that happens, opening it in any application may yield an error message and a search dialog (similar to the Final Cut Pro Offline Files dialog) asking you to locate the missing file.

Final Cut Pro reference movies contain all of the audio data from the sequence, plus any frames that needed to be rendered at the time of the export. But raw video will be pulled from the files in your Capture Scratch folder, and sections of the sequence that were previously rendered are pulled from the files in your Render Files folder. If any of those files are altered, the reference movie will become unplayable.

Reference movies are fine as long as you have no intention of taking them off the computer, and you don't plan to make changes to the files they're based on (such as re-rendering a portion of your sequence).

1   Select the *Finished* sequence.

2   Choose File > Export > QuickTime Movie.

     The QuickTime movie export Save dialog appears.

3   Name the new file *Blue_Angels_Bearcats_REFERENCE.mov* and navigate to your desired destination.

4   Set the Setting pop-up menu to Current Settings, the Include pop-up menu to Audio and Video, and the Markers pop-up menu to All Markers.

5   Deselect the Make Movie Self-Contained checkbox and click Save.

     The exported file will be a reference movie.

Exporting Project Data

There are occasions when you need to move your Final Cut Pro project information to another program or another system. Final Cut Pro accommodates this in many different ways.

Exporting EDLs

You can also export an edit decision list (EDL), which is a text file containing the time-code numbers for all the edits in your sequence. Although an EDL doesn't include effects such as filters or compositing, it can include transition effects and complex multitrack edits. EDLs were originally used to drive linear tape-to-tape editing systems that were traditionally used to perform an *online* edit, essentially recutting your show at the original full tape resolution.

This has become a very uncommon workflow, mainly because you can online nearly any format right in your Final Cut Pro Timeline, which is more reliable and takes less effort, plus you can maintain any effects including filters, titles, compositing, and everything else you might dream up.

Still, EDLs have some value because they're a very simple record of exactly what clips go in what order to create your sequence, and nearly any video-related software on the market can read an EDL and recreate the sequence it describes. Final Cut Pro can generate many of the most common EDL formats from CMX, Grass Valley, and Sony.

1   In the Browser, select *Finished*.

2   Choose File > Export > EDL.

The EDL Export Options dialog appears.

Many of the settings here are intended to work with limitations other systems have when importing EDLs (such as not being able to read filter or transition effects). Consult the facility (or user manual of the software) requesting the EDL to determine the optimal settings for your circumstances.

3   Click OK.

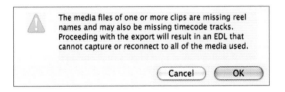

The Save dialog appears.

4   Navigate to your desired location and click Save.

It's essential that you retain the .edl extension, as some systems that read EDL files are based on antiquated file systems that depend on the extension to identify the file type.

If there are elements in your project that did not originate from tape with reel number and timecode (such as titles, generators, sound effects from a library, still images, and so on), you'll get a warning like this:

> ⚠ The media files of one or more clips are missing reel names and may also be missing timecode tracks. Proceeding with the export will result in an EDL that cannot capture or reconnect to all of the media used.
>
> Cancel   **OK**

In this example, it's the sync beep at the beginning and end of the sequence (created using Final Cut Pro generators) that's triggering the warning.

5   Click OK.

Exporting XML Files

The XML format is a very flexible data description file type and an XML file generated in Final Cut Pro contains every bit of data associated with the selected items. In addition to the obvious data about what clips go where, it includes the precise Timeline layout, all effects, generators, and so on.

The XML file is a thorough, open standards-based description of your Final Cut Pro project, and many third-party tools can read and interpret it. This allows you to, for example, send a project to Adobe After Effects,, or to another application that auto-assembles sequences or creates subtitles, and so on.

Each time Final Cut Pro is revised, the XML version is updated to include features unique to that new version (for example, an XML file created with Final Cut Pro 5 would not be able to store variable speed effects unique to Final Cut Pro 7).

Generating an XML file is easy and can be done based on any selection in the Browser; it can include clips, bins, sequences, and even effects.

1   In the Browser, select both sequences.

2   Choose File > Export > XML.

The Export XML dialog opens.

3   Leave the settings at their defaults and click OK.

A Save dialog appears.

4   Name the file *Bearcats_Finished.xml* and click OK.

The XML file is exported to the designated destination and is ready to be imported into another program or saved as an open-standards based description of your project data.

> **TIP** ▶ A Final Cut Pro XML file is one great way to open a Final Cut Pro project in an earlier version of the software. For example, if you were cutting in Final Cut Pro 7, but you wanted to share the project with someone working in Final Cut Pro version 6, simply export an XML file (use version 4 of the XML Interchange format for Final Cut Pro 6, version 3 for Final Cut Pro version 5, and so on); then have your colleague import that XML file into their older software, and your project will be automatically re-created. Of course, features unique to the new version will not be included in the exported data.

Lesson Review

1. What's the difference between a movie for Apple TV and for iPhone?
2. True or False: Share exports must be done one at a time.
3. How many files are created when using the DVD output?
4. True or False: Blu-ray Discs can be burned without a Blu-ray recorder.
5. When using the MobileMe output option, how many videos are made?
6. How can you use the Share window to access Compressor presets?
7. Name at least three ways to export audio data from a Final Cut Pro sequence.
8. What should always accompany an OMF export?
9. What's a reference movie, and how do you make one?
10. True or False: XML files contain only sequence data.

Answers

1. They're the same format, but have different frame sizes and different file sizes.
2. False. You can create a batch of share outputs and export them all at once.
3. Two. One video file and one audio file.
4. False, however, AVCHD discs can be burned on standard DVD recorders and contain Blu-ray-style HD video.
5. Three: Mobile, Medium, and Large.
6. Set the output type to Other.
7. As a mixed stereo AIFF, as a channel grouped AIFF, as a multitrack QuickTime movie, as an OMF, and as a compressed AC3 file.

8. OMF exports should always be delivered with a corresponding video file, preferably with BITC that matches the timecode in the OMF.

9. A reference movie is a tiny QuickTime file containing pointers to the media contained in the clips used in a sequence. You create one by deselecting the Make Movie Self-Contained checkbox in the QuickTime Movie Save dialog.

10. False. XML files can include any information saved in a Final Cut Pro project file including bins, clips, sequences, effects, and so on.

Working with RED Footage

More and more projects are being produced using RED cameras, and although the RED/Final Cut Pro workflow isn't complicated or difficult, there are a few specific settings and procedures of which you should be aware. This appendix covers the essentials to get you cutting your RED footage with a minimum of hassle.

There are two primary workflows commonly employed with RED footage: editing the native RED media directly (as QuickTime files), or transcoding the files to Apple ProRes during ingest. The only solid reason to stick with the original RED files is if you were planning to make a 4k digital master to print onto 35mm film. For the vast majority of users finishing on video or exhibiting digitally, transcoding the RED footage to Apple ProRes provides an excellent benefit-to-cost ratio, primarily because the resolution you sacrifice is virtually undetectable to your audience.

The benefits of transcoding are increased real-time and overall performance in Final Cut Pro, reduced disk space and bandwidth requirements, and a simplified workflow. Basically, once the files have been converted, working with RED source material is no different from editing with any other type of footage.

The only real disadvantage to transcoding is the time it takes to perform the actual conversion, which is significantly slower than just copying the raw RED data from the R3D files created in the camera into QuickTime files ready for editing in Final Cut Pro. And of course you're reducing your 4k master files down to 2k or smaller.

> **TIP** Although the default transcoding method does lock your color space and gamma settings into the files (either using the settings applied by the cinematographer in the field, or using one of several presets available in Final Cut Pro), you can work around this by creating a CinemaTools database for your RED source files and using that to generate the files sent to Color for grading. For more information on this workflow, see the Cinema Tools User Manual.

Installing the Plug-in

Regardless of which workflow you intend to follow, you must install some software to allow Final Cut Pro to read and work with the RED media. The latest version of the RED Final Cut Studio 3 Installer can be downloaded from www.red.com/support. This adds several functions to Final Cut Pro (as well as Color and all QuickTime-compatible applications) that allow you to ingest, view, edit, and output RED footage.

Managing RED Media

The files created by the RED camera are stored in folders labeled .RDM (for Red Digital Magazine). These contain the raw data (stored in .R3D files) as well as QuickTime reference movies and some other miscellaneous files. This data must be moved from the Compact Flash card or RED hard disk to a folder on your Mac.

> **NOTE** ▶ RED recommends that rather than simply copying the files using the Finder, you should use a third-party program to clone the files. This is most important if copying to older, heavily fragmented disks.

Move the entire RED volume into its own folder on your Mac. Name the folder to describe its contents.

TIP ▶ An additional copy of these files should be backed up and kept in a very safe place.

Before ingesting, rename the .RDM folders to help you keep track of which files came from which folders. Think of each folder as a reel, and each should have a distinct, specific reel name. For example, change G031_100126.RDM to Nov-10_Scene_25.RDM. The folder name is used by Final Cut Pro to determine the default name of the clips as they're ingested. Do not use the Reel filed in the Log and Transfer window.

There are a number of important guidelines regarding the arrangement of the raw RED data on your Mac hard disk:

1. Never put the contents of multiple RED volumes into a single folder. Each volume should have its own folder.

2. It's essential that each .RDM folder have a unique name.

3. Never change the name of any folders or files within the .RDM.

4. Don't nest folders of RED content within each other.

Final Cut Pro can't directly read the R3D files containing the raw footage. It can open and work with the QuickTime proxy files automatically generated by the camera; however, Apple doesn't recommend using these files for editing. These QuickTime files are reference movies, and if the link between them and the R3D files is ever broken (which can happen if either set of the files are moved in certain ways), the QuickTime files become worthless. If you made an edit using those files, there would be no way to conform it back to the actual footage.

Ingesting the Footage

Regardless of whether you plan to edit the RED footage natively, or to transcode it into ProRes, you must use the Log and Transfer window in Final Cut Pro to create files for editing.

1 In Final Cut Pro, choose File > Log and Transfer or press Command-Shift-8.

Add Volume button   Log and Transfer Settings menu

The Log and Transfer window opens.

2   Click the Add Volume button (or press Command-I), navigate to the .RDM folder containing the clips you want to ingest, and then click OK.

If the RED software has been installed, several new options appear in the Log and Transfer preferences.

3 Click the Settings pop-up menu and choose Preferences.

The Log and Transfer Preferences window opens. This is where you can choose whether to keep your footage native, or whether to transcode it. If you choose to transcode, you can select the destination format.

Staying Native

Final Cut Pro can't read the raw R3D files, but it can stuff the R3D data into a QuickTime file without any conversion. This way you still have access to all the raw data (including the color space and gamma settings saved in the file's metadata), and you can edit the footage right in Final Cut Pro.

1 In the Log and Transfer Preferences window, click the Target Format column next to the RED Digital Cinema REDCODE entry. From the pop-up menu that appears, choose Native.

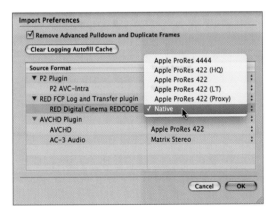

This tells Final Cut Pro in what format to store the QuickTime files it creates when you proceed with the Log and Transfer operation.

Converting to ProRes

Alternatively, you can select one of the Apple ProRes codecs from that menu, and when you proceed with the Log and Transfer process, the files will be converted into that format.

The maximum width of a ProRes image is 2048 pixels, and so when converting RED files into ProRes, the files are automatically scaled down to 2048 x 1152 for 16:9 footage and 2048 x 1024 for 2:1 footage (half their native resolutions).

The matter of which ProRes codec to choose depends on the rest of your workflow. If you're planning to match back to the raw R3D files at a later time, you might choose Apple ProRes 422 (Proxy). It's a small, lightweight file that will work great for editing, but probably doesn't have the quality to serve as a final master (unless your final output is going to be SD-sized or smaller files transmitted over the Internet—in which case the proxy codec might be sufficient).

If you plan to make the transcoded version your new master and want your final output to remain at the 2k frame size, choose one of the higher-quality versions of ProRes, such as Apple ProRes 4444 and Apple ProRes 422 (HQ). These codecs will retain much more of the fidelity of your camera original.

If you plan to make the transcoded version your new master and your final output is going to be smaller than the full 1080 HD resolution, you might consider the Apple ProRes 422 or even the Apple ProRes 422 (LT) versions. The files you generate will still be saved at 2k resolution, but will be smaller and thereby allow you to store much more footage on your drive and see better performance in Final Cut Pro. These codecs are still capable of displaying very high-quality images suitable for later conversion to SD DVD or files compressed for viewing on the web.

When converting your files to ProRes, you "bake in" the color space, gamma and other settings associated with the *look* of the image. By default, the settings applied will be the settings chosen by the cinematographer or video tech in the field. But there are a few presets you can choose to override those settings.

1   In the Log and Transfer Settings pop-up menu, choose "RED FCP Log and Transfer plugin" and choose from one of the settings in that submenu.

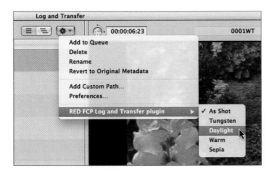

The setting you select will be applied to all the clips in a "one-light" style when the files are processed during the Log and Transfer session.

Proceeding with Log and Transfer

Once you've selected the format to which your REDCODE files will be converted, you can use any of the other features in the Log and Transfer window, including naming the files and adding other metadata, setting In and Out points, and so on.

> **TIP** Remember not to modify the Reel field in the Log and Transfer window.

Any footage added to the queue will be converted in the background and saved as QuickTime movies in your designated Final Cut Pro capture scratch folder. Clips will be added to the current logging bin, while the original files in the RDM folders remain untouched.

Editing with RED Footage

If, during Log and Transfer, you converted your RED files to Apple ProRes, there's nothing further you must do differently from editing any other project. The first time you drag one of your source clips into a sequence, say Yes to the familiar Change Sequence Settings dialog and Final Cut Pro will automatically set the sequence settings to match the clips. Depending on which codec you chose, and whether your original footage was shot as 16:9 or 2:1, the settings will appear similar to those in the following dialog.

If you converted your RED files using the *native* setting, you should still allow Final Cut Pro to automatically set the sequence settings to match the clip's settings (by dragging your first clip into the sequence and saying Yes to the Change Sequence Settings dialog).

Final Cut Pro will set the sequence compressor to the Apple ProRes 4444 codec, which will retain the 4:4:4 RGB color from the REDCODE files with no chroma subsampling.

> **TIP** Although there is a REDCODE codec, it's a read-only codec and so it can't be used as a sequence Compressor setting.

Final Cut Pro can't play 4k files. Although the full 4k data is stored in your files (and will be available when they're sent to Color for grading), your Final Cut Pro sequence frame size will automatically be set to 2k. Set the sequence to Unlimited RT, and the clips will play as if they were native to the sequence.

> **TIP** Be aware that regardless of whether you transcode your video to Apple ProRes or keep it native, the files you're creating are going to be quite large and will require a very fast storage subsystem to play back without dropping frames.

Controlling Video Quality

You can further reduce the quality to half resolution to improve playback performance by changing the Playback Video Quality setting in the Timeline RT menu.

By setting this menu to High, video will always play at the full sequence resolution (up to 2k). When set to Medium or Low quality, the video will be reduced to half resolution; so, for example, files currently playing at 2k will instead play at 1k, which will allow for more real-time effects and better overall performance.

Outputting a RED Project

At this point in the workflow, you can take full advantage of all the features in Final Cut Pro, just the same as working with any other type of source footage. The only time you have to remember that your footage came from RED source files comes when it's time to output your finished project. If you transcoded to Apple ProRes, there's nothing special to think about; you can finish in any of the ways you would with any other sort of project. However, if you kept your files native, you can use Color to output a full 4k version of your sequence as DPX files, even if you don't want to do any color correction on your files.

1   Once your project is complete, select a sequence in the Browser and choose File > Send to > Color.

2   Enter a project name in the Send to Color dialog and click OK.

    A Color project is created containing all the selected items from your Final Cut Pro sequence.

Color can process the full 4k resolution of the source clips, so any grading or other effects you do there will be processed at the files' full native resolution. Additionally, the metadata containing the color space, gamma, and other settings associated with the raw RED files is accessible and modifiable in Color, in a special tab that appears in the Primary In room.

NOTE ▶ The RED tab is installed as part of the RED Final Cut Studio 3 software installation recommended at the beginning of this appendix.

Once you've completed whatever grading or corrections you desire in Color (the details of which are beyond the scope of this book ; for more information, see *Apple Pro Training Series: Color Correction in Final Cut Studio*), you'll be ready to output your Color project.

TIP ▶ For projects intended to go to a DPX digital intermediate (typically done in preparation for printing to film), you'll probably want to work with a very simplified sequence in Final Cut Pro: no filters, motion, or speed effects, and only cuts or simple dissolves. Effects in the Final Cut Pro sequence will not be sent to Color, and therefore won't make it out to the DPX files you export from Color.

You can use Color's Geometry room to perform pan and scan, flopping, and similar motion effects.

3   In the Project Settings tab of the Color Setup room, set the Resolution Preset to match your project's native resolution and set the Render File Type to DPX.

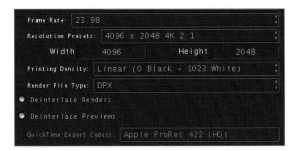

4   Use the Render Queue to output the files in your Color project.

The files will be exported at full 4k resolution.

NOTE ▶ For an expanded description of the RED/Final Cut Studio workflow, see the Final Cut Pro 7 Professional Formats and Workflows document at http://documentation.apple.com.

Index

Apple Certification
Fuel your mind.
Reach your potential.

Stand out from the crowd. Differentiate yourself and gain recognition for your expertise by earning Apple Certified Pro status to validate your Final Cut Pro skills.

This book prepares you to earn Apple Certified Pro—Final Cut Pro Level Two. Level One certification attests to essential operational knowledge of the application. Level Two certification demonstrates mastery of advanced features and a deeper understanding of the application. Take it one step further and earn Master Pro certification in Final Cut Studio.

Three Steps to Certification

1 Choose your certification path.
More info: training.apple.com/certification.

2 Select a location:

Apple Authorized Training Centers (AATCs) offer all exams (Mac OS X, Pro Apps, iLife, iWork, and Xsan). AATC locations: training.apple.com/locations

Prometric Testing Centers (1-888-275-3926) offer all Mac OS X exams, and the Final Cut Pro Level One exam. Prometric centers: www.prometric.com/apple

3 Register for and take your exam(s).

"Now when I go out to do corporate videos and I let them know that I'm certified, I get job after job after job."

—Chip McAllister, Final Cut Pro Editor and Winner of The Amazing Race 2004

Reasons to Become an Apple Certified Pro

- **Raise your earning potential.** Studies show that certified professionals can earn more than their non-certified peers.

- **Distinguish yourself from others in your industry.** Proven mastery of an application helps you stand out from the crowd.

- **Display your Apple Certification logo.** Each certification provides a logo to display on business cards, resumes and websites.

- **Publicize your Certifications.** Publish your certifications on the Apple Certified Professionals Registry to connect with schools, clients and employers.

Training Options

Apple's comprehensive curriculum addresses your needs, whether you're an IT or creative professional, educator, or service technician. Hands-on training is available through a worldwide network of Apple Authorized Training Centers (AATCs) or in a self-paced format through the Apple Training Series and Apple Pro Training Series. Learn more about Apple's curriculum and find an AATC near you at training.apple.com.

training.apple.com/certification

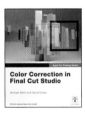

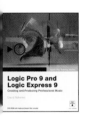

WATCH
READ
CREATE

Meet Creative Edge.

A new resource of unlimited books, videos, and tutorials from the world's leading experts.

Creative Edge is your key to staying at the top of your game—bringing you the inspiration and training you need so you can focus on what you do best—being creative.

Access any day, any time you need it. Only $24.99 per month.

creativeedge.com